The Strategist's Handbook

The Strategist's Handbook

Tools, Templates, and Best Practices Across the Strategy Process

Timothy Galpin

OXFORD

UNIVERSITY PRESS

OXFORD
UNIVERSITY PRESS

Great Clarendon Street, Oxford, OX2 6DP,
United Kingdom

Oxford University Press is a department of the University of Oxford.
It furthers the University's objective of excellence in research, scholarship,
and education by publishing worldwide. Oxford is a registered trade mark of
Oxford University Press in the UK and in certain other countries

Published in the United States of America by Oxford University Press
198 Madison Avenue, New York, NY 10016, United States of America

British Library Cataloguing in Publication Data
Data available

Library of Congress Control Number: 2023935117

ISBN 978–0–19–288520–3
ISBN 978–0–19–288528–9 (pbk.)

DOI: 10.1093/oso/9780192885203.001.0001

Printed and bound by
CPI Group (UK) Ltd, Croydon, CR0 4YY

Preface

Whether you realize it or not, you are already a strategist. For instance, you likely have decided to pursue an education to obtain knowledge and skills you bring to the job market and receive some sort of compensation. You then use that compensation to fund your lifestyle, while also potentially saving some of that income for future use. These are examples of strategies you have chosen to help you achieve your financial and other personal goals. You may have done a lot of analysis to arrive at your chosen strategies, or you may have simply used your intuition ("gut feel") to make your strategic choices. Either way, you have "done" strategy, at least at the personal level. *The Strategist's Handbook* is designed to expand your strategic skills beyond the personal level to the organizational level.

Field-Tested, Time-Tested, and Practical

The Strategist's Handbook is a collection of the best materials, insights, tools, and templates that comprise the core Strategy course taught in the undergraduate, MBA, executive MBA, and postgraduate diploma programs at the Saïd Business School, University of Oxford. Each of the best practices, pitfalls to avoid, tools, and templates presented in this book has been field-tested and refined for over three decades while working with for-profit, not-for-profit, and government organizations, across multiple industries around the globe to help them develop and implement their strategies. The guidance and tools can be applied in small, mid-sized, and large organizations. Their application just needs to be scaled accordingly. While this is a practical "how-to" book, the tools and approaches presented are based on a solid foundation of well-established theory and extensive research that is also highlighted within each chapter.

My students and clients often ask me, "What has changed in the over thirty years since you have been working with organizations on developing and implementing their strategies?" Table P.1 identifies my observations of what has changed in the discipline of Strategy and what is the same today as it was three decades ago.

Developing Strategy Expertise and Depth of Knowledge

Those new to "strategy" as well as seasoned strategy professionals can benefit from the book's contents. However, this book will not make anyone a strategy expert. Like most complex activities, the best learning is by doing. Every organization is

Table P.1 Three decades of strategy: what has changed and what is the same

What is the same?	What has changed?
• The "classic" strategy frameworks are still applicable	• The content (quantitative and qualitative data) that goes into the frameworks has changed
• Top-down strategy	• People talk more about "democratic" or "dispersed" strategy (but strategy is still not very democratic)
• 10- to 20-year strategies	• 1- to 3-year strategies
• The reasons for strategic change	• Increase in the frequency of the reasons for strategic change
• Senior management overconfidence and mistakes	• Different senior management (who are still overconfident and make the same mistakes as their predecessors)
• Strategy consultants	• More strategy consultants
• The best strategy is the one you can implement	• A greater awareness of implementation importance (but it is still difficult)
• "Culture eats strategy for breakfast" (Peter Drucker)	• Culture eats strategy for breakfast, lunch, and dinner

different and the business landscape (technologies, regulations, competitors, society, and so forth) in which they operate is constantly evolving. Consequently, developing a "strategic mindset" is an ongoing pursuit.

Intended Audience

Strategy applies to all organizations (large, medium, and small), across all sectors, including for-profit, not-for-profit, government, non-governmental organizations (NGOs), and foundations, across all geographies. Strategy is also a cross-disciplinary endeavor, requiring a broad team with varying expertise from different levels of the organization. Therefore, the best practices, pitfalls to avoid, and tools and templates presented will benefit current and aspiring senior managers, middle- and frontline managers, functional experts, and strategy consultants alike.

Overview of the Contents

The thirteen chapters and two appendices of *The Strategist's Handbook* provide time-tested "best practices," key tools and templates, and essential "lessons learned" across various aspects of strategy, including:

- predicting the organization's future operating environment
- building strategically valuable resources
- selecting high-impact strategies
- strategy execution
- managing strategic transformation
- strategic communications
- retention and re-engagement of key talent during strategic change
- aligning culture with strategy
- nonmarket strategy
- how corporate parents add strategic value
- pursuing alliances, joint ventures, mergers, and acquisitions
- shareholder activism and restructuring
- key findings from the Oxford Strategy Insights Project
- a Strategy Workbook, packed with practical exercises and field-tested tools and templates.

Legal Considerations

The guidance and tools contained throughout this text are practical and time-tested. However, the contents should not be taken in any way as authoritative legal or financial guidance. When pursuing strategy, readers should consult with qualified intermediaries, including legal counsel and financial advisers, about any aspects that may have legal or financial consequences.

The Oxford Strategy Insights Project

Appendix A presents key findings from the Oxford Strategy Insights Project, with input from 167 executives and managers across 26 industries, spanning over 30 countries, regarding their firms' strategy processes.

Strategy Workbook

Appendix B provides a Strategy Workbook containing processes, tools, and templates that can be used to facilitate effective strategy formulation and execution efforts, across industries (including for-profit, not-for-profit, and government entities), various geographies, and all sizes and stages of organizations.

The Author

Tim Galpin is Senior Lecturer of Strategy and Innovation and Director of the Post-graduate Diploma in Strategy and Innovation at the Saïd Business School, University of Oxford. His consulting clients have included numerous Fortune 500 and FTSE 100 companies. Tim has authored five previous management books that have been published in six languages and authored numerous articles for publications, including *Mergers & Acquisitions, Strategy & Leadership, Journal of Business Strategy, The Handbook of Business Strategy, World Journal of Entrepreneurship*, and *Corporate Governance*. Tim is also Contributing Editor of *Strategy & Leadership* and a member of the Editorial Advisory Board for the *Journal of Business Strategy*. Tim has been featured on CNBC, Reuters Television, and National Public Radio and has been quoted in various publications throughout the world.

Timothy Galpin
Saïd Business School, University of Oxford
timothy.galpin@sbs.ox.ac.uk
www.timgalpin.com

Contents

List of Figures

List of Tables

Introduction

Strategy in Theory and Practice

Strategy is an ancient pursuit with its roots in military strategy. In the fifth century BC, the Chinese military general Sun Tzu (Master Sun) wrote *The Art of War* (also known as *Master Sun's Military Methods*), a tome consisting of thirteen chapters devoted to various aspects of military strategy. Likewise, the Greek term *strategos*, a compound of the Greek words *stratos* (army) and *agos* (leader), refers to a leader or commander of an army.

The Evolution of Business Strategy

Beyond military strategy, over the centuries strategy has evolved in the business environment through various eras:

- *1700–1800: an "invisible hand" has control.* Adam Smith (1776) describes forces that are beyond the control of individual firms, referring to the "invisible market forces" that, through the actions of self-interested individuals, bring levels of supply and demand in a free market to equilibrium and create unintended greater social benefits and public good. The "free market" is a system in which the prices for goods and services are self-regulated by buyers and sellers negotiating in an open market without market coercions such as government regulation.
- *1800–1900: the "visible hand" appears.* The profession of management takes shape, with professional managers running multi-divisional or "M-form" corporations characterized by firms being separated into several semi-autonomous business units, typically with financial targets set by the corporate center. Many firms make large investments in manufacturing and marketing. Management hierarchies are established to plan and coordinate resources (capital, people, and equipment) across the business units (Chandler, 1977).
- *1900–30s: strategic factors emerge.* The need for a formal approach to corporate strategy was first articulated by top executives of M-form corporations (Ghemawat, 2002). In 1923 Alfred Sloan (chief executive of General Motors from 1923 to 1946) devised a strategy that was explicitly based on the perceived strengths and weaknesses of its main competitor, Ford (Sloan, 1963). In the 1930s Chester Barnard, a senior executive at AT&T, argued that managers

The Strategist's Handbook. Timothy Galpin, Oxford University Press. © Timothy Galpin (2023).
DOI: 10.1093/oso/9780192885203.003.0001

should pay especially close attention to "strategic factors," which depend on "personal or organizational action" (Barnard, 1938).

- *1939–45: the rise of "management science."* The problem of allocating scarce resources across an entire economy in wartime leads to many innovations in management science, such as operations research. First discovered in the military aircraft industry, "learning curves" become an important tool for planning, finding that labor costs decreased by a constant percentage as the cumulative quantity of aircraft produced doubled, for example. Learning effects figure prominently in wartime production planning efforts (Hartley, 1965). In the postwar era of the 1950s, the management guru Peter Drucker contended that management should not simply entail passive, adaptive behavior; rather, effective management means taking action to create desired results (Drucker, 1954).
- *1960s: planning departments are established and the SWOT framework appears.* Following Drucker's assertion about the role of active management, the 1960s see a proliferation of "planning departments" established in many large US companies (Ghemawat, 2002). The SWOT analysis (Learned et al., 1965) matching a firm's Strengths and Weaknesses with marketplace Opportunities and Threats becomes a fundamental element of strategic planning.

Paralleling the development of strategy in industry, business schools began teaching strategy and strategy consultancies were established:

- *1912: the teaching of Business Policy.* Designed to integrate knowledge gained in functional areas such as accounting, operations, marketing, and finance, Business Policy is established as a required second-year course at Harvard Business School (Ghemawat, 2002).
- *1914: Booz Allen & Hamilton.* After graduating from Northwestern University, Edwin G. Booz founded the Business Research Service, later becoming Booz Allen & Hamilton (Booz Allen & Hamilton, 2022).
- *1926: McKinsey & Co.* James O. McKinsey, a University of Chicago professor and expert on management accounting, establishes his consulting firm (McKinsey & Company, 2022).
- *1960s–70s: BCG and Bain.* The Boston Consulting Group (BCG) is established in 1963 (Boston Consulting Group, 2022) and a decade later, in 1973, a group of ten employees break away from BCG and form Bain & Company (Companies History, 2022). Subsequently, the "big four" strategy firms (Bain, BCG, Booz, and McKinsey) dominate the strategy consulting market.

Today, the concept of "strategy" is still evolving, shifting from an economic view to a value-creation view:

- *1950–2000: growth economics and "economic strategy."* Sustained economic growth of firms is paramount. The environment is characterized by relative stability in geopolitics. An international consensus forms about global trade shaped by developed democracies. "Financialization" including waves of mergers and acquisitions and the formalization of financial and accounting standards, and the concept of "shareholder value" becomes the dominant purpose of the corporation. "Economic strategy" promotes the concepts of "sustainable competitive advantage," with strategic analysis focusing on firms operating in well-established and structured industries. Internal firm resources are arranged to outperform rivals over time. The standardization of strategic decision-making tools, and a clear set of quantitative performance indicators, focus on incumbent firms from the West and North, known as the Anglo-American/European economic model (Vantresca, 2022).

- *2000–today: value economics and "value-creation strategy."* As industries converge, boundaries between industries become blurred. In addition to shareholders, multiple "stakeholders" emerge including employees, communities, and activists who have varied interests beyond financial returns. The economic environment is characterized by greater instability and uncertainty. The "global economy" takes shape, with emerging markets and economies becoming more significant to global economic activity. "Value-creation strategy" embraces the concept of "transient competitive advantage." "Value creation" begins to replace "competitive advantage" as the dominant strategic pursuit. The blurring of industry boundaries and a fundamental shift from "firms" to "ecosystems and platforms" business models gives rise to more complex market contests with varied actors. "Grounded cultural-political action" rather than asocial "economic rational action" becomes more prevalent among firms and across industries, giving rise to corporate political activity and ESG (environmental, social, and governance) organizational policies, and "nonmarket strategy" (see Chapter 9) takes a more central role (Vantresca, 2022).

Strategic Planning, Strategic Management, and Strategic Thinking

We have all heard the terms *strategic planning, strategic management,* and *strategic thinking.* However, depending upon whom you ask, they often mean different things to different people. So, let's do some level-setting about the definitions used in this text for each term.

Strategic Planning

The most prevalent descriptions of "strategic planning" characterize it as the process by which an organization differentiates itself from its competition to achieve its desired mission and goals (Mallon, 2019). For example, in his seminal work on the topic, Chandler describes strategic planning as the courses of action and allocation of resources necessary to fulfill an organization's mission and achieve its desired goals (Chandler, 1962). Moreover, strategic planning is often distinguished from "operational effectiveness," the latter being the ways in which an organization will continuously improve its business processes (Porter, 1996). Likewise, strategic planning has been differentiated from "business planning," with strategic planning encompassing mid- to long-term plans with a lifespan of several (e.g., three to five) years or longer, whereas business planning focuses on short-term, tactical time horizons such as how a firm's annual budget is allocated across areas of the business.

Researchers from disciplines as varied as management, anthropology, public administration, economics, decision sciences, and education have extensively studied strategic planning, using quantitative, qualitative, or a combination of the two research methods. Various meta-analyses (the synthesis of data from several separate studies on the same subject to determine overall trends) have found positive relationships between strategic planning and organizational performance (Boyd, 1996; George et al., 2019; Miller and Cardinal, 1994; Schwenk and Shrader, 1993). However, studies on strategic planning have been criticized for conflating correlation with causation (Poister et al., 2013). Critics argue that positive organizational performance may be attributable to strategic planning, but the outcomes may also be caused by other factors such as favorable economic conditions, faltering competition, competent leadership, or simply luck.

Strategic Management

While strategic planning focuses on courses of action, strategic management involves a broader, more systemic perspective that includes but is not limited to the organization's strategy. Like the terms *strategic planning*, *strategic management*, and *strategic thinking*, we have all heard the terms *mission*, *vision*, *values*, *goals*, *strategy*, *tactics*, and *measures*. Again, depending upon whom you ask, these terms often mean different things to different people. Accordingly, let's do some level-setting about the definitions used in this text for each of these components of a firm's strategic management system (see Figure I.1).

Mission. A mission answers the question: *what* do we do as an organization? A well-designed mission statement defines the company's primary, distinctive purpose, setting the firm apart from other similar organizations. By communicating what the firm provides to customers, the market, and/or society, a clearly articulated mission establishes the priorities of the organization (Jacopin and Fontrodona, 2009). Moreover, a mission statement promotes a set of shared expectations among employees and communicates a public persona to external stakeholders such as the community, consumers, and investors (Wheelen and Hunger, 2008). Too often a mission statement is paragraphs long, drawn out, and all-inclusive, illustrating management's attempt to be all things to all people. Such missions do nothing more

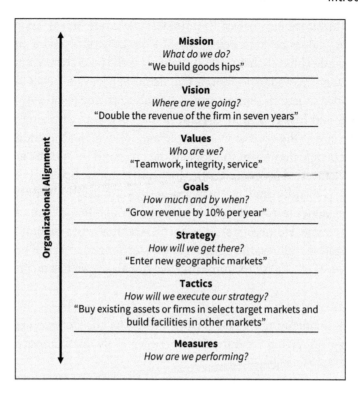

Figure I.1 Components of a firm's strategic management system

than confuse those who even take the time to read them. Therefore, clear mission statements should be short, repeatable, and easily understood by both internal and external stakeholders. An example of a clear, concise, repeatable, and enduring mission statement comes from Newport News Shipbuilding, whose mission has not changed since the company's founding in 1886 (Humes, 2016): "We shall build good ships here—at a profit if we can—at a loss if we must—but always good ships."

Vision. A clear organizational vision answers the question: *where* are we going as an organization? The benefits of an effective vision statement include (Lipton, 1996):

- providing the foundation for a range of performance measures by identifying a future organizational aspiration
- promoting organizational change
- providing the basis for a strategic plan to achieve the stated vision
- motivating individuals and facilitating the recruitment of talent
- putting decision-making in the context of vision attainment
- attracting investors.

The clear and concise vision of General Electric, during the tenure of former CEO Jack Welch, was: "We will be either number 1 or 2 in any business we are in."

Values. A firm's values answer the question: *who* are we as an organization? Organizational values refer to beliefs about standards of behavior organizational members should exhibit (Schein, 1985). Values are the basis for the development of organizational norms and expectations that define appropriate behavior by employees in particular situations. Shared values can also provide a source of motivation, commitment, and loyalty among organizational members (Morsing and Oswald, 2009). Values are at the core of who people are, influencing the choices individuals make, the people they trust, the appeals they respond to, and the way their time and energy are invested (Posner, 2010). Moreover, clearly articulated organizational values can help identify the "fit" between employees and the firm. For example, someone who values teamwork will fit much better in a firm that embodies teamwork as a core value. Numerous studies have found that when an employee's values fit the organization's values, the employee will stay longer and be more productive (Kristof-Brown et al., 2005). Example organizational core values include:

- balance—maintaining a positive work and life balance for our workforce
- diversity—respecting the differences between individuals across our organization
- teamwork—working together to solve problems and achieve organizational goals
- innovation—welcoming new and creative ideas
- integrity—acting honestly in all we do, without compromising the truth
- passion—putting our hearts and minds into our work to achieve the best results possible
- risk-taking—encouraging each other to take risks without fear of retribution for failure
- continuous learning—understanding and applying key lessons gained from our successes and our failures.

Goals. A firm's strategic goals answer the question: *how much* and by *when*? Organizational goal-setting is a crucial initial step in the strategic management of a firm. Organizational goals segment the organization's vision into more near-term achievable metrics. For example, a vision of *doubling the revenue of the company over the next seven years* can be deconstructed into annual goals of *10 percent revenue growth per year for each of the next seven years*. Thus, organizational goals provide the foundation for developing a roadmap of organizational activity (i.e., the firm's strategy), as well as providing the basis for establishing the metrics that will be used to measure progress (Ransom and Lober, 1999). Etzioni (1960) defines a corporate goal as a desired situation the organization attempts to realize or a future situation the organization collectively is trying to achieve. Commonly stated organizational goals include revenue growth, earnings, market share, innovation, customer satisfaction, and employee productivity (Doyle, 1994). The key "SMART" (Doran, 1981) characteristics of effective organizational goal-setting are:

- *Specific.* Identifies explicit performance standards (e.g., an increase or decrease of X percent).
- *Measurable.* Clear metrics can be applied.
- *Attainable.* The goal can be accomplished within the target achievement time-frame.
- *Relevant.* The goal should have importance to the future success of the organization.
- *Time-based.* Includes a target achievement date or timeframe.

Strategy. As identified above, strategy has long been described as the courses of action and the allocation of resources necessary to fulfill an organization's mission and achieve its desired goals (Chandler 1962). Therefore, an organization's strategy answers the question: *how* will we get there? In other words, how will we deliver on our mission, achieve our goals, and reach our vision? For example, "growth strategies" to achieve a vision of *doubling the revenue of the company over the next seven years* enabled by achieving a goal of *10 percent revenue growth per year for each of the next seven years* can include offering new products or services to the firm's current customers in current markets and/or entering new geographic markets with current products or services. The sorts of strategies available to organizations are discussed in detail in Chapter 3. Moreover, strategists must always remember that *the best strategy is the one you can implement.* No matter how brilliant or elegant a strategy is, it is worthless until effectively implemented (see Chapter 4).

Tactics. There is often semantic confusion surrounding the question of "what is a strategy and what is a tactic?" While strategy addresses how a firm will deliver on its mission, achieve its goals, and reach its vision, *tactics* answer the question: *how* will we execute our strategy? Therefore, tactics are a subset of a particular strategy. For example, the tactics to execute a growth strategy of "entering new geographic markets" can include "buy existing assets or firms in select target markets" and "build facilities in other new markets."

Measures. An organization's measures answer the question: *how are we performing in relation to our strategic goals?* Organizational performance can include financial, customer, business process, and innovation and learning measures (Kaplan and Norton, 2005). Historically, management focused on the use of measurement to communicate organizational financial performance to investors. However, moving from "performance measurement" to "performance-based management" requires more than simply reporting financial or operational results. Performance-based management links measurement to an organization's strategy and uses measurement as a key lever for organizational improvement (Altmayer, 2006). The extent of performance measurement a firm should conduct is a balancing act. Too few measures encourage a narrow organizational focus, whereas too many measures create confusion to the point where measures are ignored (Rumens, 2002). Robert Behn (2003) of Harvard University identifies eight key benefits of effective performance measurement:

1. *Evaluation.* How well is the department, business unit, or overall organization performing?
2. *Control.* How can we ensure management and employees are doing the right thing?
3. *Budgeting.* In which programs, people, or projects should we invest?
4. *Motivation.* How can we prompt line staff, middle managers, and collaborators to do what is necessary to improve performance?
5. *Promotion.* How can we demonstrate to stakeholders and the media we are doing a good job?
6. *Celebration.* What accomplishments are worthy of celebrating success?
7. *Learning.* What is working or not working?
8. *Improvement.* In what areas do we need to focus our improvement efforts?

Organizational alignment. As illustrated in Figure I.1, it is not enough for an organization to have clearly articulated their *mission, vision, values, goals, strategy*, and *measures*. Alignment throughout the organization from the senior team, through middle management, to front-line employees around these components of the firm's strategic management is crucial to organizational performance. Organizational alignment provides the foundation for successful strategy execution and achievement of each element, whereas misalignment about the content and aims of each of these strategic elements creates confusion on the part of all stakeholders, internal and external. Research has found that greater alignment throughout the organization around the content and aims of each strategic element has a significant positive relationship with higher revenue and EBITDA (earnings before interest, taxes, depreciation, and amortization) per employee (Jevtic et al., 2018).

Strategic Thinking

Strategy is analytical, but it is also creative, therefore "strategic thinking" requires both analysis and creativity. There are wide-ranging views about what comprises "strategic thinking" and "strategic thinkers." For example, the influential strategy authority Henry Mintzberg (1987) argued that strategic planning is an analytical process with a business plan as its outcome. Strategic thinking, on the other hand, also utilizes intuition and creativity, resulting in an integrated perspective of the enterprise including a planned strategy with ongoing experimentation during implementation of the plan and potentially "emergent strategies" as the outcome. Liedtka (1998) presents five components of strategic thinking.

- *Systems perspective*: a strategic thinker has an end-to-end systems view of how the organization creates value and understands the interdependencies within the system.
- *Intent-focused*: a strategic thinker has a long-term view of the future market and positioning of the firm over time; a sense of direction.
- *Intelligent opportunism*: within the intent-driven focus, a strategic thinker leaves room for strategies to emerge.
- *Thinking in time*: a strategic thinker connects past, present, and future. The past has predictive value. The present provides not only a foundation for the future but also a comparison of what today versus tomorrow looks like. The future provides the intent-focus.
- *Hypothesis-driven*: a strategic thinker utilizes the scientific method by generating hypotheses about possible future paths and uses data to assess and select the "best path" forward.

Similarly, Bonn (2001) presents four characteristics of "strategic thinkers."

- *Critical thinking*: ability to objectively analyze a situation and evaluate the pros and cons and the implications of any course of action.
- *Conceptual thinking*: ability to grasp abstract ideas and put the pieces together to form a coherent picture.
- *Creative thinking*: ability to generate options, visualize possibilities, and formulate new approaches.
- *Intuitive thinking*: ability to factor hunches into the decision-making equation without allowing them to dominate the outcome.

Since these are varied and nebulous skills, there is an obvious question of whether "strategic thinking" can be taught. Many business schools teach the analytical capabilities strategic thinkers require, including hypothesis development, data collection and analysis, financial and operational analysis, and so forth. However, creativity and intuition are much more difficult to "teach" in structured educational courses. Therefore, many strategic thinking skills develop over time from various experiences. Goldman (2006) presents ten experiences contributing to the development of strategic thinking expertise at the top of organizations, categorized by four levels of interaction.

- *Personal level of interaction*. Upbringing and education, general work experience, and promotion to the top management team.
- *Interpersonal level of interaction*. Being mentored and challenged by a key colleague.
- *Organizational level of interaction*. Monitoring results against benchmarks, doing strategic planning, and leading a major growth initiative.

- *External level of interaction.* Dealing with a threat to organizational survival and vicarious experiences.

Strategy Can Be Deliberate, Emergent, or a Combination of Both

Deliberate Strategy

Deliberate or planned strategy is one that is chosen by the organization's top management team. In their best-selling strategy books, Porter (1980) and Treacy and Weirsma (1995) assert that management must make choices that require trade-offs when it comes to strategy. Porter (1980) identifies three generic strategies that firms can choose based on market scope and competitive advantage:

1. *Cost leadership.* The low-cost provider across a broad market.
2. *Differentiation.* Providing product or service uniqueness across a broad market.
3. *Focus.* Consisting of two subsets by applying numbers 1 and 2 in a focused rather than broad market; (3a) being the low-cost provider in a narrow/focused market segment and (3b) providing product or service uniqueness in a narrow/focused market (see Figure I.2).

Treacy and Weirsma (1995) studied firms who they termed "market leaders" (those companies that consistently outperform their industry rivals over time). They found that each market leader chose and persisted over time with one of three strategic "value disciplines": (1) *customer intimacy* (providing extremely high levels of

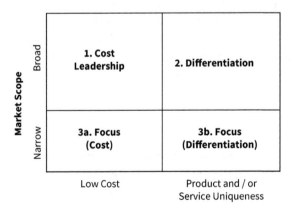

Figure I.2 Porter's generic strategies

service), (2) *product leadership* (consistently bringing new and innovative products to market), and (3) operational excellence (being the low-cost provider in their industry). The authors assert that a successful business needs to maintain at least "acceptable" levels of performance in each dimension, but management need to choose one dimension to become a market leader in their industry, and excelling in any of the dimensions requires making sacrifices in the others.

Emergent Strategy

Although "deliberate strategy" and "strategic choice" have been the dominant strategy themes implemented by numerous organizations large and small, the concept of "emergent strategy" has also been promoted by strategy authorities. The earliest and most prominent advocate of emergent strategy was Henry Mintzberg. In his discussion about the process of "crafting strategy," he asserts, "Strategies need not be deliberate, they can also emerge … strategies can *form* as well as be *formulated* … effective strategies develop in all kinds of strange ways" (1987, pp. 68, 70). Figure I.3 illustrates Mintzberg's notion of deliberate versus emergent strategy.

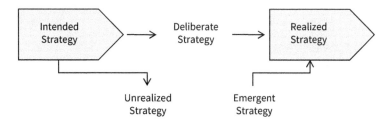

Figure I.3 Mintzberg's deliberate and emergent strategies

A Combination of Deliberate and Emergent Strategy

Although advocating an emergent approach to strategy, Mintzberg (1987, p. 69) points out that "In practice, of course, all strategy making walks on two feet, one deliberate, the other emergent. For just as purely deliberate strategy making precludes learning, so purely emergent strategy making precludes control. Pushed to the limit, neither approach makes much sense. Learning must be coupled with control." Likewise, Felin and Powell (2016, p. 80) advocate that organizations be designed to embody "dynamic capabilities … the capacity for developing new capabilities that anticipate and respond to a turbulent marketplace." However, at the same time, the authors discuss the need for "organizational integration" by providing structure to strategy development and implementation, asking, "How can we map the organization onto the full diversity of its environment, while employing structures, processes, and systems ['integrating mechanisms'] that prevent the orga-nization from disintegrating into chaos?" (p. 81). Or, as Teece (1996) suggests, "let chaos reign, then rein in chaos" (p. 86).

Traditional versus Dynamic Strategy

A "dynamic" approach to strategy (sometimes called "democratized strategy") is mainly found in small- and medium-sized organizations (e.g., those with fewer than one hundred employees). However, some larger organizations also utilize a more dynamic strategy process. Dynamic strategy is characterized by a focus on opportunity capture. Potential strategic initiatives are identified and proposed by managers and employees across the firm and at all levels of the organization, from senior executives to middle management, to front-line employees. Dynamic strat-egy is ongoing, and information comes from employee insights gleaned from their day-to-day work, continuous contact with customers, and awareness of the broader market (see Table I.1).

Table I.1 Dynamic strategy process

Focus	Opportunity capture
Who	Cross-functional and multilevel ("democratized")
When	Ongoing
How	Customer and market contact
Where	Occurs at organizational and functional boundaries

As organizations grow to become medium-sized (e.g., those with one hundred or more employees) or larger, they will often use a more traditional "top-down" strategy-setting process. Traditional strategy is characterized by a focus on plan-ning, done by the senior team (sometimes with consulting assistance), on a regular basis (e.g., annual cycle), involving detailed research (of markets, competitor posi-tioning, customer preferences, and so forth) (see Table I.2). Figure I.4 illustrates the difference between dynamic and traditional approaches to Andrews' (1971) four main strategy components: *external analysis, internal analysis, strategy selection*, and *strategy execution*.

Table I.2 Traditional strategy process

Focus	Planning
Who	Senior management, strategy team, consultants ("top-down")
When	Annual cycle
How	Detailed research
Where	Centralized/headquarters

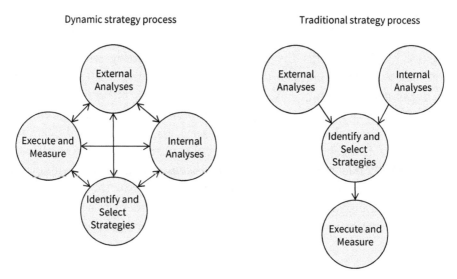

Figure I.4 Difference between dynamic and traditional approaches to Andrews' four main strategy components

Inductive versus Deductive Strategy

Inductive Strategy

Inductive reasoning starts with broad observations and data collection, subsequently using patterns identified within the observed data to form specific theories. Therefore, *inductive strategy* starts with broad observations via quantitative and qualitative data-gathering (e.g., market data, customer data, competitor data, and so forth) to detect patterns and regularities. This information is then used to identify potential strategies the organization may want to pursue (e.g., entry into new markets or launching new products or services).

Two key dangers are frequently encountered with the inductive strategy approach. The first is "analysis paralysis" due to the extreme amount of data available when attempting to identify patterns and regularities upon which the firm can base their choice of strategies to pursue. The second is pattern-matching, which leads to decisions based on what worked before. Errors tend to occur in pattern recognition, where management's "I've seen this before" bias exists, and managers might ignore disconfirming information and be confident they have recognized or understood the pattern. This leads to the possibility that the wrong strategic decision may be taken. Additional analysis of the potential strategies such as the investment required, implementation considerations, projected return on investment, and so forth can help mitigate these pitfalls and assist management in deciding upon a shortlist of strategies to implement.

Deductive Strategy

Deductive reasoning works the other way around, starting with one or more hypotheses, then collecting data to validate or invalidate each hypothesis. Thus, *deductive strategy* (a technique used by many strategic consulting firms) starts with identifying potential strategies the organization may want to pursue (e.g., entry into new markets or launching new products or services). Then, targeted quantitative and qualitative data collection (e.g., market data, customer data, competitor data, and so forth) is conducted to support or rebut each potential strategy, with management then pursuing those strategies supported by the analysis. The key risk found in the deductive strategy approach is "confirmation bias" where data is collected that lends itself to supporting the choice of management's previously favored strategies (see Figure I.5).

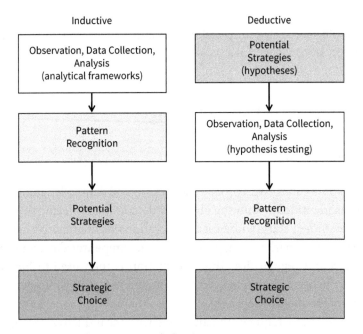

Figure I.5 Inductive versus deductive strategy

Intuition Is Part of the Strategy Process

Strategy identification and selection frequently involves overt data collection and analysis (market analysis, competitor analysis, financial analysis, operational analysis, and so on) and oftentimes a lot of it. However, beyond formal data and cold hard facts, humans have biases. Therefore, intuition or "gut feel" always plays a part in the strategy process. Early on, Mintzberg (1987) asserted that although data helps managers with strategic decision-making, personal knowledge and an intimate understanding of their business and industry also have a part to play in management's ability to choose effective strategies. Since Mintzberg's assertion, various studies have demonstrated that managers' intuition plays an integral part in the strategy process (Betsch and Kunz, 2008; Matzler et al., 2014; Pretz, 2008). Intuition, however, is not just making things up. Intuition is informed by a person's experience and observation, which are more informal and less overt sources of data collection and analysis. As Matzler and colleagues state, "Most managers would be unable to work effectively if they couldn't rely on their ability to extract relevant information from the many reports and charts they are confronted with daily. Thanks to their experience, skilled managers can 'read between the lines' and recognize patterns, rather than consider all possible information in detail" (2014, p. 34). Accordingly, use your intuition during the strategy process, but at the same time be aware of your biases.

Functional Strategies

The discussion, tools, templates, and approaches to strategy presented throughout the following chapters will focus on "firm-wide" business strategy. However, functional strategies are a key part of broader business strategy formulation and implementation. Human resources (HR), information technology (IT), marketing, operations, finance, accounting and tax, legal, and other functions contribute to the overall development, execution, and success of a firm's business strategy. Therefore, each "functional strategy" must be aligned with the business strategy. For example, if the firm's growth strategy is to enter new (for the firm) international markets, each functional strategy should be designed to help enable international market entry by answering functional-level questions, including:

- *HR*: what talent do we need to hire and what are the HR regulations and protocols in each market?
- *IT*: what technology needs to be in place in each market?
- *Marketing*: what are the differences in local promotional techniques and content in each market?
- *Legal*: what are the legal and regulatory requirements in each market?
- *Finance*: how will we fund the expansion into each market?
- *Accounting and tax*: what are the local accounting standards and tax requirements in each market?

Reasons for Strategic Change

Various reasons exist that encourage an organization to change strategy. The main reasons for a change of strategy include the following.

Underperformance. Many organizations regularly review the effectiveness of their current strategies. Some firms continuously monitor progress via "strategy dashboards" that track progress against desired strategic outcomes. Strategy dashboards are often organized by the four categories of the widely used "balanced scorecard": financial, customer, business process, and innovation and learning measures (Kaplan and Norton, 2005). Other organizations use a quarterly, half-yearly, or annual review cycle, while others use a longer review cycle. In any case, if a strategy is not delivering the projected results, management may decide it is time for a change of strategy. Table I.3 presents an example strategy review template.

Table I.3 Example strategy review template

Current strategy (key strategic initiatives)	Key performance indicators (KPIs) (is the strategy working?)	Recommendation
Superior sales and service	• Revenue growth • Customer retention • Customer feedback	• Better execution
Acquisitions	• Revenue growth • Cost synergies capture • Market share	• Update (pause to absorb completed deals)
Innovation (product, service, business model innovation)	• Revenue growth • Number of new products launched • Time to product launch	• Better execution
New target customer segment(s)	• Revenue growth • Market share • Customer feedback	• New strategy (limited current uptake)

Black swan events. The phrase is a metaphor that describes an event that comes as a surprise and has a major effect on regional or global societies, economies, and the organizations that operate within them. Example black swan events include pandemics, war, economic crashes, and natural disasters.

Change of leadership. Often when a new person takes on the top leadership role (e.g., CEO, board chair, or president) she or he will want to "put their stamp" on the organization by changing strategy.

Competitive pressures. An organization may change strategy when existing or new competition gains a market or performance advantage over the firm.

Political or regulatory requirements. New political policies or regulations that impact the industry or market in which a firm operates, or that impact only the individual firm, can create the need for strategic change.

Activist investors. Activist shareholders have become much more involved in trying to incite senior management to change the firm's strategy (see Chapter 12).

Participants and Key Activities

Strategy is a team sport (see Figure I.6), involving multiple internal and external participants who perform essential activities, including:

- *Senior executives.* Identify and communicate the firm's strategic management components (*mission, vision, values, goals, strategy,* and *measures*).
- *Internal strategy team.* Some firms (usually mid- to large-sized organizations) have established internal strategy teams who collect and analyze relevant external and internal data to assist senior management with strategy identification and selection.
- *External strategy consultants.* Assist senior management and the internal strategy team with data collection and analysis that shapes strategy identification and selection.

Figure I.6 Strategy is a team sport

- *Board of directors.* Work with senior management to approve, guide, and shape the strategic priorities of the organization.
- *Functional managers.* Provide essential functional information to help shape the organization's strategy identification and selection.
- *Middle management and employees.* Democratized strategy processes involve representatives of middle management and front-line employees, who are knowledgeable about the day-to-day operations of the business and who have continuous contact with customers, to help shape the organization's strategy.
- *Key customers.* Democratized strategy processes can also involve representatives of key customers who bring the "user's view" of the organization's products and services.
- *Activist shareholders.* Activist shareholders have become much more involved in trying to influence an organization's strategic direction (see Chapter 12).

Best Practices

Use data to mitigate personal bias. Although intuition plays a role in the strategy process, and, depending on the organization, often a prominent role, those working on the strategy process should guard against intuition turning into detrimental bias. Personal bias is unavoidable but it can limit considering strategic alternatives that may be more advantageous to the organization's future than a favorite strategy of the most senior decision-maker. You cannot *eliminate* your own or others' biases but you can use data to *mitigate* the effect of personal bias in the strategy process.

Democratize traditional strategy. Although traditional strategy is a top-down driven process conducted by the senior team (and their consultants), the top-down approach can include broader input from both internal stakeholders (middle management and employees) and external stakeholders (customers and investors). Sampling these groups for their views of potentially desirable strategies makes for a more robust strategy formulation process.

Use appropriate frameworks. A multitude of frameworks and tools exist to help with strategy formulation and implementation. However, no single strategy framework is useful in all situations. Learning how and when to use the various tools available will help expedite and augment the organization's strategy process.

Assign a "devil's advocate." A person assigned within the senior team to make the case for why a particular proposed strategy should *not* be pursued can help moderate any management biases and/or groupthink that may occur, helping management to genuinely think through the rationale for and validity of each proposed strategy.

Align all aspects of the strategic management system. Alignment throughout the organization around the firm's *mission, vision, values, goals, strategy,* and *measures* facilitates consistency throughout the organization regarding the firm's strategic intentions and how to achieve them.

Align functional strategies with the business strategy. Aligning functional strategies to enable execution of the overall business strategy facilitates business strategy success.

Potential Pitfalls

Analysis paralysis. Inductive strategy, beginning with broad data collection, identifying trends, then identifying potential strategies for the organization to take advantage of those trends, can get caught up in endless analysis rather than actual strategy identification and selection.

Confirmation bias. A deductive strategy approach, beginning with identifying potential strategies, lends itself to collecting data that merely validates a strategy management already favors.

Intuition only. Because management often believe they "know" their business, their industry, and their markets, they may discount the value of objective data collection and analysis during the strategy process.

Groupthink. In situations where a senior team is composed of members with similar experiences, from the same industry and even the same organization, throughout their careers a tendency exists among the team to fall into groupthink (quickly locking in on one viewpoint) around strategic options.

Organizational misalignment. Failing to align all areas of the organization around the firm's strategic management components (*mission, vision, values, goals, strategy,* and *measures*) and not aligning functional strategies with the overall business strategy leads to confusion and ultimately marginalizes an organization's strategic outcomes.

Key Frameworks, Tools, and Templates

Strategy frameworks and templates are useful tools that provide structure when analyzing a multitude of quantitative and qualitative information that feeds into strategic decision-making. Like the example strategy review template (Table I.3) above, throughout the subsequent chapters various frameworks, tools, and templates are presented that help structure strategy formulation and execution. Applying analytical frameworks during the strategy process serves several purposes, including:

- *Targeting information.* To facilitate focused data-gathering.
- *Organizing information.* Assisting with applying the most relevant data to various aspects of the strategy process (e.g., market data, customer data, operational data, and so on).

- *Prioritizing information.* Data should be prioritized by its importance to and potential impact on the future of the organization.
- *Analyzing information.* Structured analysis facilitates more efficient decision-making, as it enables decision-makers to focus on the most important and relevant data.
- *Communicating information.* Structured data collection and analysis facilitates more consistent and easily digestible information when communicating with various stakeholders.

Best-Practice Case Example

A description of MidTech Inc.'s approach to the strategy process in practice is summarized in Table I.4.

Table I.4 The strategy process at MidTech Inc.*

The need:

- Senior management of MidTech (a European-based, mid-sized technology company with approximately 1,500 employees who provides business software) realized that their previously accelerated growth was significantly slowing, and that existing and new competition were gaining a performance advantage over them.
- The firm operated in a rapidly changing market environment.
- The CEO decided that a new strategy was required and that the firm needed a more "inclusive, stakeholder-oriented strategy process."

The solution:

- Rather than engaging an advisory firm to assist the top management team with formulating a new strategy, senior management engaged a consulting firm to assist them with establishing a new "strategy process" that included regular strategy reviews and, in addition to the senior management team, involved middle management and employees.
- The firm implemented a "strategy dashboard" that monitored firm progress in the four areas of the balanced scorecard: financial, customer, business process, and innovation and learning measures.
- Senior management also established a "democratized strategy process" that included representatives from middle management, employees, and key customers in their quarterly strategy reviews.

The results:

- Over a subsequent five-year period after implementing their democratized strategy process, MidTech regained their revenue and market share growth trajectory by entering new geographic markets and reported higher profitability than their benchmark industry competitors.

---

* Because of non-disclosure considerations, a mid-sized technology company is referred to throughout the illustration as MidTech Inc.

Chapter Summary

- Strategy is an ancient pursuit with its roots in military strategy.
- In the business environment, strategy has evolved through various eras including the invisible hand, the visible hand, strategic factors, management science, planning departments, strategy teaching in business schools, establishment of strategy consulting firms, and from the economic view to the value-creation view.
- Strategy terms mean different things to different people. Therefore, it is essential to level-set across an organization the meaning of key terms such as *strategic planning*, *strategic management*, and *strategic thinking*, as well as each component of a firm's strategic management system including *mission, vision, values, goals, strategy*, and *measures*.
- Many strategic thinking skills develop over time from an executive's personal, interpersonal, and career experiences.
- Strategy can be deliberate, emergent, or a combination of both.
- There are key differences between traditional and dynamic approaches to strategy.
- Democratized strategy reaches beyond the senior management team by involving representatives of internal and external stakeholder groups.
- Inductive strategy starts with broad observations via quantitative and qualitative data-gathering, with the information then used to identify potential strategies the organization may want to pursue.
- Deductive strategy starts with identifying potential strategies the organization may want to pursue, then targeted quantitative and qualitative data collection is conducted to support or rebut each potential strategy.
- Intuition or "gut feel" is part of the strategy process but can result in too much personal bias driving a firm's strategy process.
- Functional strategies have a key role as a part of business strategy formulation and implementation.
- Various reasons exist that encourage an organization to change strategy, including underperformance, black swan events, change of leadership, competitive pressures, new political or regulatory requirements, and pressure from activist investors.
- There can be multiple internal and external participants involved in the strategy process, including senior executives, an internal strategy team, external strategy consultants, the board of directors, middle management and employees, key customers, and activist shareholders.
- Best practices of the strategy process include using data to mitigate personal bias, democratizing traditional strategy to garner more varied views, using appropriate frameworks for more structured strategic analysis and implementation, assigning a "devil's advocate" to mitigate groupthink, aligning

all aspects of the strategic management system, and aligning functional strategies with the business strategy to alleviate potential stakeholder confusion.
- Potential pitfalls of the strategy process include analysis paralysis, confirmation bias, intuition only, groupthink, and organizational misalignment.
- Strategy frameworks, tools, and templates are useful tools that help target, organize, prioritize, analyze, and communicate information that supports strategic decision-making.

Discussion Questions

1. What activities does your organization do well regarding its strategy process? What aspects of the strategy process could your organization perform better?
2. Who is typically involved in your organization's strategy process? Who should be involved?
3. Which approach does your organization use: dynamic or traditional strategy? Which approach should they use?
4. How often does your organization review its strategy? Should the frequency of strategy reviews change and, if so, why?
5. How does your organization monitor "strategic success"? What aspects should be monitored?
6. What are the typical reasons your organization has changed strategy? Should there be other reasons for strategic change considered in the future?

Organizational Self-Assessment

Completing the following self-assessment (Table I.5) will provide a view of how effective your organization's strategy process is.

Steps to complete the self-assessment:

1. Rate each item on a scale of 0 (poor) to 10 (excellent).
2. Make notes for each item to explain the rationale for the numerical rating.
3. Add all ten scores to get a TOTAL SCORE (maximum score = 100).

Rating scale:

0–20 = Poor (significant improvement needed)
21–40 = Below average (improvement needed in several areas)
41–60 = Average (identify areas of weakness and adjust)
61–80 = Above average (identify areas that can still be improved)
81–100 = Excellent (continuously review and refine each component for each iteration of the organization's strategy efforts)

Table I.5 Organizational self-assessment: strategy process

Component	Rating (0 = poor, 10 = excellent)	Notes/rationale
When it comes to our strategy process …		
1. We have a clear process		
2. We regularly monitor our strategic performance		
3. We have "democratized" our process		
4. We use data to mitigate personal bias in the process		
5. We use appropriate frameworks throughout the process		
6. We conduct the appropriate amount of analysis and avoid "analysis paralysis"		
7. We assign a "devil's advocate" within the senior team to make the case for why a proposed strategy should *not* be done to help moderate management biases and/or groupthink		
8. We align all aspects of our strategic management system (mission, vision, values, goals, strategy, and measures) across the organization		
9. We align functional strategies with the business strategy		
10. We would be considered "best practice"		
TOTAL SCORE		

PART I
STRATEGY FORMULATION

1

Predicting the Future

At its core, strategy is about predicting the future. Markets, consumers, geopolitics, economies, demographics, and even the weather, among many other factors, might impact an organization's future performance over time. Some factors change rapidly and some more slowly. Of course, no one can accurately, or at least consistently, predict the future environment within which a firm will operate. There are too many variables. Simple guesswork might suffice, but guessing is not the best method, unless you want to leave your organization's future performance to chance. Therefore, in this chapter we will examine the approaches, tools, best practices, and potential pitfalls of the "external analysis" element of the strategy process (see Figure 1.1).

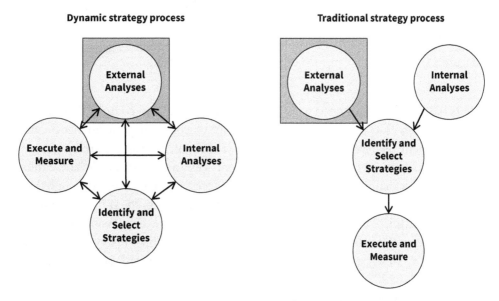

Figure 1.1 Difference between dynamic and traditional approaches to Andrews' four main strategy components: external analysis

Industry Analysis

How Much Does Industry Matter to a Company's Profitability?

Both internal and external factors matter to a company's profitability performance. But which matters most to company profitability—the industry it operates in, the country it operates in, or characteristics of the firm itself? The answer to this question

The Strategist's Handbook. Timothy Galpin, Oxford University Press. © Timothy Galpin (2023).
DOI: 10.1093/oso/9780192885203.003.0002

is often surprising. According to two different studies (McGahan and Porter, 1997; Rumelt, 1991), in developed economies, company characteristics have about three times more impact on profitability than industry factors. However, in emerging economies, company characteristics have over *twenty times* more impact than either industry or country factors (Etiennot et al., 2013) (see Figure 1.2).

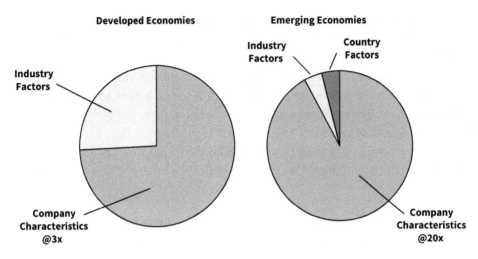

Figure 1.2 Industry, company, and country effects on profitability

It is not unusual to disagree with the data in Figure 1.2 and contend that in some regions "country factors" have an outsized impact on company performance because of government regulations that limit access to a country's market. Likewise, company owners with "connections to government" can (and often do) leverage those connections to facilitate business licensing and access to the market. Although these aspects very much exist in some countries, for the purposes of the studies mentioned above and for this text, connections with local government are classified as a "company characteristic," also known as an "internal organizational resource," discussed in Chapter 2, which addresses the topics of "internal analysis" and "strategically valuable resources."

Why Industry Analysis Matters

When it comes to firm performance, since company characteristics greatly overshadow industry factors, you might logically ask: should industry analysis even matter? Yes, because financial performance varies significantly between industries. For example, a McKinsey study spanning over forty years and twenty industries found that the top three industries—pharmaceuticals, household personal products, and software services—achieved a median return on invested capital (ROIC) of 21 percent, 18 percent, and 18 percent, respectively. Meanwhile, the bottom three industries in the same study—transportation, telecom services, and utilities—achieved a median ROIC of 8 percent, 7 percent, and 7 percent, respectively (Jiang and Koller, 2006). Therefore, the industry a firm operates in will impact overall performance because of various industry structural elements such as available suppliers, competition, common pricing practices for products and services, customer bargaining power, and so forth.

Moreover, industries progress through a "lifecycle" (Johnson et al., 2017) and the stage of the industry's lifecycle often dictates the strategy firms within the industry pursue. Table 1.1 illustrates the various stages of an industry lifecycle and the potential strategies that firms within the industry might pursue to succeed during each stage.

Industries Now Overlap

For over 200 years, commerce has transitioned through various "industrial revolutions." The first industrial revolution saw the mechanization of production and transportation through steam power. The second involved electrification, mass production, and assembly lines. The third gave rise to the adoption of computers and

Table 1.1 Industry lifecycle stages and potential strategies

Stage	Common characteristics	Potential strategies for success
Introduction	• Low rivalry among competitors • High differentiation between firms • High innovation	• Product or service innovation
Growth	• Low rivalry among competitors • High growth and weak "buyer power" • Low barriers to entry	• Greater market penetration through lower pricing and/or enhanced sales and marketing efforts
Shakeout	• Increasing rivalry among competitors • Slower growth • Some firms exit because of competitive pressures • Managerial and financial strength	• Enter new geographic markets • Access new customer segments • Introduce new products or services
Maturity	• High rivalry among competitors • Slowing growth • Standardization of products and services across the industry • Stronger "buyer power" • Higher barriers to entry barriers	• Diversify into new industries • Merge or acquire for market share growth and/or cost efficiencies
Decline	• Extreme rivalry among competitors • Many firms exit because of extreme competitive pressures and declining growth • Lack of available financing	• Diversify into new industries if funding is attainable • Merge for survival via cost efficiencies • Sell the firm

automation. Now, "industry 4.0" is building upon the technology introduced in the third revolution. The fourth revolution is characterized by extensive data analytics, machine learning, and the embedding of technology into everyday products such as automobiles, appliances, and energy, changing the way we use, produce, and deliver all manner of products and services, giving rise to and accelerating "industry convergence" (Marr, 2018).

Consequently, defining a company's industry is not as clear as it once was because industries now overlap. For example, is Airbnb a technology company or a hospitality firm? What about Uber? Airbnb competes with hotels and Uber with taxis, but their shares trade in the realm of tech firms. Amazon? The firm's shares trade in the stratospheric valuation range of tech firms, but Amazon competes with all varieties of retailers, as well as "cloud-providing" tech companies. Same for Tesla, with its shares trading as a tech firm but competing with automobile manufacturers including Ford, Nissan, GM, Honda, Toyota, BMW, Mercedes, and so forth. Why should it matter how we define these firms? Because the industry a firm competes in plays a significant role in the "external analysis" upon which to base strategic decisions. Identifying industry competitors, trends, suppliers, consumers, regulations, and so on all feed into predicting a firm's potential future operating environment.

Identify, Prioritize, and Analyze Variables that Matter Most to Your Industry and Organization

Myriad variables shape a firm's current and future external environment. However, there are simply too many variables to consider them all. Therefore, prioritizing the variables that will matter most to a firm's future operating environment is key to making any external analysis manageable. Moreover, the prioritization may change as time horizons extend. For example, the cost of jet fuel in the near and medium term will impact airline companies' decisions about the composition of their fleet, choice of routes, and ticket pricing, whereas the potential longer-term future development of alternative aircraft power systems including battery, solar, and hydrogen will shape different strategic decisions for airlines.

External Strategic Analysis Identifies a Firm's Future Opportunities and Threats

SWOT (Strengths, Weaknesses, Opportunities, Threats) is an archetypal overarching strategic analysis tool widely used across industries as part of numerous firms' strategic analysis efforts. The framework encompasses both the external factors and internal characteristics of an organization (Learned et al., 1965). The "OT"

	Opportunities	Threats
External Factors	The external trends that present potential areas that the organization can take advantage of in the future such as population growth, increasing spending power of customers, or the availability of new technologies.	The external factors that present potential damage or hindrances to the organization's future, such as increased competition, shifting customer preferences, or disruption of raw materials supply.
Internal Factors	Strengths	Weaknesses

Figure 1.3 SWOT framework: external factors

Note that a common mistake made when conducting strategic analysis using the SWOT framework is to confuse "opportunities" (future external conditions) with "strategies" (actions firms can take). To mitigate this confusion, in the context of the SWOT analysis a useful synonym for "opportunities" is "trends" that identify and quantify potential future developments that the organization can capitalize on. For example, trends such as regional population growth, increasing spending power of consumers in a particular country, or the advancement of new technologies present "opportunities" (future external conditions) for an organization, whereas many people during their "opportunities identification" portion of the SWOT analysis identify "strategies" or "how" the firm can take advantage of the identified trends (e.g., enter the region, establish a presence in the country, or install the new technology). Remember, the selection of strategies such as these comes a bit later in the strategy process (see Chapter 3).

(Opportunities and Threats) elements address the external aspects of the SWOT analysis (see Figure 1.3).

While the SWOT framework is often used on its own, additional "sub-frameworks" can be applied to conduct a more granular analysis of an organization's external and internal strategic factors. Two of the most popular strategic analysis frameworks that feed into the external "opportunities" and "threats" elements of the SWOT analysis are the Five Forces industry analysis and the PESTEL analysis.

The Five Forces Industry Analysis

The Five Forces model (Porter, 1979) examines five industry elements that impact an organization's performance relative to other organizations in the same industry. Conducting a Five Forces analysis provides data that feeds into the external "OT" (Opportunities and Threats) elements of a SWOT analysis, helping management understand where a firm fits in the industry landscape, how it currently competes within the industry, and how it might position itself in the future. In a follow-up piece to his original Five Forces article, Porter (2008) emphasized that understanding the overall industry structure as well as the competitive forces at play is a vital element of effective strategic decision-making to develop an effective competitive organizational strategy. He states, "Understanding the competitive forces, and their underlying causes, reveals the roots of an industry's current profitability while providing a framework for anticipating and influencing competition (and profitability) over time" (p. 80). The five industry forces identified by Porter are:

Competitive rivalry: identifies the industry competitors and examines the intensity of market competition. Considerations include the number of competitors, the capabilities, and the market share of each. Competitive rivalry is often greater when an industry is growing, or when there are only a few industry players who control most of the market, or when customers are easily able to switch to a competitor's offering with little effort or cost. Price wars are a key dynamic of elevated competitive rivalry. Useful data for this portion of the Five Forces analysis includes the number of competitors, diversity of competitors, industry concentration and market share, industry growth, pricing and quality differences between competitors, brand loyalty, and customer switching costs.

Bargaining power of suppliers: examines how much power a business' suppliers have and the potential ability of suppliers to raise their prices. The number of suppliers of raw materials and potential alternatives for obtaining a firm's inputs are key considerations. The fewer suppliers that exist, the more bargaining power each supplier maintains. Therefore, it is advantageous to firms in the industry when there are multiple suppliers. Common data analysis regarding this force includes the number and size of suppliers, the uniqueness of each supplier's products or services, and potential alternatives to current suppliers.

Bargaining power of buyers: assesses the power of consumers to impact industry pricing, quality, and service offerings. The fewer the number of consumers, the more power they possess, especially if there are a high number of sellers and it is easy and not costly for consumers to switch between vendors. Conversely, buyer power is lower when they purchase small amounts of products and when a seller's product is unique compared to those of its competitors. Typical data analysis regarding this force includes the number of customers, the average size of customer purchases, differences between the offerings of various competitors, price sensitivity, the availability of alternative products and services, and switching costs for buyers to purchase goods or services from a competitor.

Threat of new entrants: considers how easy or difficult it is for new competitors to join an industry. The easier it is for new competitors to enter an industry, the higher the risk of existing competitors' market shares to diminish. Barriers to the entry of new competition include incumbents' cost advantages, access to inputs, economies of scale, and established brand identity. Typical data collected for this analysis includes barriers to entry, economies of scale, brand loyalty, capital requirements to enter the industry, and switching costs for buyers to purchase goods or services from new entrants.

Threat of substitute products or services: this force examines the availability of alternative products or services to what the industry competitors provide. Key data collection elements include the number of potential substitutes available, the cost of substitute products or services, and switching costs for buyers to purchase substitute goods or services.

Advantages and Disadvantages of the Five Forces Analysis

One advantage of the Five Forces framework is the widespread applicability of the analysis across industries, as each force (competitors, suppliers, buyers, potential substitutes, and possible new entrants) exists, at least to some extent, in all industries. A second advantage is the enduring nature of the Five Forces. Each of the forces existed within all industries long before Porter categorized them, and each force will be a part of competitive industries for centuries to come. The primary disadvantage of the Five Forces analysis is due to industry convergence and overlap (see the discussion of industry 4.0 above), making the clear identification of and data collection about industry competitors, buyers, suppliers, new entrants, and substitutes much more problematic than when industry boundaries were more easily delineated.

Criticisms of the Five Forces Analysis

One criticism of the Five Forces framework is that it fails to explain "strategic alliances" within industries. Consequently, almost two decades after Porter's seminal article, Brandenburger and Nalebuff (1996) introduced the concept of a "sixth force" they called "complementors," which provide products and services that are best used in conjunction with a product or service from another provider. Alliances and cooperation between microchip producers and computer manufacturers, airlines and hotel chains, charging station providers and electric vehicle manufacturers, and e-reader makers and book publishers are all examples of complementors. A second criticism is that the Five Forces is a market analysis, whereas "nonmarket forces" also impact various industries and the firms that compete within them. Nonmarket forces include governmental regulations and the influence of the media and citizen groups (see Chapter 9).

External Analysis beyond the Industry

Beyond the five industry forces, myriad other external factors exist that can also affect future organizational performance and strategic decision-making. The PESTEL framework (Aguilar, 1967) provides six categories of external factors, helping management target useful data and identify trends that can contribute to the external "OT" (Opportunities and Threats) elements of a SWOT analysis. The six categories of the PESTEL framework are:

Political: includes factors that can be used to determine the extent to which various governments and their policies may influence an industry or a company. For example, a newly introduced governmental trade policy can change a firm's access to the market, impacting the future revenue of the company either by opening access (presenting an "opportunity" to grow revenue) or preventing previously allowed access (creating a "threat" by reducing future company revenue). Political factors include government policies, political stability, corruption, trade policies and restrictions, tax policies, and labor laws.

Economic: these factors assess the state of global, regional, and local economic activity and performance that directly impact a company currently and in the future. For instance, rising inflation affects the cost of raw materials, labor costs, and the pricing of a firm's products and services. Additionally, inflation affects consumer purchasing power and can change customer demand. Economic factors include economic growth and decline, exchange rates, cost of capital, consumer disposable income, and unemployment rates.

Social: considers factors that impact consumer lifestyle trends and preferences, workforce concerns, and regional and local cultural dynamics. Social factors are particularly important to an organization's future marketing efforts, revenue growth, and workforce profile. Social factors include population growth rates, age and gender distributions, career attitudes, workforce employment and working environment preferences, lifestyle attitudes, and cultural norms and behaviors.

Technological: these factors include the innovations and developments in information, communication, production, transportation, and distribution technologies, all of which can affect an organization's operations, costs, revenue, and competitive positioning. Technological factors include global, regional, and local levels of innovation, automation, research and development activity, and consumer adoption rates of new technologies.

Environmental: encompasses factors concerned with the ecological aspects affecting an organization. This category is fundamental to certain industries such as agriculture, energy, and tourism. Environmental factors can present opportunities for future firm market share and revenue growth, as well as creating threats to the firm by adding costs or reducing revenue. Technological factors include weather patterns, climate shifts, regional and local environmental policies and regulation, and consumer preferences regarding environmental impact.

Legal: these factors include matters that can impact an organization's talent profile, access to raw materials, imports and exports, taxation, and consumer interaction. Moreover, legal elements often differ between regions and individual countries. Legal factors include employment laws, antitrust regulations, consumer protection, intellectual property, and health and safety protocols.

Advantages

The PESTEL analysis offers several advantages. First, the framework provides a broader understanding of the business environment a firm operates in beyond the five industry forces. Second, the six component categories are applicable across all industries and geographies, although some categories are more relevant to some industries. Third, like the five industry forces, the six PESTEL categories endure over time. The six categories existed well before they were included in the framework, and each category will remain a part of all organizations' external environments for the foreseeable future. Fourth, a PESTEL analysis enables management to identify future trends that present both opportunities for revenue growth, service improvement, and cost reduction, as well as threats in the form of lower revenue or higher costs. Finally, a PESTEL analysis also helps develop management's broad strategic thinking capabilities.

Disadvantages

The PESTEL analysis also has several potential disadvantages. There is a danger of oversimplifying the data collection and using insufficient data for strategic decisions. Conversely, management can easily get caught in "analysis paralysis" given the enormous amounts of data available within each of the six categories. Therefore, prioritization of data collection and analysis is crucial to conducting an efficient and effective PESTEL analysis. Moreover, management assumptions about the trajectory and importance of future trends within each category may be incorrect. Finally, the pace of change within each of the six categories makes it difficult to accurately anticipate future developments upon which to base strategic decisions.

Identifying Potential Futures

Often, multiple future developments may occur within each of the Five Forces and PESTEL categories. Some identified developments may advance more quickly or more slowly than anticipated, while some may not occur at all. Therefore, "scenario planning" (Ramírez et al., 2017) is a key tool to help management prioritize potential future developments identified by both the Five Forces and PESTEL analyses upon which to base strategic decisions. Effective scenario planning entails:

Table 1.2 Example probability-weighted scenario planning

	Key elements/ characteristics (from PESTEL analysis)	Probability (%)	Impact on the business (1=low, 10=high)	Probability-weighted impact*
Scenario 1: Increased environmental regulation	• New environmental regulation introduced in the next 24 months	80%	4	3.2
Scenario 2: Economic downturn	• Global economic downturn in the next 12 months	50%	10	5.0
Scenario 3: New industry entrants with new technology	• Disruptive technology introduced in the next 36 months	100%	8	8

* Multiply the impact on the business by the probability percentage.

(1) identifying several potential future developments within all or a subset of the Five Forces and PESTEL categories, (2) determining the probability of each development, and (3) choosing strategies to capitalize on the potential opportunities or minimize the threats presented by the most probable scenarios. Table 1.2 illustrates a probability-weighted scenario planning example.

Macro and Micro Trends

The word "trend" is found in numerous business reports, academic papers, strategic analyses, and strategic plans (Peloso, 2020). A common definition of a trend is the identification of societal changes and developments (Kjaer, 2014). Identifying trends presenting "opportunities" an organization can capitalize on, as well as those that pose potential "threats" to the organization's future, is fundamental to external strategic analysis. A Five Forces analysis helps identify trends across the five industry elements of the framework, while a PESTEL analysis helps identify trends that can impact a firm beyond the industry it operates in. However, various subsets of trends exist (Haberman, 2016), including:

Fads. Common in the fitness, clothing, food, and beauty products industries. A
  fad is something that quickly becomes popular and often disappears just as
  quickly, often lasting a year or less (e.g., seasonal clothing styles), but may
  continue a bit longer.
Micro and macro trends. Although there is no clearly defined timeline that separates a fad from a trend, trends last longer and occur on a much wider
  scale than fads. Regarding timing, a micro trend typically lasts from three to

five years (e.g., hairstyles), while a macro trend lasts longer, in the five- to ten-year timeframe or longer (e.g., new exercise or diet approaches). From a scale perspective, a micro trend is often popular among a particular segment of the population (e.g., new clothing designs in Europe), but a macro trend is popular across the broader population (e.g., the use of social media). It takes longer for macro trends to become broadly popular. However, once they do develop across a wider population, macro trends gain the staying power to create long-lasting shifts in the market.

Megatrends

Fads are short in duration and often narrow in scope, trends last longer and their scope is broader, whereas megatrends are enduring, take years to progress, and impact the entire world. According to the Copenhagen Institute for Future Studies (2022), "Megatrends are the probable global future, and express what we know with great confidence about the future." Current megatrends include aging populations in various regions, accelerating technologies across industries, and the urbanization of societies around the world.

Black Swans

A "black swan" event is a metaphor describing a surprise occurrence that has a major regional or global societal and economic effect. Taleb (2007) identifies three attributes of black swan events: (1) the event is unpredictable, (2) the event has widespread societal and/or economic ramifications, and (3) there is "hindsight bias" as after the event has occurred people assert that it was explainable and predictable. There is often debate about whether certain events should be classified as "black swans," but examples of widely acknowledged black swan events include the bursting of the dotcom bubble, the 9/11 attacks, the financial crash of 2008–9, the Covid-19 pandemic, and the war in the Ukraine. While by definition black swan events are unpredictable, organizations can and should have contingency plans in place as there is a high likelihood that black swan events will occur at some point in the future, which will have a major impact on firms' operating environment.

Participants and Key Activities

There can be multiple internal and external participants involved in a firm's strategic external analysis who perform essential activities, including:

- *Senior executives.* Bring extensive knowledge and experience regarding industry dynamics, priorities, and trends.

- *Internal strategy team.* Identify, prioritize, collect, and regularly monitor external data to ascertain trends that will affect the future opportunities for and threats to the organization.
- *External strategy consultants.* Assist senior management and the internal strategy team with industry, market, and nonmarket data collection and analysis that shapes the organization's strategy identification and selection.
- *Board of directors.* In addition to senior management, board members bring extensive knowledge and experience regarding the dynamics, priorities, and trends within and outside the industry.
- *Functional managers.* Provide essential information about functional trends (talent profiles, technology trends, legal developments, and so forth) within and outside the industry to help shape the organization's strategy identification and selection.
- *Middle management and employees.* As part of a "democratized" strategy processes (see the Introduction), management and employees throughout the organization can provide extensive knowledge of market dynamics, competitor information, and customer preferences.
- *Key customers.* Also, as part of a "democratized" strategy process (see the Introduction), customers can provide extensive knowledge of market dynamics, competitor information, and consumer preferences.
- *Activist shareholders.* In addition to senior management and board members, activists can also bring extensive knowledge and experience regarding the dynamics, priorities, and trends within and outside the industry (see Chapter 12).

Best Practices

Prioritize data. Not all categories of the Five Forces or PESTEL frameworks will be equally important to your industry or firm. Companies operating within "mature" industries, characterized by incumbent firms having all or most of the market share, often prioritize the "competitive rivalry" category of their Five Forces analysis. Industries in transition such as the automobile industry find that "new technologies" and "new entrants" are the most important aspects of their Five Forces analysis. The energy industry, which is seeing a major shift to renewables, focuses on the "environmental" and "social" areas of the PESTEL analysis. Likewise, not all data within a particular category of each framework will be equally important to a firm's strategic analysis. For example, understanding the magnitude and timeframes of shifting demographic trends such as aging populations in many countries is highly important to the future of firms in the travel, investment, and healthcare industries.

Regularly update the data. All elements of the Five Forces and PESTEL analyses are in a continuous state of flux. Moreover, the introduction of new technologies, changing customer preferences, and shifting industry dynamics continues to accelerate.

Therefore, firms need to constantly assess their external operating environments to stay abreast of new developments.

Use multiple data sources. Diverse sources of data will provide more valuable strategic insights. Sources of external data include government statistics, current and former employees, customers of the firm, customers of competitors, market research reports, management intuition, industry journals, employees from adjacent industries, and so forth.

Apply the 80/20 rule. In any of the Five Forces and PESTEL categories, it is easy to spend 80 percent of your time trying to find and analyze 20 percent more data. Because external analysis is concerned with predicting the future, no amount of data will enable management to accurately foretell the future environment within which the organization will operate. Hence, strategic decisions must be made based upon often limited and what may seem like insufficient data.

Potential Pitfalls

No prioritization. Simply identifying a "laundry list" of items under each Five Forces or PESTEL category can be useful to generate an overview of the external strategic factors that may positively or negatively impact an organization's future. However, not all factors will have an equal impact on a firm's future. Therefore, a much better approach is to prioritize the key external factors that are determined to have the biggest effect on the firm's potential direction and performance. Furthermore, a list of the key external factors will often vary from firm to firm even within the same industry. Prioritization of external factors can be based on various criteria such as the potential to increase or decrease the firm's costs, hinder or enhance operations, diminish or improve the pool of available talent, decrease or increase revenue, reduce or expand the availability of raw materials, and so forth.

One-off analysis. Strategic external factors are not stagnant and shift over time. Some factors will change quickly, while others evolve more slowly. In any event, external strategic analysis should be updated periodically or even continuously to stay abreast of changes to the organization's external environment.

Using qualitative information only. Using qualitative information such as customer feedback or commentary from industry experts is useful. However, quantitative data such as demographic statistics, population growth, financial analysis, market share statistics, and so forth is often more helpful to identify the significant trends that management should consider when determining the organization's future direction.

Analysis paralysis. With so much data available, it is easy to get caught up in endless data collection and analysis, never leading to any action. At some point, management must use the data to make strategic decisions, and not view data analysis as an end in and of itself.

Intuition only. Because management often believe they "know" their business, their industry, and their markets, they may discount the value of objective data collection and analysis about the organization's operating environment.

Key Frameworks, Tools, and Templates

Below are descriptions of key templates used to conduct external strategic analysis. These tools are included in Appendix B.

SWOT. Examines both the external (Opportunities and Threats) and internal (Strengths and Weaknesses) factors pertinent to an organization's strategic decision-making.

Five Forces. Examines key industry dynamics across five categories (Competitors, Suppliers, Customers, Substitutes, and New Entrants).

PESTEL. Examines key external factors beyond industry dynamics across six categories (Political, Economic, Social, Technological, Environmental, and Legal).

Scenario planning. Combines with the Five Forces and PESTEL analyses to identify potential future scenarios and their probability-weighted impact on the organization.

Best-Practice Case Example

A description of Global Mining Plc's approach to external strategic analysis in practice is summarized in Table 1.3.

Table 1.3   The external strategic analysis process at Global Mining Plc*

The need:

- Senior management of Global Mining Plc (a worldwide mining company) understood that the changing external operating environment would present future opportunities and threats to the firm.
- A rigorous assessment of future external trends was required as part of their strategy process.

The solution:

- The firm's internal strategy team conducted an analysis of external trends that were deemed most important to the company's future strategic direction.
- The economic, social, and environmental elements of the PESTEL analysis revealed that the accelerating shift to EVs (electric vehicles) and renewable energy would increase the demand for rare earth metals used in battery technology.
- Consumer preferences, pending governmental regulation, EV sales projections, and renewable energy growth statistics were all collected, analyzed, and presented to the senior management team.

The results:

- The senior team determined that the company needed to create a "future-focused portfolio" by acquiring various rare earth mining assets.

---

* Because of non-disclosure considerations, a worldwide mining company is referred to throughout the illustration as Global Mining Plc.

Chapter Summary

- At its core, strategy is about predicting the future.
- Simple guesswork about the organization's future external environment might suffice, but guessing is not the best method, unless you want to leave your organization's future performance to chance.
- The industry a firm operates in will impact overall company performance because of various industry structural elements.
- Industries progress through a "lifecycle," and the stage of the industry's lifecycle often dictates the strategy firms within the industry can pursue.
- For over 200 years, industry has transitioned through various "industrial revolutions."
- The fourth revolution has given rise to an accelerating "industry convergence"; consequently, defining a company's industry is not as clear as it once was because industries now overlap.
- Myriad variables shape a firm's current and future external environment.
- SWOT (Strengths, Weaknesses, Opportunities, Threats) is an archetypal overarching strategic analysis tool widely used across industries as part of numerous firms' strategic analysis efforts.
- While the SWOT framework can be used on its own, additional "sub-frameworks" can be applied to conduct a more granular analysis of an organization's external strategic factors, including the Five Forces industry analysis and PESTEL analysis.
- The Five Forces model examines five elements (Competitors, Suppliers, Customers, Substitutes, and New Entrants) that impact an organization's performance relative to other organizations in the same industry.
- Conducting a Five Forces analysis provides data that feeds into the external "OT" (Opportunities and Threats) elements of a SWOT analysis.
- Beyond the five industry forces, myriad other factors exist external to an organization that can also affect management's strategic decisions.
- The PESTEL framework examines key external factors beyond industry dynamics across six categories (Political, Economic, Social, Technological, Environmental, and Legal), which can also contribute to the external "OT" (Opportunities and Threats) elements of a SWOT analysis.
- Some developments identified within the six PESTEL categories may advance more quickly or more slowly than anticipated, while some may not occur at all.
- Scenario planning is a key tool to help management prioritize potential future developments identified by a Five Forces and PESTEL analysis.
- A common definition of a trend is the identification of societal changes and developments.
- A fad is something that quickly becomes popular and often disappears just as quickly.
- Trends last longer and occur on a much wider scale than fads.

- A micro trend typically lasts from three to five years and is often popular among a particular segment of the population, whereas a macro trend lasts longer and is popular across the broader population.
- Megatrends are enduring, take years to progress, and shift the world.
- A "black swan" event is a metaphor describing a surprise occurrence that has a major regional or global societal and economic effect.
- There can be multiple internal and external participants involved in a firm's strategic external analysis who perform essential activities, including senior executives, the internal strategy team, external strategy consultants, board members, middle management and employees, key customers, and activist shareholders.
- Best practices of external strategic analysis include prioritizing data, regularly updating data, using multiple data sources, and applying the 80/20 rule.
- Potential pitfalls of external strategic analysis include no prioritization of data, one-off analysis, using qualitative information only, analysis paralysis, and relying on management intuition only.
- Key tools that help structure external strategic analysis are Five Forces, PESTEL, and scenario planning.

Discussion Questions

1. What activities does your organization do well regarding its external strategic analysis?
2. What aspects of external analysis could your organization perform better?
3. Who is typically involved in external strategic analysis? Who should be involved?
4. How often does your organization conduct external analysis? Should the frequency of external analysis change and, if so, why?
5. What external data collection and analysis does your organization prioritize? What should be prioritized?

Organizational Self-Assessment

Completing the following self-assessment (Table 1.4) will provide a view of the effectiveness of your organization's external strategic analysis process.

Steps to complete the self-assessment:

1. Rate each item on a scale of 0 (poor) to 10 (excellent).
2. Make notes for each item to explain the rationale for the numerical rating.
3. Add all ten scores to get a TOTAL SCORE (maximum score = 100).

Table 1.4 Organizational self-assessment: external strategic analysis

Component	Rating (0 = poor, 10 = excellent)	Notes/rationale
When it comes to external strategic analysis …		
1. We regularly monitor our organization's external operating environment		
2. We prioritize external environment data that is most important to our organization		
3. We collect external data from multiple sources		
4. We involve various stakeholders		
5. We use both quantitative and qualitative data		
6. We conduct an appropriate amount of analysis and avoid "analysis paralysis"		
7. We use structured frameworks such as the Five Forces and PESTEL		
8. We use probability-weighted scenario planning		
9. We have contingency plans in place for the occurrence of "black swan" events		
10. We would be considered "best practice"		
TOTAL SCORE		

Rating scale:

0–20 = Poor (significant improvement needed)
21–40 = Below average (improvement needed in several areas)
41–60 = Average (identify areas of weakness and adjust)
61–80 = Above average (identify areas that can still be improved)
81–100 = Excellent (continuously review and refine each component for each iteration of the organization's strategy efforts)

2

Building Strategically Valuable Resources

Both internal and external factors matter to a company's strategic decisions and subsequent performance. As identified in Chapter 1, two separate studies (McGahan and Porter, 1997; Rumelt, 1991) found that in developed economies internal organizational attributes have about three times more impact on profitability than industry factors. Meanwhile, a third study found that in emerging economies organizational characteristics have more than twenty times more impact on firm performance than either industry or country factors (Etiennot et al., 2013). With this significant impact in mind, in this chapter we will examine the approaches, tools, best practices, and potential pitfalls of the "internal analysis" element of the strategy process (see Figure 2.1).

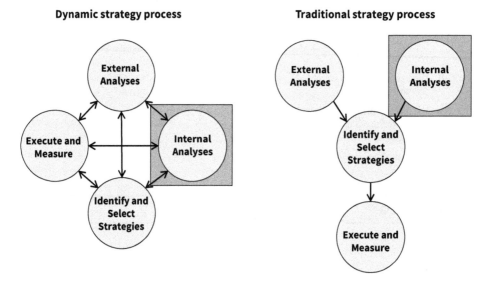

Figure 2.1 Difference between dynamic and traditional approaches to Andrews' four main strategy components: internal analysis

Organizational Resources

Defining an organization's resources is not as clear as it once was because organizational boundaries have become porous. For example, "platform" companies such as Airbnb and Uber own the technology that customers use to access their services. However, other essential resources include the Uber drivers and owners of properties listed on Airbnb—resources that are not "internal" to either organization.

The Strategist's Handbook. Timothy Galpin, Oxford University Press. © Timothy Galpin (2023).
DOI: 10.1093/oso/9780192885203.003.0003

Likewise, auto manufacturers such as GM, Ford, BMW, Mercedes, Honda, and Toyota rely on multitudes of parts suppliers that provide essential components but are not owned by the auto company. These and similar examples raise key questions, including: What exactly is a resource of the firm? Who controls the resource? Must all resources be "owned" by the firm to be "strategically valuable"? We will now explore these questions.

Strategically Valuable Resources

The resource-based view (RBV) proposes that management should look inside the firm to find sources of competitive advantage (Wernerfelt, 1984). According to RBV theory, internal resources are given the major role in helping companies achieve higher organizational performance. There are two key assumptions of RBV theory:

- *Heterogeneity.* Resources organizations possess differ from one company to another. If organizations had the same amount and mix of resources, they could not employ different strategies to outcompete each other.
- *Immobility.* Resources are not mobile and do not move from company to company, at least in the short run. Because of this immobility, companies cannot replicate rivals' resources and implement the same strategies.

Two fundamental types of resources exist: tangible and intangible. Tangible assets are physical things such as land, buildings, machinery, equipment, and capital. Physical resources can easily be bought in the market so they present little advantage to companies in the long run because rivals can soon acquire identical assets. Intangible assets are everything else that has no physical presence but can still be possessed by the company. For example, brand reputation, intellectual property, supplier relationships, organizational culture, and business processes are all intangible assets. Unlike physical resources, many intangible assets are built over a long time and are something that other companies cannot buy from the market. RBV theory argues that intangible resources usually stay within a company and are the main source of competitive advantage (Wernerfelt, 1984).

Building upon RBV theory, Prahalad and Hamel (1990) described the concept of "core competencies," proposing that firms can differentiate themselves from their competition by developing an integrated set of unique and valuable capabilities (a combination of tangible and/or intangible assets) that are difficult for other firms to imitate. Besides being a differentiator, how a firm organizes around a unified set of capabilities provides a source of strategic competitive advantage. Separately, each capability is valuable. However, the principal competitive advantage is found in the integrated combination of capabilities a firm employs in a particular area, making them hard to separate and difficult for other firms to duplicate (Porter, 1996). How then does a firm know if a particular core competency provides competitive

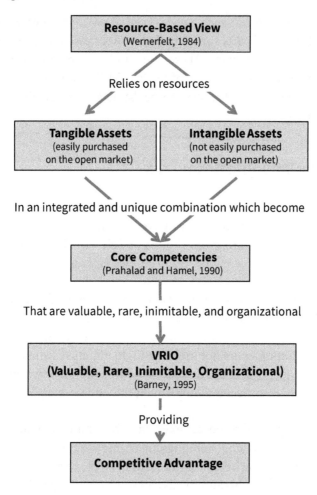

Figure 2.2 Resource-based view of core competencies that
provide competitive advantage

advantage? Since its introduction by Barney (1995), the VRIO (valuable, rare, inimitable, organizational) framework has become a standard test of how well a particular
core competency does or does not provide competitive advantage to a firm (Knott,
2015). Figure 2.2 illustrates the RBV as core competencies, which fulfill the VRIO
criteria, leading to competitive advantage.

Resources versus Competencies

To avoid confusion, it is useful to differentiate between resources and competencies. On the one hand, "resources" are *what firms have* and can be segmented into
four categories (physical, financial, human, and organizational). On the other hand,
"competencies" (which are often also called "capabilities") are *what firms do* and can
also be segmented into the same four categories (see Table 2.1).

Table 2.1 Resources versus competencies

Resources—what we have (nouns)	Category	Competencies (also can be called capabilities)—what we do (verbs)
• Machines, buildings, raw materials, patents, databases, computer systems	Physical	• Manage processes, produce products, serve customers
• Cash, investors, creditors	Financial	• Raise funds, manage cash flows, invest capital
• Managers, employees, partners, suppliers, customers	Human	• Train, develop, motivate, influence, innovate
• Structure, culture	Organizational	• Make decisions, share information, manage culture

Threshold versus Distinctive Competencies

When considering the value of a firm's resources, it is essential to identify "threshold" competencies and "distinctive" competencies. Threshold competencies are required to compete in the industry, provide competitive parity, are essential for organizational survival, and are possessed by many competitors. Meanwhile, distinctive competencies are required to win in a competitive market, provide competitive advantage, create organizational success, and are possessed by one or just a few firms in the market (Johnson et al., 2017). For example, every airline possesses threshold competencies including flight scheduling, aircraft maintenance, and ticket sales. However, Southwest Airlines has built an organizational culture that is a distinctive competency. Espoused by co-founder Herb Kelleher, the firm's ethos is "the business of business is people." Southwest puts this ethos into practice by placing its employees first, recognizing that treating its employees well creates happy customers, which results in operational and financial success including 85 percent of employees saying that they are proud to work for Southwest, having the lowest number of customer complaints in the industry, and forty-four consecutive years of profitability in a notoriously unprofitable industry (Robertson, 2018). Therefore, successful firms identify and leverage their distinctive competencies.

Transient Competitive Advantage

The RBV originally advanced the concept that by developing strategically valuable resources that fulfill the VRIO criteria, an organization can establish a "sustainable competitive advantage." In his seminal article on the topic, Ghemawat (1986, p. 54) asserts, "Sustainable advantages fall into three categories: size in the targeted market, superior access to resources or customers, and restrictions on competitors' options. Note these options are nonexclusive. They can, and often do, interact. The more, the better." For example, Walmart enjoyed competitive advantage because of the firm's size in the market and superior access to resources by seamlessly embedding vendors into their supply chain; further, by continually offering the lowest-cost merchandise, they restricted competitors' options who struggled to match Walmart's pricing. Although long-lasting, Walmart's competitive advantage began to erode when faced with the online retail model pioneered by Amazon, whose size in the market and access to resources and customers through their platform model (bringing multiple sellers and buyers together in one marketplace) restricted competitors' options (including Walmart's options). This was caused by the "network effect" of capturing a large share of the online retail market, establishing high "switching costs" for both sellers and buyers.

Because of examples such as Amazon's impact on Walmart, the concept of "transient competitive advantage" has replaced sustainable advantage as the new strategy mantra. In her influential article on the subject, McGrath (2013, p. 64) declares, "The field of strategy needs to acknowledge what a multitude of practitioners already know: Sustainable competitive advantage is now the exception, not the rule. Transient advantage is the new normal … any competitive advantage, whether it lasts two seasons or two decades, goes through the same cycle." McGrath calls this cycle "the wave of transient advantage" which entails: launch, ramp up, exploit, reconfigure, and disengage. She states, "When advantages are fleeting, firms must rotate through the cycle much more quickly and more often" (p. 64).

Internal Strategic Analysis Identifies a Firm's Strengths and Weaknesses

As discussed in Chapter 1, the SWOT framework includes both the external factors and internal characteristics of an organization (Learned et al., 1965). The "SW" (strengths and weaknesses) elements address the internal aspects of the SWOT analysis (see Figure 2.3).

Although the SWOT framework can be used on its own, supplementary "subframeworks" can be applied to conduct a more granular analysis of an organization's internal strategic resources. Two of the most popular strategic analysis frameworks that feed into the internal "strengths" and "weaknesses" elements of the SWOT analysis are the value chain analysis in combination with the VRIO analysis.

The Value Chain Analysis

The value chain model (Porter, 1985) is an end-to-end view of an organization's operational and support activities. A firm's operational activities along their value chain can include sourcing raw materials, manufacturing and production, logistics

	Opportunities	Threats
External Factors		
	Strengths	**Weaknesses**
Internal Factors	The internal attributes of an organization that are most valuable to the implementation and realization of its strategy.	The internal attributes of the organization considered to be limitations, faults, or defects that may prevent the implementation and realization of its strategy.

Figure 2.3 SWOT framework: internal factors

and distribution, marketing and sales, and after-sales service. A firm's support activities can include human resources, information technology, finance, procurement, legal, accounting, and tax, among others. Conducting a value chain analysis identifies the resources along the chain that are organizational strengths or weaknesses. Data to support the categorization of a firm's resources into "strengths" or "weaknesses" can include cost, customer ratings, and the contribution of each resource to the firm's revenue generation, among others.

Although the value chain analysis was originally designed to assess the activities of manufacturing firms, the framework can also be applied to services organizations including legal, consulting, accounting, information technology, education, government agencies, and other service providers. A service organization's "raw materials" are their professional staff. The firm's "production" is the training and development of staff and the tools and processes they use to perform their work. The "distribution" activity of the firm is the staff's delivery of client services. Professional services organizations also maintain support functions including human resources, information technology, finance, and so forth. Like manufacturing companies, data to support the categorization of a service organization's resources into "strengths" or "weaknesses" can include cost, customer ratings, the contribution to the organization's "mission fulfillment," and the contribution of each resource to the firm's revenue generation, among others.

The VRIO Analysis

The VRIO framework (Barney, 1995) consists of four key criteria about a resource or capability to determine its strategic value to the organization:

1. **Value**: Does the resource/capability enable the firm to improve its efficiency or effectiveness?

2. **Rarity**: Is control of the resource/capability in the hands of one or only a few firms?
3. **Inimitability**: Is it difficult for other firms to imitate, and will there be significant cost disadvantages to a firm trying to obtain, develop, or duplicate the resource/capability?
4. **Organization**: Is the firm organized in such a way that it is ready and able to exploit the resource/capability?

The VRIO analysis is often combined with the value chain analysis. The firm's operational or support capabilities along their value chain that fulfill all four VRIO criteria are sources of competitive advantage. Table 2.2 presents an example VRIO analysis matrix for a firm's capability to integrate their mergers and acquisitions.

The four VRIO criteria also interact. For example, resources that are "inimitable" are often "rare" among competitors because they are hard for other firms to copy or acquire. As discussed earlier, intangible resources are often the most inimitable as they typically cannot be purchased on the open market. Key characteristics that make resources inimitable are:

- *Complexity.* The resource consists of internal and external linkages. An example is an auto manufacturer's supplier network and embedding those suppliers into the firm's enterprise resource planning (ERP) system.

Table 2.2 VRIO analysis for capability—integrating mergers and acquisitions (M&A)

M&A post-transaction integration		
VRIO criteria	Fulfills VRIO?	Rationale
Value: Does the resource/capability enable the firm to improve its efficiency or effectiveness?	YES	• Projected deal synergies (improved firm efficiency and effectiveness) are realized through effective post-deal implementation.
Rarity: Is control of the resource/capability in the hands of a relative few?	YES	• Most firms only focus on the transaction rather than an integrated M&A approach spanning pre- and post-transaction capabilities.
Inimitability: Is it difficult to imitate and will there be significant cost and/or time disadvantage to a firm trying to obtain, develop, or duplicate the resource/capability?	YES	• An M&A integration competency is hard to duplicate because of the effort, time, and cost involved in building the capability.
Organization: Is the firm organized in such a way that it is ready and able to exploit the resource/capability?	YES	• An M&A integration capability requires a firm to organize around an integrated end-to-end M&A process, applying all the relevant skills, knowledge, tools, and talent required for transaction completion and post-transaction value creation.

- *Ambiguous.* It is difficult for other firms to discern the characteristics and linkages of the resource. A firm's superior customer service process that blends skilled service personnel with an automated customer management system and a service-oriented organizational culture is an example of an ambiguous resource.
- *Historical.* The resource is built over time. A firm's reputation for providing high-quality and long-lasting products is an example of a resource that is built over time.
- *Cultural.* The resource is embodied in the firm's culture, such as a culture of innovation that enables the firm to regularly offer new products and services.

Developing and Managing Strategically Valuable Resources

The "care and feeding" of strategically valuable resources will make them even stronger and more valuable. Once identified, a strategically valuable resource must be built or bought (if the firm doesn't currently possess the identified resource), maintained, or even enhanced. There are several methods firms use to build, develop, and manage strategically valuable resources. Options include hiring new talent, training staff for skill enhancement, integrating resources (e.g., service staff using specialized technology), connecting resources (e.g., embedding suppliers in the firm's ERP system), upgrading resources with regular investment in new equipment and technologies, redesigning organizational processes, and acquiring resources through mergers and acquisitions.

Participants and Key Activities

There can be multiple internal and external participants involved in a firm's strategic internal analysis who perform essential activities, including:

- *Senior executives.* They have extensive knowledge and experience regarding the firm, its priorities, and its capabilities to support the organization's strategic priorities. They allocate investment to develop and manage strategically valuable resources.
- *Internal strategy team.* They identify, prioritize, collect, and regularly monitor internal data to ascertain organizational resources that will affect the firm's future capabilities to pursue identified strategies.
- *External strategy consultants.* They assist senior management and the internal strategy team with internal data collection and analysis that shapes the organization's strategy identification and selection.

- *Board of directors.* In addition to the senior management of the organization, board members bring extensive knowledge and experience regarding strategically valuable resources within the industry and from other industries.
- *Functional managers.* They provide essential information about the organization's functional resources (talent profile, technology capabilities, financial status, and so forth) that will affect the firm's future capabilities to pursue identified strategies.
- *Middle management and employees.* As part of a "democratized" strategy processes (see the Introduction), management and employees throughout the organization can provide extensive knowledge of the firm's core capabilities.
- *Key customers.* As part of a "democratized" strategy processes (see the Introduction), customers can provide extensive knowledge of the firm's core capabilities.
- *Activist shareholders.* In addition to senior management and board members, these bring extensive knowledge and experience regarding strategically valuable resources within the industry and from other industries (see Chapter 12).

Best Practices

Prioritize data. Not all categories of the value chain or VRIO frameworks will be equally important to your industry or firm. For example, the components of your value chain will depend upon which industry you operate in, whether the organization is a manufacturer of goods or provider of services, and the operating model of the organization. Likewise, the data used to determine whether a resource is valuable (the "V" of VRIO) will depend on whether the resource helps reduce costs or increase the revenue of the firm.

Regularly update the data. Certain elements of the value chain and VRIO analyses may shift over time. For example, the introduction of new technologies, reconfigured organizational processes, the addition of new talent to the organization, and mergers and acquisitions will change the characteristics of various firm resources. Therefore, firms need to constantly monitor their internal resources to identify how they evolve over time.

Use multiple data sources. Diverse sources of internal data will provide more valuable strategic insights. Sources of internal data include current employees, customers of the firm, management intuition, and operational measures such as cost, cycle time, and headcount.

Apply the 80/20 rule. As with the external analysis, it is easy to spend 80 percent of the time trying to analyze 20 percent more internal data. Because organizational capabilities are continually evolving, collecting 100 percent of the data about internal resources is not possible. Therefore, strategic decisions must be made based upon often limited and what may seem like insufficient data.

Potential Pitfalls

No prioritization. Simply listing a firm's resources is insufficient as not all resources will have an equal impact on its current and future performance. Consequently, a better approach is to prioritize the key firm capabilities that will have the biggest effect on the firm's future direction and performance. Prioritization of internal factors can be based on several criteria such as the potential to increase or decrease the firm's costs, decrease or increase revenue, reduce or expand access to raw materials, and so forth.

One-off analysis. Valuable resources are not stagnant and shift over time. Some resources will change quickly, while others evolve more slowly. In any event, internal strategic analysis should be updated periodically or even continuously to monitor the state of an organization's strategically valuable resources.

Using qualitative information only. Using qualitative information such as feedback from customers and employees is useful. However, quantitative data such as costs, operational productivity, revenue contribution, and so forth is extremely helpful to identify and monitor the firm's strategically valuable resources.

Analysis paralysis. With so much operational data available even for small organizations, it is easy to get caught up in endless internal data collection and analysis, never leading to any action. At some point, management must use the data to make strategic decisions and not view internal data analysis as an end in and of itself.

Intuition only. Because management often believe they know their organization, they may discount the value of objective data collection and analysis of the organization's operations and capabilities.

Key Frameworks, Tools, and Templates

Below are descriptions of key templates used to conduct the internal strategic SWOT analysis. These tools are included in Appendix B.

SWOT. Examines both the external (opportunities and threats) and internal (strengths and weaknesses) factors pertinent to an organization's strategic decision-making.

Value chain. Provides an end-to-end view of an organization's operational and support activities, enabling management to understand the current and potential linkages between organizational activities, as well as identifying potentially strategically valuable resources of the firm.

VRIO. Used in conjunction with the value chain framework to assess various organizational resources to determine which resources are "strategically valuable" (the resources that fulfill the four VRIO criteria).

Best-Practice Case Example

A description of Specialist Consulting Plc's approach to internal strategic analysis in practice is summarized in Table 2.3.

Chapter Summary

- Two separate studies found that in developed economies internal organizational attributes have about three times more impact on profitability than industry factors. Meanwhile, a third study found that in emerging economies organizational characteristics have more than twenty times more impact on performance than either industry or country factors.
- Defining an organization's resources is not as clear as it once was because organizational boundaries have become porous.
- The RBV proposes that management should look inside the firm to find sources of competitive advantage.
- Two fundamental types of resources exist: tangible and intangible.
- Building upon RBV theory, the concept of core competencies proposes that firms can differentiate themselves from their competition by developing an

Table 2.3 The internal strategic analysis process at Specialist Consulting Plc*

The need:

- Because of the increasingly global nature of their client's operations, management of Specialist Consulting Plc (a specialist project management consulting firm) based in the United Kingdom realized that their future growth strategy depended upon being able to deliver services across the globe.
- A rigorous assessment of the firm's global service capabilities was required as part of the firm's strategy process.

The solution:

- Management conducted an analysis of the firm's delivery capability and presence in key markets into which their clients were rapidly expanding.
- They found that two client markets were undergoing rapid growth: the Middle East and Africa.
- The firm's value chain analysis revealed that the firm did not possess the core capability (local market knowledge) or the capacity (no staff located in each region) required to effectively deliver their services to clients.
- Based on the firm's growth potential in each market identified by the external strategic analysis, combined with the need for local staff in each region identified by the internal analysis, management decided to establish and staff local offices in each region.
- As part of the on-boarding process of staff in each region, management put in place extensive project management process and skills training for the newly hired staff.

The results:

- Not only was the firm able to provide "on-the-ground" regional services to their international clients but it also acquired local clients in each region.

---

* Due to non-disclosure considerations, a project management consulting firm is referred to throughout the illustration as Specialist Consulting Plc.

integrated set of unique and valuable capabilities that are difficult for other firms to imitate.

- On the one hand, "resources" are *what firms have*. On the other, "competencies" (which are often also called "capabilities") are *what firms do*.
- "Threshold competencies" are required to compete in the industry and are possessed by many competitors, whereas "distinctive competencies" are required to win in a competitive market and are possessed by one or just a few firms in the market. Successful firms identify and leverage their distinctive competencies.
- The RBV originally advanced the concept that an organization can establish a "sustainable competitive advantage." However, the concept of "transient competitive advantage" has replaced sustainable advantage as the new strategy mantra.
- Two of the most popular strategic analysis frameworks that feed into the internal strengths and weaknesses elements of the SWOT analysis are the value chain and VRIO analyses.
- The value chain model is an end-to-end view of an organization's operational and support activities.
- Although the value chain analysis was originally designed to assess the activities of manufacturing firms, the framework can also be applied to services organizations including legal, consulting, accounting, information technology, education, government agencies, and other service providers.
- The VRIO framework consists of four key criteria that assess a resource or capability to determine its strategic value to the organization (valuable, rare, inimitable, and organizational).
- There are several methods firms use to build, develop, and manage strategically valuable resources.
- There can be multiple internal and external participants involved in a firm's strategic internal analysis who perform essential activities.
- The best practices of internal strategic analysis include prioritizing data, regularly updating the data collected, using multiple data sources, and applying the 80/20 percent rule.
- The potential pitfalls of internal strategic analysis include no prioritization, one-off analysis, using qualitative information only, analysis paralysis, and relying on management intuition only.
- Key tools that help structure internal strategic analysis are SWOT, value chain, and VRIO.

Discussion Questions

1. What activities does your organization do well regarding its internal strategic analysis?

2. What aspects of internal analysis could your organization perform better?
3. Who is typically involved in internal strategic analysis? Who should be involved?
4. How often does your organization conduct internal analysis? Should the frequency of internal analysis change and, if so, why?
5. What internal data collection and analysis does your organization prioritize? What should be prioritized?
6. Does your organization know its "strategically valuable resources"?
7. Does your organization build, develop, and manage strategically valuable resources? How? Should your organization provide more "care and feeding" to the identified strategically valuable resources?

Organizational Self-Assessment

Completing the following self-assessment (Table 2.4) will provide a view of the effectiveness of your organization's internal strategic analysis process.

Steps to complete the self-assessment:

1. Rate each item on a scale of 0 (poor) to 10 (excellent).
2. Make notes for each item to explain the rationale for the numerical rating.
3. Add all ten scores to get a TOTAL SCORE (maximum score = 100).

Rating scale:

0–20 = Poor (significant improvement needed)
21–40 = Below average (improvement needed in several areas)
41–60 = Average (identify areas of weakness and adjust)
61–80 = Above average (identify areas that can still be improved)
81–100 = Excellent (continuously review and refine each component for each iteration of the organization's strategy efforts)

Table 2.4 Organizational self-assessment: internal strategic analysis

Component	Rating (0 = poor, 10 = excellent)	Notes/rationale
When it comes to internal strategic analysis …		
1. We regularly monitor our organization's internal resources		
2. We prioritize internal resource data that is most important to our organization		
3. We collect internal data from multiple sources		
4. We involve various stakeholders		
5. We use both quantitative and qualitative data		
6. We conduct an appropriate amount of analysis and avoid "analysis paralysis"		
7. We use structured frameworks such as the value chain and VRIO		
8. We know which are our strategically valuable resources		
9. We continually develop and manage our strategically valuable resources		
10. We would be considered "best practice"		
TOTAL SCORE		

3
Selecting High-Impact Strategies

Moving from strategic analysis to strategy selection is where analytics meets creativity in the strategy process. Whether using a traditional or more dynamic strategy approach, the data collected during external and internal strategic analysis should inform management's strategic decision-making. As discussed in the previous two chapters, the analytics of strategy include external data analysis (growth rates in different regions, demographic shifts, technological developments, and so forth) and internal data analysis (operational costs, service quality, productivity, revenue contribution, and so on). These analyses provide answers to two key strategic questions:

1. Where and what are the largest and most likely future external developments and market opportunities?
2. What internal resources do we have, and might we need, to take advantage of the future developments and market opportunities identified?

In any strategy process (whether dynamic or traditional), analytical data (both formal and intuitive) informs the potential strategies management identify and the strategic choices they make. While drawing upon external and internal analytical data, developing an array of potential strategies is also a creative exercise. Moving from external and internal analyses to making strategic choices combines data analysis and creativity (see Figure 3.1). Therefore, in this chapter we will examine the approaches, tools, best practices, and potential pitfalls of identifying potential strategies and selecting high-impact priority strategies for the organization to pursue (see Figure 3.2). Although the strategy process identified in Figures 3.1 and 3.2 is depicted as linear, in practice the process is iterative and overlapping, involving feedback loops between external and internal analysis, management intuition and creativity, and strategy identification and selection.

"Strategic Ideation" Combines Analysis with Creativity to Identify Potential Strategies

As illustrated in Figures 3.1 and 3.2, data from the firm's external and internal strategic analysis is used while generating potential strategies. Example categories of strategic initiatives include launching new products and services, new market entry, greater penetration in current markets, retrenchment (cost reduction), and business process redesign, among others. Typical goals for various initiatives include revenue

The Strategist's Handbook. Timothy Galpin, Oxford University Press. © Timothy Galpin (2023).
DOI: 10.1093/oso/9780192885203.003.0004

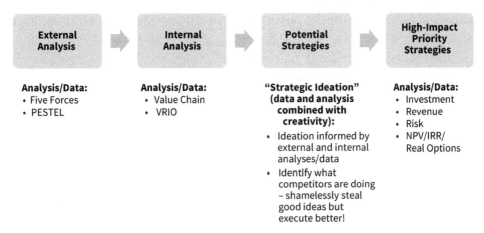

Figure 3.1 Moving from strategic analyses to strategy selection

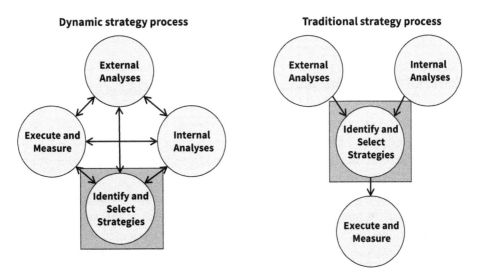

Figure 3.2 Difference between dynamic and traditional approaches to Andrews' four main strategy components: identify and select strategies

growth, market share expansion, cost reduction, and service improvement (Jackson, 2017). The key deliverable from this activity is a list of potential strategic initiatives, with specific goals identified for each.

To generate a list of potential strategies, management should draw upon the external and internal strategic data collected to inform the "strategic ideation" process. For example, a potential strategy might be to establish and expand the firm's international presence, with associated market share and revenue growth goals. External data including growth rates of various markets, demographic projections in each potential market, and consumer spending power forecasts for each market should inform management's decision about whether international expansion is generally worthwhile and, if so, which markets are most attractive to enter. Likewise, internal data about the firm's capacity (financing ability and the number of staff, for example) as well as the firm's capability (knowledge and skills) to expand internationally should also be considered. Combining external and internal data with the collective experience and creativity of the management team (and potentially others in the organization in a more "democratized" strategy process) will yield different possibilities for entering selected markets. Potential market entry strategies include variations of exporting, licensing, joint ventures, mergers and acquisitions, or greenfield approaches. These entry options will be discussed in more detail below. Moreover, an assortment of strategic frameworks can be used to help management bring together external and internal data with management intuition and creativity to identify potential strategies. Several of these frameworks are discussed in more detail below.

Wild Ideas

In addition to identifying potential strategies that are realistic pursuits for your firm (such as increased market penetration, new market entry, or adding new products and services), generating "wild ideas" stretches the creative element of the strategic ideation process by identifying thought-provoking, albeit not yet viable, potential very long-term strategies. In fact, what were once science fictions are now or fast becoming everyday products and services, including air travel, space tourism, pocket-sized audio and video communication devices, and robotics. Other "wild ideas" currently being pursued by firms in various industries include fusion power, wireless electricity, and quantum computing, all of which are in various stages of development. Identifying the "wild ideas" that are being pursued in your industry or adjacent industries will position your firm to take advantage of the new markets they open as those ideas become viable.

Mapping Implementation Priorities

Most strategic plans are composed of multiple cross-functional initiatives, each involving high-stakes competitive challenges (Canales and Caldart, 2017). Because of resource limitations (people, time, and capital), most firms cannot pursue more than three to five major strategic initiatives at any one time. For example, a study of 1,800 global executives found that 64 percent of respondents reported they have too many conflicting priorities, and 56 percent said allocating resources in a way that really supports the strategy is a significant challenge, especially when companies chase a wide set of initiatives (Leinwand and Mainardi, 2011). Therefore, management must target the few highest-impact priority initiatives and identify any others that need to be abandoned or deferred. Figure 3.3 provides a strategic priorities

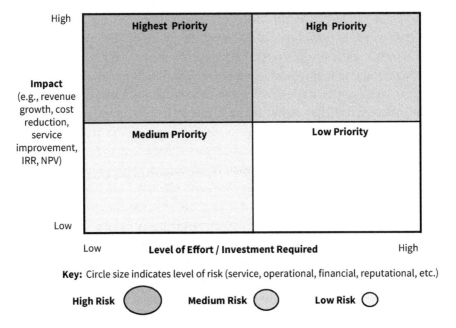

Figure 3.3 Strategic priorities map

map (Galpin, 2018) that can be used to rank the list of potential strategic initiatives generated, based on three dimensions: impact (such as revenue growth, cost reduction, and service improvement), level of effort and/or investment required (talent, time, and financial investment), and potential risk (service, operational, financial, and reputational).

Comparing Strategies Based on Financial Projections

Besides comparing potential strategies based upon the expected impact of each on service, competitive positioning, or market share, common methods used to compare potential strategies based upon their projected financial value creation include net present value, internal rate of return, and real options (Koller et al., 2020). Net present value (NPV) is used to calculate the total current value of a project's future cash flows. The basis of NPV is to project an investment's (such as a new market entry strategy) future cash outflows and inflows, discount all the future cash flows back to the present day (based on the cost of the firm's capital), and then add them together. The resulting number is the investment's NPV. A positive NPV means that, after considering the time value of money, the company will make money if it proceeds with the strategy. However, there are drawbacks to calculating a potential strategy's NPV as the assessment rests heavily on assumptions and estimates including investment costs, the "discount rate" (the cost of the firm's capital) used, and projected revenue growth. Thus, considerable room for error exists.

NPV and internal rate of return (IRR) are closely related concepts in that NPV and IRR are trying to answer two related but separate questions. The question answered by NPV is: what is the projected total amount of money (expressed as an amount of dollars, pounds, yen, euros, and so forth) the firm will make if it proceeds with a particular strategy (after considering the time value of money)? Meanwhile, the question answered by IRR is: if the firm proceeds with the strategy, what would be the equivalent annual rate of return (expressed as a percentage) the firm would achieve? IRR is often used to compare dissimilar strategies—those with different lifespans and amounts of investment required. As with NPV, considerable room for error exists when calculating IRR as similar assumptions and estimates are required.

Fundamentally, real options are the right but not an obligation for management to initiate, defer, abandon, or expand a firm's strategic investments. The term "real" is used because the expression applies to decisions about investing in tangible business initiatives (rather than financial instruments). For example, a real options analysis might assess the NPV of the option to expand a company's operations in a particular market versus the NPV of an alternative option to leave the market by selling the firm's business in that market and realize the "exit value." The option determined by the analysis to achieve the higher NPV is the prudent choice. To gain a better understanding of these methods, any strategist would benefit from the full texts and courses available that cover the topics of valuation and corporate finance in detail.

Participants and Key Activities

There can be multiple internal and external participants involved in strategy execution who perform essential activities, including:

- *Senior executives.* Identify potential strategies. Define strategy prioritization criteria and determine the shortlist of high-priority strategies to pursue.
- *Internal strategy team.* Assist senior management with identifying potential and priority strategies. Apply the designated comparison criteria to assess the projected impact and financial value creation of each potential strategy.
- *External strategy consultants.* Assist senior management and the internal strategy team with identifying potential strategies and applying designated comparison criteria to assess the projected impact and financial value creation of each potential strategy.
- *Board of directors.* Work with senior management to approve, guide, and shape the strategic priorities of the organization.
- *Functional managers.* Provide essential information about the organization's functional resources (talent profile, technology capabilities, financial status, and so forth) to help determine which strategies are most viable to pursue.

- *Middle management and employees.* As part of a "democratized" strategy processes (see the Introduction), management and employees throughout the organization can assist with identifying potential strategies.
- *Key customers.* As part of a "democratized" strategy processes (see the Introduction), customers can also assist with identifying potential strategies.
- *Activist shareholders.* In addition to the senior management and board members, these also assist with identifying potential strategies and priority strategies (see Chapter 12).

Best Practices

Keep the list of priority strategies short. Identifying a shortlist (e.g., three to five) of priority strategies for implementation enables management and the broader organization to allocate sufficient resources and attention to each strategic priority.

Use data. Information from both the external and internal strategic analyses should support the strategy identification and selection process.

Combine data with creativity. The external and internal data in combination with management intuition should inform "strategic ideation" to generate a list of potential strategies.

Identify "wild ideas." Potential strategies that are unachievable today will likely be commonplace tomorrow. Identifying "wild ideas" during the strategic ideation process will enable the firm to start positioning itself today to pursue the very long-term strategies of the future.

Apply rigor in selecting priority strategies. Rigorous selection criteria, such as impact versus investment, should be identified to triage the list of potential strategies down to a shortlist of priority strategies. Rigor helps mitigate management bias toward selecting personally preferred strategies that may or may not fulfill the strategy selection criteria identified.

Potential Pitfalls

Relying on analysis only. Although important to the strategy process, data alone will not produce a comprehensive set of potentially high-impact strategies. Therefore, management's creativity, experience, and intuition should be combined with the external and internal data to produce a more wide-ranging list of potential strategies.

Relying on creativity and intuition only. Relying primarily on experience and intuition can quickly cause a management team to base their strategic decisions on personal biases. Bias is unavoidable, but using external and internal data to inform the strategic ideation and strategy selection processes will produce a more realistic and achievable set of strategies.

Ignoring "wild ideas." Not generating wild ideas constrains the creative element of the strategic ideation process and limits management's strategic thinking.

Key Frameworks, Tools, and Templates

There are several useful tools that can help structure an organization's strategy identification and selection process. Below are descriptions of key templates that can be used to prepare for and conduct strategy identification and selection discussions and decisions. Several of these tools are included in Appendix B.

Ansoff's Growth Matrix (Ansoff, 1957). This classic two-by-two framework provides firms with four categories of growth strategies:

(1) Additional market penetration in existing markets with existing products and services. Achieved through additional marketing, increased sales efforts, lower prices, or industry consolidation via mergers and acquisitions.
(2) Entering new geographic markets or serving new customer segments with existing products and services.
(3) Offering new products and services in existing markets.
(4) Diversification by adding new "business units" that offer new products and services in new markets not currently served.

Market entry options map. This framework identifies five market entry options, each having its own considerations including how much strategic and operational control management desire in each market, the financial and human capital investment required to enter each market, and the potential financial, reputational, and legal risk to the firm upon entering each market. The five entry options are:

(1) Export (direct or indirect) by selling products and shipping them to international markets. E-commerce has become an important enabler of direct selling and exporting. For example, eBay and Amazon vendors sell their merchandise and ship it across international borders. Indirect exports entail goods being sold through an intermediary such as an agent or distributor, allowing you to take advantage of the local knowledge of the agent or distributor. The advantages of exporting are low investment and low risk. However, disadvantages include low control of intermediaries' fulfillment and service, trade barriers, tariffs, transport costs, and vulnerability to exchange rate fluctuations.
(2) Licensing through allowing a second-party company in another market to use your brand and intellectual property in return for royalties. Franchising is one form of licensing. For example, licensed outlets make up most of Starbucks outlets in international markets such as AmRest Holdings having the license to operate Starbucks in the Czech Republic, Hungary, Poland,

Romania, Bulgaria, and Slovakia. The advantages are that licensing provides low-investment market access and thus lower financial risk. Disadvantages include low control over the licensee (depending upon the licensing agreement), exposure to brand image risk (if the licensee engages in harmful activities such as wrongful treatment of staff, offering poor service, or providing low-quality goods), and potentially enabling the licensee to become a future competitor (by learning your processes and procedures and then setting up their own competing entity).

(3) Joint venture (JV) by creating a third company or operating entity with another partner. The two firms become joint owners of the third entity, with both contributing financial investment, staff, and other resources to the entity. A JV enables you to take advantage of the partner's infrastructure, local knowledge, and reputation. It is critical to ensure both companies' strategic goals are aligned. JVs may be the only method of entry into some markets, depending on local regulations that require a local partner for your firm to operate in the market. An example is Danone's joint venture with China Mengniu Dairy to form Danone China. The advantage is that JVs allow for closer control of the business compared to licensing because of joint ownership of the entity. The disadvantages include a higher investment of capital and/or other resources than exporting or licensing and potential organizational culture clashes between the partners who form and own the JV.

(4) Mergers or acquisitions (M&As) through buying all (a stock purchase) or part (an asset purchase) of a local company. An example is the Coca-Cola acquisition of AdeS (the soy-based fruit beverages business of Unilever Group) in Latin America, enabling Coca-Cola to instantly gain a 54 percent market share of soy-based drinks sales in the region. Advantages of M&As include high control (of strategic and operational decisions), instant access to the acquired company's market and network, limiting any conflict-of-interest risk or misaligned strategic objectives as may be the case in JVs, and, in the case of asset purchases, acquiring the parts of a company you desire and not buying those you don't want. The disadvantages are higher investment and in stock purchases the acquirer often takes on all existing and future liabilities and risks of the acquired firm.

(5) Greenfield, by setting up a wholly owned local subsidiary. Greenfield investment is a long game and presents numerous challenges including local staff recruitment, regulatory compliance, and understanding local market nuances. An example is the package producer DS Smith, which builds and operates manufacturing and distribution facilities in several international markets. The advantages include the highest control as local operations and company culture are built from the ground up, and no conflict-of-interest risk or misaligned strategic objectives with other entities. The disadvantages are high investment, high risk because of the challenges involved, and extending the time to get up and running within a market.

Often businesses don't just choose and follow one market entry strategy; they employ an incremental approach. For example, you can start with licensing, move to a JV, then do a full acquisition. A staged approach increases your business' involvement in the market gradually over time. Likewise, you can begin in one city or region of large markets to test, learn, then expand to the broader market.

Market entry profile map. A systematic market entry profile begins with a "business environment assessment." The environmental factors of various markets are identified and assessed on a five-point scale from 1 (low market attractiveness) to 5 (high market attractiveness). Business environment factors commonly rated for each market include:

- ease of doing business
- regulations
- rule of law (such as contract enforcement)
- corruption
- competition
- human capital/local talent.

A subsequent "total business environment score" is then assigned to each market by adding the individual factor scores. The markets with the highest total scores have the most favorable business environments.

A systematic market entry profile should also include a "market access assessment" by assigning a rating for each access factor on a five-point scale from 1 (low market attractiveness) to 5 (high market attractiveness). Market access factors commonly rated for each market include:

- partners
- proximity
- e-commerce
- distribution channels
- retail landscape
- infrastructure (ports, roads, internet, etc.).

A subsequent "total market access score" is then assigned to each market by adding the individual factor scores. The markets with the highest total scores have the most favorable market access.

Finally, using a market entry profile map to combine the business environment and market access assessment scores completes the structured market entry profile. The total "business environment" score for each market is plotted on the vertical axis of the map, and the total "market access" score for each market is plotted on the horizontal axis. The plotting of each market's rating ranks the overall attractiveness of each market from highest to lowest.

CAGE Distance Framework. An alternative to the market entry profile map is the CAGE Distance Framework (Ghemawat and Siegel, 2011), which can be used to ascertain differences or "distances" between countries across four dimensions that companies should address when identifying and implementing international strategies. The four dimensions of the framework are:

- *cultural*, which includes language, customs, values, norms, work systems, traditions, religion
- *administrative*, including trade agreements, colonial ties, currency, legal system, governmental policies, political hostility, visa and work permit requirements, and corruption
- *geographic*, involving physical distance, common land borders, time zones, transportation, and communication
- *economic*, composed of per capita income, cost of labor, availability of human resources, and economic size.

PATH Framework. Yet another alternative to the market entry profile map and the CAGE Distance Framework to assess a country's market attractiveness is the PATH Framework. The four dimensions of the framework are:

- *political*, which includes governmental policies, political stability, corruption, and regulation
- *administrative*, covering trade agreements, currency, legal system, and visa and work permit requirements
- *transportation and infrastructure*, encompassing ports, roads, telecommunications, and internet access
- *human resources*, including demographics, cost of labor, workforce skills and education, and labor laws.

New products and services options map. Like the market entry map, this framework identifies five options for offering new products and services, each having its own considerations including how much strategic and operational control management desire over the development and sales of each new product or service, the financial and human capital investment required to obtain and offer each new product or service, and the potential financial, reputational, and legal risk to the firm. The five options are:

(1) Non-equity alliance, through an agreement with another firm to share resources (product R&D, cross-marketing and sales, technical and operational knowledge, and so forth) without creating a separate entity or sharing equity. Non-equity alliances are more informal than an equity alliance. The advantages are low investment and low risk, and the partnering firms can

"test the relationship" (strategic, operational, and cultural fit). However, disadvantages include low control and low commitment on the part of both entities.

(2) Equity alliance, when one firm purchases equity in another entity (a partial acquisition), or each firm purchases equity in each other (a cross-equity transaction). In both arrangements, the holder of equity does not have controlling interest in the other entity and therefore does not make strategic or operational decisions for the firm in which they hold equity. The advantages are lower investment than an acquisition, potential financial gain for the investing entity, and like non-equity alliances the partnering firms can "test the relationship" (strategic, operational, and cultural fit). The main disadvantage is lower control than is provided by an acquisition.

(3) JV by creating a third company or operating entity with another partner. The two firms become joint owners of the third entity, with both contributing financial investment, staff, and other resources to the entity. The advantage is that JVs allow for closer control of the business compared to licensing because of joint ownership of the entity. The disadvantages include a higher investment of capital and/or other resources than exporting or licensing and potential organizational culture clashes between the partners who form and own the JV.

(4) Mergers or acquisitions (M&As) through buying all (a stock purchase) or part (an asset purchase) of a local company. Advantages of M&As include high control (of strategic and operational decisions), instant access to the acquired company's market and network, limiting any conflict-of-interest risk or misaligned strategic objectives as may be the case in JVs, and, in the case of asset purchases, acquiring the parts of a company you want and not buying those you don't desire. The disadvantages are higher investment and in stock purchases the acquirer often takes on all existing and future liabilities and risks of the acquired firm.

(5) Greenfield, by setting up a wholly owned local subsidiary. Greenfield investment is a long-term effort and presents numerous challenges including local staff recruitment, regulatory compliance, and understanding local market nuances. The advantages include the highest control as local operations and company culture are built from the ground up, no conflict-of-interest risk or misaligned strategic objectives with other entities. The disadvantages are high investment, high risk because of the challenges involved, and extending the time to get up and running within a market.

Like entering a new market, often businesses don't just choose and follow one product or services diversification strategy. They frequently employ an incremental approach such as starting with a non-equity alliance, then moving to an equity alliance, and ultimately do a full acquisition. A staged approach increases your firm's exposure to potentially promising new product offerings over time. For example, "corporate venture capital" has become a popular approach for long-standing legacy firms in industries such as energy and banking. This approach is characterized by a legacy firm establishing numerous non-equity and equity alliances with start-up and early-stage firms that have developed innovative offerings that may present promising future additions to the legacy firm's product and service portfolio ("greentech" energy and "fintech" banking, for example). Then, as a particular new technology gains broader appeal with consumers, the legacy firm will raise its stake in the partner firm by moving from a non-equity to equity alliance, increase its ownership percentage of the partner firm in an equity alliance, or ultimately acquire controlling interest in the partner firm, thus adding a new offering to the legacy firm's product or service portfolio over which it now has strategic and operational control.

Innovation landscape map. A key tool to generate strategies for technology and/or business model innovation. The framework consists of a two-by-two matrix with new and existing "business models" on the vertical axis and new and existing "technical competencies" on the horizontal axis, segmenting innovations into four quadrants (Pisano, 2015):

- *Routine.* Innovations that fall into the existing business model and existing technical competencies quadrant.
- *Disruptive.* Innovations that segment into the new business model and existing technical competencies quadrant.
- *Radical.* Innovations that segment into the existing business model and new technical competencies quadrant.
- *Architectural.* Innovations that segment into the new business model and new technical competencies quadrant.

Four levels of innovation matrix. A key framework to generate strategies for product or service innovation. The template identifies four "levels of innovation" (Miner, 2010):

- *Level one.* New features on existing products or services.
- *Level two.* Advancement of existing products and services.
- *Level three.* Evolutionary products and services.
- *Level four.* Revolutionary products and services.

The platform ecosystem. The framework can be used to identify potential new business models (Alstyne et al., 2016). The model consists of "producers" (Uber drivers, eBay sellers) on one side of the "platform" and "consumers" (Uber riders, eBay buyers) on the other side. The platform itself consists of "interface providers" for the platform (mobile devices are providers of the interface for Facebook, for example) and "owners" of the platform who control the platform's intellectual property and who mediate who may participate on the platform (Meta owns Facebook).

The value net. The model can be used to identify potential collaborative arrangements for a firm with four other entities (Brandenburger and Nalebuff, 1996):

- *Customers.* Such as arrangements between firms and their frequent customers, including membership discounts and special offers not available to non-members.
- *Suppliers.* Auto parts producers and auto manufactures agreeing to specific design standards, for example.
- *Competitors.* Such as several shoe stores in the same shopping center sharing advertising expenses to draw customers to the shopping center.
- *Complementors.* Providers of products and services best used in combination with a product or service from another provider, such as alliances and cooperation between microchip producers and computer manufacturers or airlines and hotel chains.

Strategy canvas. This framework is used to identify "blue ocean" opportunities for a firm to create and capture uncontested market space, while avoiding competing with rivals in areas they are strongest in (Kim and Mauborgne, 2005). For example, Southwest Airlines has used a "car travel" model to create strategic differentiation by offering frequent departures, with no frills (food or seat selection) at a lower cost than other airlines.

Strategic priorities map. This two-by-two framework is used to rank the list of potential strategic initiatives generated, based on three dimensions: impact (such as revenue growth, cost reduction, service improvement), level of effort and/or investment required (talent, time, and financial investment), and potential risk (service, operational, financial, reputational, and so forth).

Best-Practice Case Example

A description of Petrochemical Inc.'s approach to strategy identification and selection in practice is summarized in Table 3.1.

Chapter Summary

- Moving from strategic analysis to strategy selection is where analytics meets creativity in the strategy process.
- While drawing upon external and internal analytical data, developing an array of potential strategies is also a creative exercise.
- Combining external and internal data with the collective experience and creativity of the management team (and potentially others in the organization in a more "democratized" strategy process) will yield a broad array of possible strategies.

Table 3.1 Strategy identification and selection at Petrochemical Inc.*

The need:

- Senior management of Petrochemical Inc. (a global petrochemical company) realized that historically their strategy identification and selection process was primarily based on the personal biases of senior team members.
- Although the senior team possessed extensive industry experience that informed their strategy generation and selection process, the team wanted a more structured process to identify and select strategies.
- One of the executives noted that the company had always been adept at generating numerous initiatives but had never been very good at prioritizing them. Therefore, the team needed an effective process to prioritize strategic initiatives.

The solution:

- With the help of the internal strategy department, the senior team applied structured strategy generation tools including Ansoff's matrix, the market entry profile map, the value net, and the four levels of innovation, the team identified more than 30 potential strategic initiatives, which they knew were too many to effectively implement.
- The team used the strategic priorities map to rank their potential initiatives based on the projected impact, investment, and risk of each.

The results:

- From the over 30 potential strategic initiatives generated, 5 high-impact priority strategies were identified: customer service improvement, acquisitions, new geographic market entry, sourcing and purchasing efficiency, and reduction of administrative costs.
- By prioritizing their strategies, management avoided a key pitfall they had encountered in the past: having too many priorities.
- The prioritization exercise was not without its conflicts. As the CEO noted, "Not everyone had their favorite initiative selected as one of the priorities. This is a key learning for us, how to accept that we cannot do everything and that our personal 'pet project' may not be a priority for the company overall."
- The next step was to effectively implement the five priority strategies (see Chapter 4).

---

* Because of non-disclosure considerations, a global petrochemical company is referred to throughout the illustration as Petrochemical Inc.

- In addition to identifying potential strategies that are realistic pursuits for your firm, generating "wild ideas" stretches the creative element of the strategic ideation process by identifying thought-provoking, albeit not yet viable, potential very long-term strategies.
- Because of resource limitations (people, time, and capital), most firms cannot pursue more than three to five major strategic initiatives at any one time.
- Therefore, management must target the few highest-impact priority initiatives and identify any others that need to be abandoned or deferred.
- Besides comparing potential strategies based upon the expected impact of each on service, competitive positioning, or market share, common methods used to compare potential strategies based upon projected financial value creation include net present value, internal rate of return, and real options.
- There can be multiple internal and external participants involved in strategy execution who perform essential activities, including senior executives, the

internal strategy team, external strategy consultants, board members, middle management and employees, key customers, and activist shareholders.

- The best practices in strategy identification and selection include keeping the list of high-impact priority strategies short, using both external and internal data, combining data with creativity, identifying "wild ideas," and applying rigor in selecting priority strategies.
- Potential pitfalls in strategy identification and selection include relying on analysis only, relying on creativity and intuition only, and ignoring "wild ideas."
- Key tools that help structure strategy identification and selection are Ansoff's growth matrix, the market entry options map, the market entry profile map, the new products and services options map, the innovation landscape map, the four levels of innovation matrix, the platform ecosystem, the value net, the strategy canvas, and the strategic priorities map.

Discussion Questions

1. What activities does your organization do well during strategy identification and selection? What strategy identification and selection activities could the organization perform better?
2. For your organization, who is typically involved in strategy identification and selection, both from internal staff and external advisers? Who should be involved?
3. What key strategy identification and selection tools and templates does your organization use? What others should they use?
4. Does your organization identify a manageable list of high-impact priority strategies to pursue, rather than have too many strategic initiatives? What could they do better to identify a shortlist of priority strategies?
5. Does your organization identify "wild ideas" that stretch the strategic thinking of the organization and that may provide future very long-term potential strategies?
6. What "wild ideas" can you identify that your organization might take advantage of as the ideas become viable?

Organizational Self-Assessment

Completing the following self-assessment (Table 3.2) will provide a view of how effectively your organization conducts strategy identification and selection.

Steps to complete the self-assessment:

1. Rate each item on a scale of 0 (poor) to 10 (excellent).
2. Make notes for each item to explain the rationale for the numerical rating.
3. Add all ten scores to get a TOTAL SCORE (maximum score = 100).

Rating scale:

0–20 = Poor (significant improvement needed)

21–40 = Below average (improvement needed in several areas)

41–60 = Average (identify areas of weakness and adjust)

61–80 = Above average (identify areas that can still be improved)

81–100 = Excellent (continuously review and refine each component for each iteration of the organization's strategy efforts)

Table 3.2 Organizational self-assessment: strategy identification and selection

Component	Rating (0 = poor, 10 = excellent)	Notes/rationale
When it comes to strategy identification and selection …		
1. External data informs our process		
2. Internal data informs our process		
3. Creativity and intuition inform our process		
4. We "democratize" our process		
5. We use key tools and templates to structure our process		
6. We compare strategies based on financial projections such as NPV, IRR, and real options		
7. We identify a manageable shortlist of high-impact priority strategies to pursue		
8. We identify "wild ideas" that stretch the strategic thinking of the organization		
9. We monitor our "wild ideas" to identify future very long-term potential strategies		
10. We would be considered "best practice"		
TOTAL SCORE		

PART II

STRATEGY EXECUTION

4

The Best Strategy Is the One You Can Implement

Analyzing and planning strategy is an important component of company success. However, any experienced executive understands, and has likely learned the hard way, that the full potential value of even the most well-designed strategy is only achieved through effective implementation. Thus, strategists must always remember that *the best strategy is the one you can implement*. No matter how brilliant or elegant a strategy is, it is worthless until effectively implemented.

Supporting the experience of numerous management teams, research has found that poor execution often squanders the value companies anticipate from innovative and potentially valuable strategic initiatives. For example, a survey of senior executives from 197 companies worldwide, with sales exceeding $500 million, found that companies typically lose well over a third (37 percent) of their strategies' potential value because of poor execution (Mankins and Steele, 2005). Another study involving interviews of over 130 executives found that 80 percent of leaders feel their company is good at crafting strategy but only 44 percent at its implementation (Jansen, 2016).

Consequently, the process of strategy execution needs to be a management priority. To make this point, Oxford Professor Thomas Powell compares strategy execution to climbers of Mount Everest who, "must consider strategy execution, both during the climb and while planning the climb ... Success in climbing Everest does not depend on choosing the right path, but on the climber's capacity to deal with the conditions of the actual climb" (Powell, 2017, p. 165). Common issues encountered during "the climb" of strategy execution include poor execution management, a lack of management attention to execution, misalignment between strategy and organizational culture, inadequate cross-functional coordination, and insufficient implementation tracking and measurement. Therefore, in this chapter we will examine the approaches, tools, best practices, and potential pitfalls of strategy execution (see Figure 4.1).

Structured Execution Is Key to Maximizing a Strategy's Full Value

To minimize the likelihood of mismanagement, companies need a repeatable process that provides an integrated and actionable approach to effective strategy execution. A pragmatic model consisting of five steps is presented in Figure 4.2. An early

The Strategist's Handbook. Timothy Galpin, Oxford University Press. © Timothy Galpin (2023).
DOI: 10.1093/oso/9780192885203.003.0005

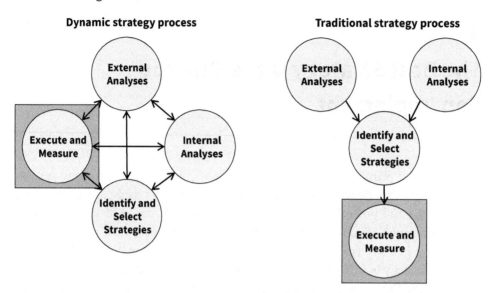

Figure 4.1 Difference between dynamic and traditional approaches to Andrews' four main strategy components: strategy execution

version of the Strategy Execution Model in Figure 4.2 originated some thirty years ago as a framework to improve strategy implementation at several UK firms. In the ensuing decades, following the principles of action-based research (French, 2009), the model has been applied and refined in numerous organizations across various industries and geographies.

Managers can apply the process in Figure 4.2 to strengthen the strategy execution competence of their organization and learn valuable lessons from each application. As the former chairman and CEO of Honeywell International Larry Bossidy emphasizes, "Execution is a specific set of behaviors and techniques that companies need to master to build competitive advantage. It's a discipline of its own" (Bossidy and Charan, 2002).

A Five-Step Strategy Execution Process

Establish an "Implementation Infrastructure"

As they grow, organizations quickly become beset with information and coordination blockages between functional "silos," slowing down and even bringing some cross-functional strategic initiatives to a stop. As a rule, the larger a firm becomes, the more formidable the obstacles to strategy execution become (Galpin, Hilpirt, and Evans, 2007). To surmount the roadblocks, a "strategy implementation infrastructure" facilitates coordination across silos, enabling the organization to implement strategic initiatives with greater speed and agility. A typical implementation infrastructure consists of three core entities:

Figure 4.2 Five-step strategy execution model

- *Executive steering team.* A team of executives who provide sponsorship, implementation oversight, impasse resolution, investment decisions, implementation go/no-go decisions, and leading the alignment of the organization's culture with the desired strategy.
- *Implementation program management team.* Led by an "implementation program manager" (sometimes called a "transformation lead" or "transformation manager"), this team is responsible for overall implementation program management, facilitating daily coordination across functional silos, project milestone and results tracking, and ongoing implementation communications.
- *Implementation task forces.* One task force per strategic initiative, plus a cultural alignment team, each staffed cross-functionally. These teams design implementation plans, coordinate with other task forces, produce deliverables, and manage implementation milestones and due dates.

Executives of Petrochemical Inc., having experienced missteps and coordination issues in their previous strategy execution efforts, put this three-part infrastructure in place. They established five cross-functional task forces to oversee, coordinate, plan, and manage the implementation of the company's priority initiatives, along with a sixth task force to manage the alignment of the company's culture. There was some grumbling by several members of the executive team who felt that the company already had a sufficient day-to-day management structure in place to run the company, and that all the relevant parties would coordinate with one another during implementation. When presented with data and examples from past strategic implementation efforts that struggled with missed timelines, poor communication between teams, and budget overruns, the skeptics accepted the new coordination approach. The next stage was to incorporate practices that promoted agility throughout the new implementation infrastructure.

Apply "Agile Implementation Management"

Successful strategy execution requires an "agile implementation management" process, which includes ongoing coordination between teams, issues identification, decision-making, and course corrections (Mihalache, 2017). A study of 2,000 organizations found that "highly successful agile [strategic] transformations delivered around 30 percent gains in efficiency, customer satisfaction, employee engagement, and operational performance; made the organization five to ten times faster; and turbocharged innovation" (McKinsey & Company, 2021, p. 3). From the opposite view, without frequent coordination within and between strategic initiatives chaos becomes more likely, implementation will quickly lose momentum and grind to a standstill. Each of the implementation teams described above—steering committee, program management, and task forces—must work in concert to keep the execution process on track. Weekly review meetings between the task force heads, and led by the program management team, should:

- review progress from the previous week
- identify any obstacles encountered
- address any cross-functional coordination required
- specify key actions for the upcoming week
- identify decisions needed from the steering committee essential to implementation progress.

Effective agile program management incorporates five key principles:

- *80/20 rule for decision-making.* Managers often spend 80 percent of their time trying to obtain 20 percent more information before making decisions, therefore "80 percent information" is sufficient to decide, implement, and adjust.
- *Push most decisions down to the implementation task forces.* More "material" decisions—large capital expenditures or major personnel impacts—should be raised to the steering committee for rapid resolution. The longer decision-making takes, the greater the chance of losing implementation momentum.
- *Staggered implementation.* To build momentum, achieve "quick wins," publicize them, and congratulate the successful teams.

- *Simplify tracking and reporting.* Develop and install a streamlined implementation tracking "dashboard," including one-page summaries for each task force and for the overall implementation program.
- *Apply implementation learning to future planning and ongoing execution.* Continuous customer and employee feedback is essential to adapt implementation actions as needed.

The implementation infrastructure at Petrochemical Inc. was managed using these agile principles. Cross-functional implementation coordination meetings were held weekly, which included the program management team and the leader of each task force. The meeting agenda focused on five key items for each task force to report: progress made since the previous week, any obstacles encountered, cross-functional coordination needed, key actions for the upcoming week, and key decisions required from the steering committee. After each weekly meeting, any major decisions required to keep the execution process moving—large capital expenditure, significant systems, or operational changes—were taken by the program management team to the steering committee for rapid decision within 72 hours to either approve, disapprove, or request modifications. At Petrochemical Inc. the process went smoothly, and after just a few weeks into the implementation process one of the executives commented, "I thought this process was going to be much too cumbersome and administrative. But, because of all the cross-functional coordination requirements we've identified already, without the process we would already be off track and behind schedule." As the agile process progressed, detailed implementation action plans were developed.

Develop Detailed Implementation Action Plans

Consistency of program management tools helps streamline the implementation process and maintain a focus on priorities, including ongoing decision-making, customer and employee feedback, and required implementation modifications (Longman and Mullins, 2004). An organization's toolkit should include program planning and coordination software, issue logs, and budget tracking templates. While "agile" adjustments will inevitably need to be made throughout implementation, using a shared set of program planning and management tools across teams to develop detailed implementation plans provides a visible roadmap to guide the direction of strategy execution. These plans include key actions, timelines, budgets, and accountabilities.

Several effective project management tools and templates were in use at Petrochemical Inc. However, the company's application of those tools and templates was not uniform. So, a key role of the program management team was to ensure the tools and templates were applied consistently by the implementation task forces to develop their action plans.

From their experience, the senior team of Petrochemical Inc. had learned that culture can derail even the best-managed initiatives. So, in addition to the agile management process and consistent program management approach, they needed a pragmatic method to align the organization's culture with the strategic initiatives.

Align Organizational Culture with Strategy

Over seventy-five years ago, the eminent psychologist Kurt Lewin asserted that, "There is nothing more practical than a good theory" (Lewin, 1943), and two basic theories underlie the shaping of behavior: personality theory and behavioral theory. Personality theory suggests that the sources of a person's behavior are characteristics of the person themselves, their values, beliefs, and attitudes (Phelps, 2015). However, behavior theory is vastly more practical when applied to aligning organizational culture with strategy. Behavioral theory asserts that rather than being driven by a person's attitudes and beliefs, individual behavior is driven by a person's environment (Skinner, 1953). Therefore, altering an organization's internal environment can incentivize desired workforce behaviors and organizational culture (Selznick, 1957).

Using the principles of behavioral theory, through the deliberate redesign of various "cultural levers" such as communications, training, and rewards, management of Petrochemical Inc. was able to effectively foster workforce behaviors that supported implementation of the five priority strategic initiatives, including improved teamwork across functions, enhanced customer service, and better cross-cultural communications during international acquisitions. Initially during the cultural alignment process employees pushed back when key elements of their environment, such as goals, metrics, pay, and rewards, were altered. The senior team at Petrochemical Inc. persevered when faced with resistance to required changes to the "cultural levers," and once results began to materialize and early successes were communicated, employees embraced the new culture. Chapter 8 describes in detail how organizational culture can be aligned with strategy.

Build Momentum and Continually Adjust

Two key activities have a major impact on building and maintaining momentum for successful strategy execution: visible "quick wins" and continuous communication. Initially implementing quick-win actions—those that can be put in place within thirty to sixty days of execution launch—demonstrates early progress. The quick wins should be closely followed by staggered implementation of medium-term (six to twelve months) and long-term (one year and beyond) actions. However, momentum from quick wins and ongoing execution is only achieved by making implementation actions visible through continuous communication, via multiple channels to all stakeholders, including board members, customers, and employees (see Chapter 6).

As implementation begins and momentum builds, adjustments need to occur. No implementation goes exactly according to plan, and unforeseeable events—economic shifts, competitor actions, and technology changes—will create the need for continual course corrections (Borchardt, 2011). Consequently, as stated previously, an agile program management approach is essential to address ongoing implementation adjustments along "the climb" of strategy implementation.

Petrochemical Inc.'s management took advantage of "quick wins" achieved—such as the early streamlining of processes, a small acquisition and consolidating fragmented customer service activities into one function—to build momentum for longer-term actions. Moreover, through the weekly progress updates and decision-making process, the company was able to continually adjust implementation actions, aligning them with inevitable market and economic shifts. Petrochemical Inc.'s strategy execution efforts were not without issues. However, as implementation progressed, management at Petrochemical Inc. grew confident that the carefully coordinated work of structured strategy execution was worth the effort. The entire execution process took place over five years, with the measures used to track and report progress all showing positive impact across the four key areas of the balanced scorecard used by Petrochemical Inc.—financial, customer, business process, and organizational learning and development (Kaplan and Norton, 2005).

Strategy Execution as VRIO

As discussed in Chapter 2, the valuable, rare, inimitable, organizational (VRIO) framework (Barney, 1995) is a standard test of how well a particular core competency does or does not provide competitive advantage to a firm. Using the VRIO criteria, Table 4.1 compares firms who approach strategy primarily as planning versus those that address strategy as planning and integrated execution. As identified in Table 4.1, strategy as primarily planning does not fulfill the VRIO criteria, whereas strategy as planning and integrated execution does meet each of the criteria.

Participants and Key Activities

There can be multiple internal and external participants involved in strategy execution who perform essential activities, including:

- *Senior executives.* Identify the shortlist of high-priority strategies to pursue, sponsor and oversee the implementation process, assign resources (budget and people) to the implementation process, and deliver regular communications regarding strategy selection, implementation requirements, and progress.

Table 4.1 VRIO: strategy as primarily planning versus planning and integrated execution

Strategy as primarily planning

VRIO criteria	Fulfills VRIO?	Rationale
Value: Does the resource/capability enable the firm to improve its efficiency or effectiveness?	NO	• Research has found that poorly managed strategy execution results in significant unrealized potential value.
Rarity: Is control of the resource/capability in the hands of a relative few?	NO	• Numerous firms focus more on planning than execution, resulting in poor implementation.
Inimitability: Is it difficult to imitate, and will there be significant cost and/or time disadvantage to a firm trying to obtain, develop, or duplicate the resource/capability?	NO	• Firms can source strategic planning capability from consultants, but execution capability needs to be internal to the organization.
Organization: Is the firm organized in such a way that it is ready and able to exploit the resource/capability?	NO	• Many companies employ in-house strategic planning teams, but lack execution capability.

Strategy as planning and integrated execution

VRIO criteria	Fulfills VRIO?	Rationale
Value: Does the resource/capability enable the firm to improve its efficiency or effectiveness?	YES	• Research has found that integrated, well-managed strategy execution can result in on average 37% more realized value.
Rarity: Is control of the resource/capability in the hands of a relative few?	YES	• Most firms focus on planning strategy, rather than building an integrated strategy execution capability.
Inimitability: Is it difficult to imitate, and will there be significant cost and/or time disadvantage to a firm trying to obtain, develop, or duplicate the resource/capability?	YES	• An integrated strategy execution competency is hard to duplicate because of the effort, time, and cost involved.
Organization: Is the firm organized in such a way that it is ready and able to exploit the resource/capability?	YES	• An integrated approach to strategy execution requires a firm to organize around a coordinated process, applying all the relevant skills, knowledge, tools, and talent required for implementation and value creation.

- *Internal strategy team.* Collect and analyze relevant external and internal data to assist senior management with strategy identification and selection.
- *External strategy consultants.* Assist senior management and the internal strategy team with data collection and analysis that shapes strategy identification and selection.
- *Internal implementation program manager.* Sometimes called a "transformation lead" or "transformation manager," this role has responsibility for day-to-day management and cross-functional coordination of the strategy implementation process (project budgeting, milestone-setting and tracking, issues identification and resolution, and regular results measurement, tracking, and reporting).
- *Implementation task forces composed of internal operational and functional managers and employees.* Provide specialized expertise and input throughout the strategy execution process (communications, operations, sales, customer service, information technology (IT), human resources (HR), marketing, legal, finance).
- *External program management, operational and functional consultants.* Assist internal resources with strategy implementation program management and functional expertise required during strategy execution (communications, operations, IT, HR, marketing, legal, finance, and so forth).
- *Board of directors.* Work with senior management to approve, guide, and shape the strategic priorities of the organization.
- *Functional managers and employees.* A broad base of functional management and employees help the firm's strategy execution efforts with functional support, including talent allocation, legal matters, financial investment, and so forth.
- *Middle management and employees.* Democratized strategy processes involve representatives of middle management and front-line employees who help shape the organization's strategy formulation. A broad base of middle management and employees also needs to participate in the firm's strategy execution efforts at the front-line level.
- *Shareholders.* Activist shareholders have become much more involved in trying to influence an organization's strategic direction (see Chapter 12).

Best Practices

Keep the list of priority strategies short. Identify a shortlist (three to five) of priority strategies for implementation to enable the organization to allocate sufficient resources and attention to each strategic priority.

Assign a strategy implementation program coordinator to each priority strategy. The implementation activities for each priority strategy should be overseen and coordinated by an "implementation program coordinator" who is responsible for driving detailed implementation planning, cross-functional coordination, progress tracking and reporting, and day-to-day implementation adjustments as required.

Apply agile management methods. No strategy execution effort will progress exactly as planned. Therefore, regular (daily or weekly) adjustments to implementation actions will be required as the process unfolds.

Align organizational culture with strategy. Organizational culture is a key determinant of success or failure for firms' strategy execution efforts. Therefore, utilize an actionable culture-management model to facilitate aligning organizational culture to support strategy execution.

Build momentum with quick wins. Demonstrate early progress with even small implementation actions. This builds momentum and sets the stage for more complex and longer-term execution activities.

Potential Pitfalls

Not allocating the required resources. Strategy implementation requires the allocation of people and budget to accomplish required milestones including training, communications, and implementation program management.

No overt cross-functional coordination. Most major strategic change initiatives (new markets, new products or services, new operational processes, and new organizational structures) are cross-functional in nature, with elements of IT, HR, legal, operations, marketing, service, and so forth. Consequently, an implementation program manager should be put in place to ensure cross-functional coordination on a regular (day-to-day, week-to-week) basis.

Discounting the value of regular strategy execution tracking and reporting. The adage of what gets measured gets managed applies to any strategy execution effort. Regular tracking of both progress against milestones of the implementation plan and results achieved throughout the implementation process is essential to focus all stakeholders (board, investors, senior executives, management, and employees) on the strategic priorities of the organization.

Key Frameworks, Tools, and Templates

There are several key tools that help facilitate an organization's strategy execution process. Below are descriptions of key templates used to prepare for and conduct strategy implementation. These tools are included in Appendix B.

Strategic priorities map. Plots potential strategies on a matrix based on each potential initiative's predicted impact, level of effort and invest required, and potential risk.

Project planning tool. Software designed to plan major implementation program tasks, start and end dates, budgets, contingencies, and task ownership.

Implementation workstreams status tracker. Electronic tracking of key strategy execution workstreams' status—those that are on schedule, at risk, or behind schedule.

Implementation results dashboard. Electronic tracking of strategy execution program results by measurement category (financial, customer, business process, and organizational learning and development).

Best-Practice Case Example

A description of Petrochemical Inc.'s approach to strategy execution in practice is summarized in Table 4.2.

Table 4.2 Strategy execution at Petrochemical Inc.*

The need:
- As described in Chapter 3, the senior team of Petrochemical Inc. (a global petrochemical company) identified more than 30 potential strategic initiatives, which they knew were too many to effectively implement.
- From the over 30 potential strategic initiatives generated, 5 high-impact priority strategies were identified: customer service improvement, acquisitions, new geographic market entry, sourcing and purchasing efficiency, and reduction of administrative costs.
- They now needed an effective strategy execution process to implement their 5 priority strategies.

The solution:
- An implementation program management infrastructure was put in place consisting of a steering committee, an implementation program team led by an implementation manager, and a series of implementation task forces.
- The implementation infrastructure was managed using agile principles, including rapid decision-making and project management tools and templates.
- Various culture levers were deliberately redesigned to align the organization's culture with the desired strategic initiatives.
- Visible implementation "quick wins" were established and communicated to build momentum.
- Balanced measures were regularly used to track and report implementation progress.

The results:
- Over a 5-year implementation period Petrochemical Inc. grew faster, gained market share, and reported higher profitability than their benchmark industry competitors.

---

* Because of non-disclosure considerations, a global petrochemical company is referred to throughout the illustration as Petrochemical Inc.

Chapter Summary

- The best strategy is the one you can implement.
- Research indicates that poor execution often squanders the value companies anticipate from innovative, valuable strategic initiatives.
- The process of strategy execution needs to be a management priority.

- To minimize the likelihood of mismanagement, companies need a repeatable process that provides an integrated and actionable approach to effective strategy execution.
- Following the principles of action-based research, a five-step strategy execution model is presented that has been applied and refined in numerous organizations across various industries and geographies.
- To begin the process, potential strategic initiatives should be identified, along with goals for each.
- Management must target the few highest-priority initiatives and identify any others that need to be abandoned or deferred.
- To surmount organizational roadblocks caused by functional "silos," a strategy implementation infrastructure facilitates coordination across silos, enabling the organization to implement strategic initiatives with greater speed and agility.
- Successful strategy execution requires an "agile implementation management" process, which includes ongoing coordination between implementation teams, issues identification, rapid decision-making, and course corrections.
- Using a shared set of program planning and management tools across teams to develop detailed implementation plans provides a visible roadmap to guide the direction of strategy execution.
- Using the principles of behavioral theory, through the deliberate redesign of various "cultural levers," management can effectively foster workforce behaviors that support chosen strategic initiatives.
- Two key activities have a major impact on building and maintaining momentum for successful strategy execution: visible "quick wins" and continuous communication.
- Strategy as primarily planning does not fulfill the VRIO criteria, whereas strategy as planning and integrated execution does meet each of the criteria.
- Best practices of strategy execution include keeping the list of priority strategies short, assigning a strategy implementation program manager to each priority strategy, applying agile management methods, aligning organizational culture with strategy, and building momentum with quick wins.
- Potential pitfalls of strategy execution include not allocating the required resources, no overt cross-functional coordination, and discounting the value of regular strategy execution tracking and reporting.
- Key strategy execution frameworks, tools, and templates include the strategic priorities map, project planning software, implementation workstreams status tracker, and implementation results dashboard.

Discussion Questions

1. What activities does your organization do well during strategy execution? What strategy execution activities could the organization perform better?

2. For your organization, who is typically involved in strategy execution, both from internal staff and external advisers? Who should be involved?
3. What key implementation program management tools and templates does your organization use? What others should they use?
4. What strategy execution measures does your organization have in place? Are the measures sufficient? If not, what other measures should the organization put in place?
5. Does your organization do a good job of establishing and communicating quick wins to build momentum for strategy execution? What could they do better?

Organizational Self-Assessment

Completing the following self-assessment (Table 4.3) will provide a view of how effectively your organization performs strategy execution.

Steps to complete the self-assessment:

1. Rate each item on a scale of 0 (poor) to 10 (excellent).
2. Make notes for each item to explain the rationale for the numerical rating.
3. Add all ten scores to get a TOTAL SCORE (maximum score = 100).

Rating scale:

0–20 = Poor (significant improvement needed)
21–40 = Below average (improvement needed in several areas)
41–60 = Average (identify areas of weakness and adjust)
61–80 = Above average (identify areas that can still be improved)
81–100 = Excellent (continuously review and refine each component for each iteration of the organization's strategy efforts)

Table 4.3 Organizational self-assessment: strategy execution

Component	Rating (0 = poor, 10 = excellent)	Notes/rationale
When it comes to strategy execution …		
1. We use a clear shortlist of prioritized strategies		
2. We apply a robust implementation program management process		
3. Our operating and functional management understand their roles and are fully involved		
4. We manage cross-functional efforts well		
5. We assign an implementation / transformation program manager to each strategic initiative		
6. We use effective project management tools and templates		
7. We align "cultural levers" to support our strategic priorities		
8. We regularly track and report progress		
9. We would be considered "best practice" in our strategy execution		
10. We continually evaluate and improve our strategy execution process		
TOTAL SCORE		

5

Managing Strategic Transformation

The vagaries of an interconnected global economy, rapidly developing new technologies, and constantly shifting customer preferences continue to create an ever more complex operating environment for management to navigate. Correspondingly, strategies have also become even more complex. Rapid business expansion across numerous geographic borders, adding multiple new products and services to a firm's portfolio, implementing new technologies, or creating new business alliances, partnerships, and combinations through mergers and acquisitions all require significant transformation to an organization's operating model, placing substantial demands on workforces to regularly change their ways of working. Therefore, strategy execution must be treated as nothing less than a far-reaching transformation management effort across the organization.

The discipline of "change management," regarded as a set of activities that realigns organizations so they can effectively address the economic, technological, and other forces transforming their marketplaces, presents significant challenges to a firm's leadership during the strategy execution process (Galpin, 1996b; Kotter, 1996). Major strategic initiatives visibly and dramatically transform the configurations and environment of a company. "Big Change" (Franklin, 2013) is an apt term to describe what often happens during strategy execution. Indeed, technological, operational, and organizational changes introduced by implementing new strategies now come far more quickly and are more significant than those to which most organizations are accustomed. Therefore, management need to apply proven concepts and tools of effective organizational transformation management.

Whether a company's strategy has been designed to grow revenue or market share in existing markets, introduce new products, gain access to new customers, or expand into new markets, to assume that a strategy that looks good on paper will ensure easy implementation is naive. Likewise, as investors and other stakeholders learn of a firm's new strategy, the pressure on management to deliver on their strategic promises intensifies. In short, the transformation required during strategy implementation presents a management challenge unlike any other. However, even with all the material written about organizational transformation over the past three decades, it is surprising that many executives who are ultimately responsible for making their strategies work still fail to see the link between strategy execution and the fundamentals of effective transformation management.

The Strategist's Handbook. Timothy Galpin, Oxford University Press. © Timothy Galpin (2023).
DOI: 10.1093/oso/9780192885203.003.0006

Organizational Dynamics Created by Strategy Execution

Because of senior management's affinity to the financial, operational, and techno-logical aspects of their organizations, transformation dynamics are often overlooked during the strategy formulation process and are further ignored as implementation gets underway. Table 5.1 lists the common organizational dynamics encountered during strategic transformation. These dynamics should be expected, as they show up with full force once strategy implementation begins.

Seven Fundamentals of Strategic Transformation Management

Because strategic transformation produces significant organizational dynamics, actions aimed at managing transformation help mitigate the risks created and stack the odds in favor of making the firm's desired strategy work. Seven fundamentals of transformation management facilitate the process:

1. Apply defined, clear implementation leadership
2. Address "me" issues quickly
3. Provide extensive communication
4. Ensure a focus on customers
5. Make tough decisions
6. Create focused initiatives
7. Manage resistance at every level

Identify and Apply Defined, Clear Implementation Leadership

In any transformation effort, leadership is important in providing clear direc-tion for the move into an uncertain future. Unfortunately, however, exceptional

Table 5.1 Organizational dynamics during strategic transformation

• Aggressive financial targets	• Accelerated timelines
• Increased customer expectations	• Intense investor scrutiny
• Organizational restructuring	• Politics and positioning
• Cultural obstacles	• Workforce "me issues"
• New workforce skill requirements	• Retention of key talent
• Communication issues	• Employee motivation

leadership is frequently difficult to find during major transformation efforts. Too often, management who should be "transformation champions" opt for playing politics instead of providing visible leadership to the organization. This tendency only makes it more difficult for people to get resolution of their "me issues" described below that generate so much uncertainty and low morale across the workforce. When people see top managers merely jockeying for political position during a strategic transition, with little or no focus on the business, its customers, or its employees, the seeds of a failed strategy are sown. Ensuring that someone oversees strategy implementation and defining clear lines of authority helps mitigate the political game-playing.

Often entailing cross-functional coordination, new technologies, shifting lines of authority, and redesigned operational processes, strategic transformation must be managed as a very large and complex project. Accordingly, unless a specific person (the "implementation program manager" or "transformation manager" identified in Chapter 4) is accountable for the project's success, the implementation effort will be stymied by delays, false starts, and confusion. To be successful, the person in charge needs several key characteristics:

- Exceptional project leadership, project management, and project coordination skills.
- Clout with and respect from (the two do not always go hand in hand) the broader organization.
- Solid decision-making ability.
- A knack to lead and facilitate productive and efficient meetings that include various constituencies.
- An exceptional multitasker.
- Extremely organized.
- Consensus builder.
- Can create positive relationships with varied stakeholders at all levels of the organization.
- Effective communicator.
- Detail oriented, while also seeing the "big picture."
- Ability to recognize and solve problems quickly.

Like a camera's lens, the implementation manager should be able to zoom in quickly on the details and just as comfortably zoom out to view the broader picture. Both views are essential to efficient and effective strategy execution problem-solving, decision-making, and direction-setting. It is often a tall order for many organizations to identify a person that possesses all of these characteristics to lead strategy implementation efforts, but identifying and allocating the right person for the role is a key component of strategy execution success.

Address "Me Issues" Quickly

During the earliest stages of any strategic transformation effort, once people become aware of what is happening, they begin to grapple with the newly introduced uncertainty. Consequently, the foremost topic to become a matter of great concern among the workforce at all levels of the organization, from executives to front-line employees, is personal uncertainty, their "me issues." Before people become focused on making required operational, service, or technological changes, they consider the personal impacts, including:

- Will this affect my pay?
- Will I potentially be put out of a job?
- To whom will I be reporting?
- Will my role change?
- Do I have the required new skills?
- Does this impact my advancement opportunities?
- Will I have to move locations?

Rather than business issues, these questions take precedence and are the real issues in the minds of managers and employees. Moreover, executives, managers, and front-line employees keep asking these questions until they get answers, and the time that the workforce spends worrying about these questions is time that is not being spent on running the business or implementing the desired strategy.

Productivity, morale, and performance inevitably decline at all organizational levels during transformation efforts, and these declines can be especially vexing during major strategic transformation efforts. Patterns of decline (decreased customer service, for example, or lower levels of operational and financial productivity) for senior managers, middle managers, and employees are staggered over time as a strategy execution effort unfolds (see Figure 5.1).

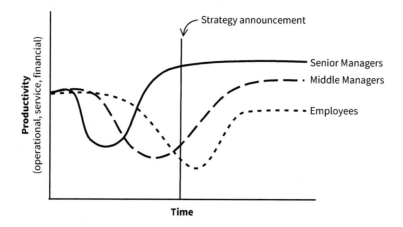

Figure 5.1 Staggered pattern of productivity loss during organizational transformation

The pattern illustrated in Figure 5.1 comes about because senior managers are the first to know about the organization's new or revised strategy, especially in organizations that employ a traditional top-down strategy approach, and they get their "me issues" answered first. Next, middle managers are informed, and finally employees are filled in. Furthermore, the staggered knowledge that results has tangible implications. Specifically, senior managers stop communicating about what is going on, as they are informed and know where they stand on the "me issues." So senior management relax, believing that the difficult work of strategy formulation and announcement is behind them. As a result, executives place lower priority on ongoing implementation management, too often taking the attitude that "they have been told about the new strategy, so everyone just needs to get back to work." Executives forget that many middle managers and employees are just learning about the new strategy and the changes required, and are only now receiving information that executives were informed of some time ago. The bottom line is that senior managers must manage strategy execution based on where most of the organization is, not based on where they themselves are.

When seeing the staggered productivity loss curves in Figure 5.1, people often ask, "Why does the employee productivity curve never return to previous levels?" The key reason is that when management do a poor job of managing implementation effort and the associated transformation dynamics, people decide to leave the organization. Moreover, the exodus is most prevalent among key talent—those individuals that are most important to the success of the organization. A survey conducted by the American Management Association found that typically 25 percent of top-performing employees in an organization leave within ninety days of a major transformation event (Withenshaw, 2003). Your best players find a new team first because they are marketable and can leave. This results in what is known as "the cesspool syndrome" (Bedeian and Armenakis, 1998), characterized by the best talent leaving an organization with average and below-average talent left behind to run the business—a situation no organization wants to find itself in.

Slow movement through the strategy implementation process prolongs the period of unrest and uncertainty, giving employees more time to dwell on their personal issues, all the time distracting them from maintaining peak productivity and performance. Implementing changes quickly, but not recklessly, clears up uncertainty and leaves less time for a decline in productivity to develop. Thus, both the depth and the duration of the productivity drop illustrated in Figure 5.1 are mitigated. Fast-track implementation, conducted at prudent but not reckless speed, also ensures that the expected gains of a new strategy will be realized as soon as possible. Cost reduction and growth enhancements can be significant and should be accelerated. Accelerating the implementation timetable by even one month can generate millions of dollars in cost savings, revenue improvement, or both.

Here is an easy-to-grasp example. Let's assume that the management of a 1,000-person organization want to implement new strategic initiatives (expansion into new geographic markets, customer service improvement, and major operational cost reduction) aimed at lowering costs and increasing growth. These strategies will require various changes to operations, organizational structure, and technology. Upon learning about the strategies, the 1,000 managers and employees talk about the impending changes for just 1 hour per day instead of doing their job. They discuss questions like "What organizational changes will they make? Will there be layoffs? What processes will be redesigned? What will the changes mean for our pay and benefits? Will we be asked to move?"—among many others. At five days per week, 5,000 hours of productivity (operational, service, and financial output) are lost each week. At an average of four weeks per month, 20,000 hours of productivity are lost each month. Data demonstrates that the typical strategy implementation period in most companies takes at least twenty-four months, and often much longer (see Appendix A). Therefore, with 20,000 hours of productivity lost per month, in this example at least 480,000 hours of productivity are lost during a twenty-four-month implementation period.

Moreover, unlike the example above, managers and employees typically do not discuss their concerns about changes for just 1 hour per day, and the conversations do not occur only before or after work or at lunch. People are distracted by the implementation for major portions of the workday, every day, until their "me issues" are resolved and the implementation effort is effectively complete. In fact, the US Department of Labor reports that an individual's normal productivity drops by as much as 3.6 hours per day during a major organizational transition (Withenshaw, 2003). Therefore, the productivity loss in the above example can be as much as 1.7 million hours over a prototypical twenty-four month implementation period.

The bottom line: at best, prolonged strategy execution causes a deep and lengthy drop in workforce productivity. At worst, because of the significant productivity drop and loss of key talent, extended implementation often results in a strategy that misses projected cost reduction, productivity improvement, or growth targets. Strategy execution conducted with prudent, not reckless, speed is the best way to prevent protracted and substantial drops in organizational productivity, an exodus of key talent, and ultimately a failed strategy. The typical benefits of strategy execution conducted with prudent speed include:

- better cash flows
- improved workforce productivity
- quicker go to market
- greater workforce confidence regarding the organization's direction, strategic focus, and management decision-making
- faster workforce acceptance of the new strategy
- higher levels of employee engagement and motivation
- better customer relations and communications.

Provide Extensive Communication

Communication is a major factor contributing to successful transformation efforts and is critically important during strategy execution. Strategic transformation creates a setting of great uncertainty. Rumors and speculation abound throughout the organization. Clear and constant communication throughout the implementation process provides answers and dispel rumors.

Beyond seeking answers to their immediate personal "me issues," the workforce also needs to know about the operational, technology, and financial implications of the new strategy because these matters will have a direct impact on their personal situations. When the workforce does not receive regular and repeated messages about the direction of the company, about why the changes are happening, about who is involved, about how implementation will unfold, and about the time frame that has been created for meeting goals, they perceive leadership, direction, and control to be lacking. Clear, consistent, and frequent communication (at least weekly and perhaps more often), even when it only takes the form of brief updates on progress, goes a long way toward building the commitment of middle managers and employees during implementation. The most frightening message during strategic transformation is silence, which must be avoided at all costs. How to reduce the rumor mill that often flourishes during major transformation efforts through effective communication is covered in Chapter 6.

Ensure a Focus on Customers

Any kind of major organizational transformation requires that a company become introspective. Once a chosen strategy has been announced, the focus of the organization turns inward to its operations, technology, and people. As a result, many organizations experience lower sales, as well as increased complaints about customer service, problems organizations cannot afford. The spotlight is on the new strategy, and stakeholders including analysts, managers, employees, and customers want to see the strategy in action and the results created. When sales and service suffer, people immediately question the viability of the new strategy. Moreover, customers may begin to flee to competitors in the belief that service has been abandoned or impaired by the new strategy.

If during strategic transformation the organization loses sight of the market, then sales and service (the points of contact with the customer) become the most vulnerable areas. For example, studies by Bain, KPMG, and Watson Wyatt have all found that customer defections are a major reason why major strategic transformation efforts such as implementing a merger or acquisition fail to deliver projected value (Miles and Rouse, 2012). Throughout strategy implementation management must ensure that the organizations' critical contact with customers is protected. During strategic transformation efforts managers should pay particular attention to maintaining the standards of sales and service that customers expect and install specific mecha-nisms to sustain good relationships with customers. Exceptional care of customers during early implementation of strategic transformation can include special initia-tives like short-term sales incentives, additional training and information for service personnel at help desks and call centers, and special advertising aimed at commu-nicating to customers that there is a continued commitment to service throughout the implementation of a new strategy. Actions to boost sales and service must be overtly planned and quickly executed.

Make Timely, Tough Decisions

A transformation of any consequence requires tough decisions to be made, such as organizational restructuring, operational redesign, and changing workforce roles and responsibilities. Often, however, managers do not want to frighten the orga-nization with too much transformation and unwisely delay these tough decisions. However, making timely, tough decisions keeps strategy execution moving for-ward and on track. In fact, decision-making has been found to be a key factor in implementation success (Cleary, Hartnett, and Dubuque, 2011; Lundqvist, 2012).

During strategic transformation, it is almost impossible for senior management to be perceived by everyone as totally fair. The difficult issues that must be dealt with during implementation include organizational structure, reporting channels, spans of control, roles and responsibilities, identification of positions, and selection of people. Seldom are there easy, clear-cut answers in these areas, but senior man-agement must make decisions quickly (with prudent speed), implement them, and abide by them. Otherwise, the organization rapidly perceives that top management is unorganized and indecisive, and that strategy execution lacks leadership. Delay-ing a decision in the hope that the perfect solution eventually will surface is itself a poor decision.

Create Focused Initiatives

When a new strategy is formulated and decided upon, each functional area (finance, systems, human resources, operations, marketing, and so on) often launches its own implementation actions and proceeds with the best of intentions. Unfortunately, however, go-it-alone managers and employees in specific areas unintentionally create harm that is manifested in several ways:

- The actions of specific areas that are uncoordinated leave the impression that the overall implementation effort is disjointed.
- Because the functionally specific efforts are uncoordinated, they often overlap, resulting in duplication of effort and inefficiency.

- Divergent activities allow important details to fall through the cracks between functions, never to be recovered.
- The aims, timing, and outcomes of uncoordinated actions often wind up in conflict with one another.

In any transformation initiative, tolerance of divergent activities can seriously hinder success. Even though various functional areas may be taking specific actions, all the elements of strategy execution must be synchronized. As identified in Chapter 4, strategy execution should be managed as a fully coordinated project with a visible project management structure.

Manage Resistance to Transformation at Every Level

People resist transformation and, as emphasized throughout this chapter, the degree of organizational transformation involved in strategy execution is often significant. Consequently, the extent of strategic transformation frequently fosters substantial resistance that may seem insurmountable and can destroy even the best-planned implementation effort.

Resistance is prevalent throughout a long history of writings about strategic organizational transformation. Seven decades ago, Lawrence (1954, p. 49) wrote in the *Harvard Business Review*,

> One of the most baffling and recalcitrant of the problems which business executives face is employee resistance to transformation. Such resistance may take several forms, persistent reduction in output, increase in the number of "quits" and requests for transfer, chronic quarrels, sullen hostility, wildcat or slowdown strikes, and, of course, the expression of a lot of pseudo-logical reasons why the transformation will not work. Even the pettier forms of this resistance can be troublesome.

Likewise, in a cross-industry study conducted by Clemons, Thatcher, and Row (1995) of why major transformation efforts have failed in large companies, the researchers found that the failures were unrelated to the technical aspects of organizations. In general, companies have the skill (or can hire it) to implement the technical aspects of transformation efforts. Rather, the authors contend, a major reason for failure is what they call "political risk," which they describe as the risk that changes will not be completed because of organizational resistance, or because of the progressive fading of commitment to the transformation effort. They contend that when resistance is substantial, organizations falter at both the development and the implementation of a transformation project. Peck (1995), who also studied major transformation projects, identifies "organizational resistance" as the top barrier to success and reports that 92 percent of respondents identified resistance as the main problem transformation efforts encountered. This finding is supported by

Longo (1996), who notes, in writing about the difficulty of transformation efforts, "the number one source of difficulty with implementation is the disregard for, or misunderstanding of, the resistance to transformation" (p. 69).

However, rather than an insurmountable obstacle, when viewed differently workforce resistance can assist with strategic transformation efforts. For example, Ford and Ford (2009, p. 100) state,

> It's true that resistance can be irrational and self-serving. But like it or not, it is an important form of feedback. Dismissing it robs you of a powerful tool as you implement transformation. It takes a strong leader to step up and engage when a transformation effort meets with pushback. If you can gain understanding, and learning from behaviors you perceive as threatening, you will ultimately deliver better results.

Moreover, Bateh, Castaneda, and Farah (2013, p. 113) assert,

> In the context of transformation management research, the issue of resistance occupies a crucial place. Organizations should be aware of the human element and its implications for the success of all transformation management decisions. The success of transformation management depends upon the organizational structure, availability of resources, vision and mission of the organization, and employees' willingness to work towards the transformation related goals. Managers who ignore this last element guarantee themselves an uphill battle, if not a sure failure.

Even with all the information about resistance to transformation that has been made available, there is still much misunderstanding among managers at all levels about the causes of and actions to address people's resistance to transformation. One reason for the continued confusion can be attributed to the education and training that most managers receive. Although the situation is shifting, many MBA programs and management training courses still focus primarily on the "hard" (technical, operational, financial, and analytical) aspects of business, dealing only in a cursory way with organizational transformation. As a result, management training does a poor job of addressing how to work through resistance encountered during major strategic transformation efforts. Another reason is that managers' practical experience during the strategy formulation process, often with a particular focus on analytics, merely serves to reinforce their training and education while undermining their ability to gain a sound understanding of why and how people resist transformation during implementation and what to do about it.

If an organization's strategy is to be implemented successfully, then resistance to transformation must not be allowed to remain a mystery to management. To simplify matters, Figure 5.2 presents a straightforward, three-level "Resistance Pyramid" (Galpin, 1996b) illustrating the key reasons for people's resistance during transformation efforts and the actions management can take to address resistance at each level. Although resistance to transformation can never be fully eliminated, the actions identified at each level in Figure 5.2 go a long way toward mitigating workforce resistance. The three levels represent a progressive hierarchy of the reasons why transformation is resisted. The base level, "not knowing," represents people's lack of knowledge about the new strategy and implementation requirements. The middle level, "not able," represents people's lack of ability to perform the tasks made necessary to effectively implement the desired strategy. The top level, "not willing," represents people's personal reluctance to make the effort to transform. Moreover, each level of the Resistance Pyramid suggests a tangible action for managing resistance. At the base level of "not knowing," what is required is communication to first make people aware of the desired strategy and subsequently to keep them informed about the implementation effort. At the middle level of "not able," what is required is training and skill-building. At the top level of "not willing," what is required is performance management consisting of setting clear team and individual goals, measuring performance against the established goals, providing feedback and coaching about team and individual progress, and providing rewards and recognition for achieving set targets.

It is important to recognize that resistance is natural and not necessarily an indication that something is going wrong with the implementation. Figure 5.3 illustrates the "20-60-20 rule." Predictably, about 20 percent of the workforce, the "enablers," will be supportive of the changes taking place, and management should engage this group to assist with implementation. On the other end of the spectrum, about 20 percent of the workforce, the "resistors," will be very much against changes taking place. Management can try to get resistors on board with the needed changes, but this is a difficult group, and they often take an inordinate amount of time to deal with. The most important group for management to focus much of their attention on is the "undecided" group in the middle 60 percent. They are your "swing vote" and, most importantly, this group is the majority who ultimately will or will not

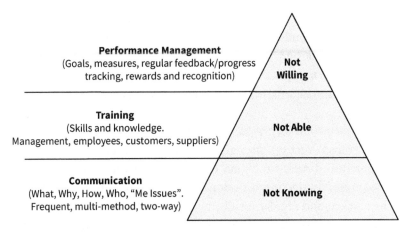

Figure 5.2 The Resistance Pyramid: addressing resistance with action

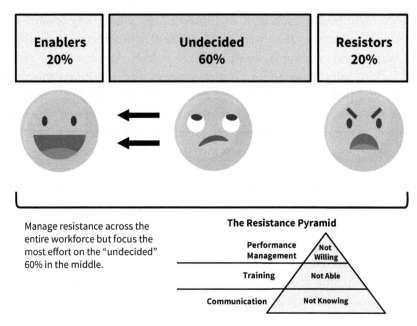

Figure 5.3 The 20-60-20 rule
Images by rawpixel.com on Freepik.

implement the desired changes effectively by either aligning with the enablers or the resistors.

Participants and Key Activities

There can be multiple internal and external participants involved in managing strategic organizational transformation who perform essential activities, including:

- *Senior executives.* Allocate resources to implementation management, deliver communications, set performance goals, oversee the implementation process, and make key decisions including personnel changes, capital expenditures, and organizational redesign.
- *External transformation consultants.* Assist with planning and crafting transformation communications, organizational redesign, and workforce training and development.
- *Internal implementation program manager.* Sometimes called a "transformation lead" or "transformation manager," this role has responsibility for day-to-day management and cross-functional coordination of the strategy implementation process (project budgeting, milestone-setting and tracking, issues identification and resolution, and regular results measurement, tracking, and reporting).
- *Implementation task forces composed of internal operational and functional managers and employees.* Provide specialized expertise and input throughout

the strategy execution process (communications, operations, sales, customer service, information technology (IT), human resources (HR), marketing, legal, finance, and so forth).

- *Middle management and employees.* Strategic transformation efforts require broad representation of middle management and front-line employees who participate in the firm's strategy execution efforts at the functional and front-line level.

Best Practices

Put as much focus on strategic transformation management as on strategy formulation. Many organizations devote significant resources to internal and external strategic analysis during strategy formulation, while strategy execution and strategic transformation management is an afterthought. Successful strategy implementation and transformation management require management focus and resource allocation not just during strategy formulation, but also throughout execution.

Rigorously apply the seven fundamentals of transformation management. As described above, seven fundamentals facilitate successful strategic transformation: clear implementation leadership, address "me" issues quickly, provide extensive communication, ensure a focus on customers, make tough decisions, create focused initiatives, and manage workforce resistance at every level.

Potential Pitfalls

Skimping on transformation management actions. Applying some of the seven fundamentals of transformation management is helpful, but not sufficient. For instance, management may ensure a focus on customers during implementation and create focused initiatives to implement various aspects of the desired strategy. However, if management ignore workforce "me issues" and do not provide regular communications, organizational productivity will suffer.

Not addressing each level of the Resistance Pyramid. For example, it is valuable when management address the "not knowing" level of the Resistance Pyramid by communicating regularly. However, if management don't put in place the performance management elements to address the "not willing" level of the pyramid, much of the workforce will still resist making required changes.

Key Frameworks, Tools, and Templates

There are several key tools that help manage strategic transformation. Below are descriptions of key templates used to prepare for and manage strategic transformation. These tools are included in Appendix B.

The Resistance Pyramid. Illustrates the key reasons for people's resistance to transformation and the actions management can take to address resistance at each level of the pyramid.

Communications planning matrix. Used to develop a detailed communications plan addressing all stakeholders that the strategy execution effort will impact (see Chapter 6).

Retention and re-engagement matrix. Used to develop a detailed plan to retain and engage each key group or individual identified as essential to the success of the strategy implementation effort (see Chapter 7).

Best-Practice Case Example

A description of Petrochemical Inc.'s approach to managing strategic transformation in practice is summarized in Table 5.2.

Table 5.2 Managing strategic transformation at Petrochemical Inc.*

The need:

- As described in Chapters 3 and 4, from over 30 potential strategic initiatives, senior management of Petrochemical Inc. (a global petrochemical company) identified 5 high-impact priority strategies: customer service improvement, acquisitions, new geographic market entry, sourcing and purchasing efficiency, and reduction of administrative costs.
- An implementation program management infrastructure was put in place consisting of a steering committee, an implementation program team led by an implementation manager, and a series of implementation task forces.
- Knowing they would inevitably encounter workforce resistance to the changes being implemented, management needed to effectively prepare for and manage the strategic transformation process.

The solution:

- The senior team applied the seven fundamentals to facilitate successful strategic transformation by assigning clear implementation leadership, addressing "me" issues quickly, providing extensive communication, ensuring a focus on customers, making tough decisions, creating focused initiatives, and managing workforce resistance at every level.
- Using the Resistance Pyramid, management identified key actions to address employee resistance at each level of the pyramid: (1) communications to address the workforce "not knowing" about the strategic changes and the rationale for them, (2) training to help those in the workforce who were "not able" to implement the required changes, and (3) performance management to address members of the organization who were "not willing" to make the required changes.

The results:

- Employee engagement was assessed each year during the 5-year implementation period, with the firm's engagement scores increasing each year and exceeding industry and cross-industry benchmarks.
- Moreover, business results included Petrochemical Inc. growing faster, gaining market share, and reporting higher profitability than their benchmark industry competitors.

---

* Because of non-disclosure considerations, a global petrochemical company is referred to throughout the illustration as Petrochemical Inc.

Chapter Summary

- Strategy execution must be treated as nothing less than a far-reaching transformation management effort across the organization.
- The discipline of "transformation management" presents significant challenges to a firm's leadership during the strategy execution process.
- To assume that a strategy that looks good on paper will ensure easy implementation is naive.
- Transformation dynamics are often overlooked during the strategy formulation process and are further ignored as implementation gets underway.
- Seven fundamentals of transformation management facilitate the strategic transformation process: clear implementation leadership, address "me" issues quickly, provide extensive communication, ensure a focus on customers, make tough decisions, create focused initiatives, and manage workforce resistance at every level.
- In any transformation effort, leadership is important in providing clear direction for the move into an uncertain future, therefore ensuring someone oversees strategy implementation and defining clear lines of authority helps mitigate political game-playing.
- Unless a specific person (the "implementation program manager" identified in Chapter 4) is accountable for the project's success, the implementation effort will be stymied by delays, false starts, and overwhelming confusion.
- Like a camera's lens, the implementation manager should be able to zoom in quickly on the details and just as comfortably zoom out to view the broader picture.
- When learning of strategic transformation, the foremost topic of concern among the workforce at all levels of the organization, from executives to front-line employees, is personal uncertainty, their "me issues" (my pay, my role, my job, and so forth).
- Productivity, morale, and performance almost always decline at all organizational levels during transformation efforts, with the US Department of Labor reporting that an individual's normal productivity drops by as much as 3.6 hours per day during a major organizational transition.
- A survey conducted by the American Management Association found that typically 25 percent of top-performing employees in an organization leave within ninety days of a major transformation event, resulting in what is known as "the cesspool syndrome" characterized by the best talent leaving an organization with average and below-average talent left behind to run the business.
- Slow movement through the strategy implementation process prolongs the period of unrest and uncertainty, giving employees more time to dwell on their personal issues.
- Fast-track implementation, conducted at prudent but not reckless speed, clears up uncertainty and leaves less time for a decline in productivity to develop.

- Communication is a major factor contributing to successful transformation efforts and is critically important during strategy execution.
- The most frightening message during strategic transformation is silence, which must be avoided at all costs.
- How to reduce the rumor mill, which often flourishes during major transformation efforts, through effective communication is discussed in Chapter 6.
- Once a chosen strategy has been announced, the focus of the organization turns inward to its operations, technology, and people, therefore many organizations experience lower sales, as well as increased complaints about customer service.
- During strategic transformation efforts managers should pay particular attention to maintaining the standards of sales and service that customers expect and install specific mechanisms to sustain good relationships with customers.
- A transformation of any consequence requires tough decisions to be made, such as organizational restructuring, operational redesign, and changing workforce roles and responsibilities.
- Making timely, tough decisions keeps strategy execution moving forward and on track, and decision-making has been found to be a key factor in implementation success.
- When a new strategy is formulated and decided upon, each functional area (finance, systems, HR, operations, marketing, and so on) often launches its own implementation actions and proceeds with the best of intentions.
- In any transformation initiative, tolerance of divergent activities can seriously hinder success, therefore all the elements of strategy execution must be synchronized.
- People resist transformation and as emphasized throughout this chapter the degree of organizational transformation involved in strategy execution is often significant.
- Research identifies "organizational resistance" as the top barrier to implementation success and that 92 percent of respondents identified resistance as the main problem transformation efforts encountered.
- A three-level "Resistance Pyramid" illustrates the key reasons for people's resistance during major transformation efforts and the actions management can take to address resistance at each level.
- Although resistance to transformation can never be fully eliminated, the actions identified at each level of the Resistance Pyramid go a long way toward mitigating workforce resistance.
- About 20 percent of the workforce will be "enablers" of strategic transformation, 20 percent will be "resistors," and the most important group for management to focus much of their attention on is the "undecided" group in the middle 60 percent.

- Best practices of managing strategic transformation include putting as much focus on strategic transformation management as on strategy formulation and rigorously applying the seven fundamentals of transformation management.
- Potential pitfalls of strategic transformation include skimping on transformation management actions and not addressing each level of the Resistance Pyramid.
- Key tools and templates to help manage strategic transformation include the Resistance Pyramid, the communications planning matrix, and the retention and re-engagement matrix.

Discussion Questions

1. What activities does your organization do well to manage strategic transformation? What transformation management activities could the organization perform better?
2. For your organization, who is typically involved in managing strategic transformation, both from internal staff and external advisers? Who should be involved?
3. What key transformation management tools and templates does your organization use? What others should they use?
4. What transformation management measures does your organization have in place? Are the measures sufficient? If not, what other measures should the organization put in place?
5. Does your organization apply the seven fundamentals of transformation management during strategy execution efforts? What could be done better to apply each fundamental?

Organizational Self-Assessment

Completing the following self-assessment (Table 5.3) will provide a view of how effectively your organization manages strategic transformation.

Steps to complete the self assessment.

1. Rate each item on a scale of 0 (poor) to 10 (excellent).
2. Make notes for each item to explain the rationale for the numerical rating.
3. Add all ten scores to get a TOTAL SCORE (maximum score = 100).

Rating scale:

> 0–20 = Poor (significant improvement needed)
> 21–40 = Below average (improvement needed in several areas)
> 41–60 = Average (identify areas of weakness and adjust)

Table 5.3 Organizational self-assessment: managing strategic transformation

Component	Rating (0 = poor, 10 = excellent)	Notes/rationale
When it comes to managing strategic transformation …		
1. We apply defined, clear implementation leadership		
2. We address "me" issues quickly		
3. We provide extensive communication		
4. We ensure a focus on customers		
5. We make tough decisions		
6. We create focused initiatives		
7. We manage resistance at every level of the Resistance Pyramid		
8. We use skilled transformation management resources		
9. Senior management are visibly involved in managing strategic transformation		
10. We put as much (or more) focus on managing strategic transformation as on strategy formulation		
TOTAL SCORE		

61–80 = Above average (identify areas that can still be improved)

81–100 = Excellent (continuously review and refine each component for each iteration of the organization's strategy efforts)

6

Communicate Even If There Is Nothing to Tell

"Customers will complain … A lot of us will be out of a job … The new strategy won't work …" Unfortunately, these are familiar phrases uttered by countless employees across numerous organizations when they learn of strategic changes management wants to make. When asked where they first heard these statements, employees often say, "in the lunchroom," "at the coffee machine," or "I saw it in our group text messages." In other words, they heard them through the rumor mill, damaging strategy execution before it even gets started. Therefore, throughout strategic transformation efforts, management need to provide effective communications so that rumors are not the main source of information. Unfortunately, however, ineffective strategic communications seem to be the rule rather than the norm. For example, in a survey of 124 executives and managers representing 21 various industries (Galpin and Herndon, 2014), 90 percent of respondents identified communication as important to the success of major transformation initiatives such as mergers and acquisitions (M&As). However, in another survey of 337 executives and managers from 31 industries, only 6 percent of respondents reported that their M&A communications are done well (Galpin, 2020). Why does this gap exist? The top ten reported reasons strategic transformation communication is ineffective are (Galpin and Herndon, 2014):

1. Insufficient resources
2. Too slow
3. Inadequate senior management attention
4. Not all stakeholders were communicated to
5. Did not customize messages for each stakeholder group
6. The messages were inconsistent
7. Launched too late
8. Not well planned
9. Not frequent enough
10. Ended too early

As early as three decades ago, management research and writing identified communications as a key component of effective organizational transformation. For example, according to May and Kettelhut (1996, p. 9), "Open communication and

The Strategist's Handbook. Timothy Galpin, Oxford University Press. © Timothy Galpin (2023).
DOI: 10.1093/oso/9780192885203.003.0007

collaboration are essential [to effective transformation]. Open communications clarify expectations and reduce ambiguity." Haslett (1995) also emphasizes communication as a key first step in any transformation effort. Jack Welch, former CEO of General Electric, offers a real-life example of employing communication to lower resistance. In his interview with Sherman (1993, p. 84), he comments, "How do you bring people into the transformation process? Start with reality. Get all the facts out. Give people the rationale for transformation, laying it out in the clearest, most dramatic terms. When everybody gets the same facts, they'll generally come to the same conclusion. Only after everyone agrees on the reality and resistance is lowered can you begin to get buy-in to the needed changes." Longo (1996, p. 69) also emphasizes that companies generally do a poor job of communicating transformation to their people: "The second biggest problem [beyond a lack of involvement] is communication. Getting people to buy into [transformation] isn't easy because people put little stock in what management is selling. Senior managers dilute, filter, and distort information." Moreover, a survey of 403 human resources professionals of manager level and above conducted by the Society for Human Resource Management (2007) found that the top two reported obstacles faced during major organizational changes were employee resistance and communication breakdown.

Beyond the transformation management research, unfortunately, experience also demonstrates that organizations need to do a better job of communicating, not only initially but also throughout their strategy execution efforts. For example, a large technology hardware manufacturer decided to pursue a strategy of providing technology services in addition to their hardware product lines. As the strategy implementation process unfolded, the firm's director of communications sent out information about the implementation process only when there was "something important" to tell people, such as which tech services the firm would be offering to clients or what internal job openings were available in the newly formed services business. This practice of not communicating until there is something important to tell meant that the announcement of the new strategy and communications about the implementation of the strategy were separated by several months. However, the director of communications continually insisted that managers and employees in the firm were receiving enough information, and that they did not want to be bothered by too many communications. About three months into the implementation process, top management held a "middle-management strategy update briefing," which included a question-and-answer session. The first question put to the senior team by one of the middle managers in attendance was "How can I tell the people in my department what they need to do to support the new services business, when I have heard nothing about what is going on?" This question was immediately echoed by three other managers. These managers went on to say that there had been a grand announcement of the new strategy, but they had heard nothing since. After this meeting, a weekly implementation communications schedule was put in place.

An Interpersonal Communication Model, with an Organizational Communication Application

The Johari Window (Luft and Ingham, 1955) is a well-established model of building effective one-to-one interpersonal communication that can be applied to an organizational context, helping management develop and deliver effective strategic communications. The Window was originally developed to improve individual interpersonal interactions by assessing the ways in which people give and receive information. It is a grid divided into four regions that represent different types of information during communication (see Figure 6.1). The basic concept of the Johari Window is that open, two-way communication can enhance interpersonal effectiveness. Within the broader context of organizations, the Johari Window can improve organizational effectiveness also through open, two-way communication; but first, it's important to understand how the model works on a personal level.

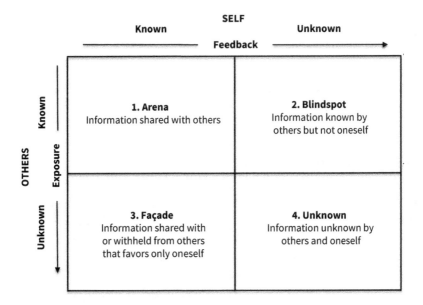

Figure 6.1 The Johari Window

Region 1: The Arena

The Arena is the area of shared information. When people share information and understand each other, their interpersonal relationships tend to be better. The larger the Arena, the more shared information, and the more effective, productive, and mutually beneficial an interpersonal relationship is likely to be.

Region 2: The Blindspot

The Blindspot involves information that is known by others but not oneself. The Blindspot can damage interpersonal relationships because it's almost impossible to truly understand people's actions and points of view without knowing why they behave and think the way they do.

Region 3: The Façade

The Façade hinders interpersonal effectiveness in that the information in this area favors only oneself. Information in the Façade protects people from others knowing negative things about them. People might not share such information simply because they're apathetic. But more often, it can be because they desire power and control.

Region 4: The Unknown

The Unknown involves information that is unknown by others and oneself. The area of the unknown has the most potential for creativity if all parties are willing to work together to bring that information to light.

Organizational Implications

During organizational transformation senior managers may try to keep information from those in lower-level positions for the same reasons that people keep information from each other in personal relationships: fear, power, or apathy. This creates a small organizational Arena and a large organizational Façade.

A large Façade favors senior management and puts everyone else in the organization at a disadvantage. This often leads people to distrust, dislike, and even sabotage of strategic initiatives. In addition, a Blindspot can form when senior management are unaware of other stakeholders' (e.g., middle management, front-line employees, customers, and so forth) views about the strategic transformation effort.

The Johari Window can be adapted to facilitate strategic transformation by enhancing organizational communication (see Figure 6.2). During strategic transformation it is vitally important for management to expand the Arena along the two axes, Feedback and Exposure, which are pivotal to effective organizational communication. Exposing more information to stakeholders expands the "organizational arena" (the area of shared information) along the vertical axis and increasing feedback expands the Arena along the horizonal axis. Moreover, by expanding the organizational arena management simultaneously reduces the organizational Blindspot, Façade, and Unknown.

Figure 6.2   Strategic transformation Johari

A Four-Phase Process

Table 6.1 depicts four phases of a strategic transformation communication process. Phase 1 is "awareness-building," which includes announcing the effort to all stakeholders, explaining the details, and identifying and addressing any workforce issues that may surface such as employees worrying that there may be layoffs. Phase 2, "implementation action," entails rolling out changes, providing training in new skills, roles, and processes, providing performance feedback to management and employees, and adjusting implementation as required. Phase 3 focuses on communicating "progress status" by identifying early "quick wins" and regularly monitoring and reporting progress. Phase 4, "follow-up," involves measuring and reporting success, and applying organizational learning to subsequent strategic transformation efforts. Although depicted as linear for clarity of discussion, it should be noted that these phases are not necessarily sequential. They often overlap as strategy execution unfolds.

Build a Comprehensive Transformation Communications Plan

A well-designed strategic transformation communications plan includes multiple touchpoints across various stakeholder groups. The plan clarifies communication timing, roles, and responsibilities throughout a transformation effort. The communications planning matrix (see Figure 6.3) is a helpful tool to identify each key element (stakeholders, goals, key messages, vehicles, timing, and accountabilities) of a strategic transformation communications plan.

Table 6.1 Four phases of communication during strategic transformation

Phase	Scope	Purpose
Phase 1: Awareness-building "This is what is happening."	Organization-wide	• Provide the "big picture." • Link transformation initiatives with strategy. • Reaffirm the organization's values. • Announce senior management involvement and support. • Give specific information about the process. • Identify and address workforce issues.
Phase 2: Implementation action "This is what we are doing."	Project-specific	• Roll out changes. • Provide skills, roles, and process training. • Provide performance feedback to management and employees. • Adjust implementation as required.
Phase 3: Progress status "This is how it's going."	Project-specific	• Identify "quick wins." • Monitor and report progress.
Phase 4: Follow-up "This is what we learned."	Organization-wide	• Measure and report success. • Apply organizational learning to subsequent strategic transformation efforts.

Identify Key Stakeholders

The first step in using the matrix is to identify key internal and external stake-holders, which may include middle managers, front-line employees, customers, suppliers, shareholders, and communities in which the organization operates. To tailor communications to each group, it is important to identify the interests of various stakeholders. Most people want to know what's in the proposed changes for them. They want to know how their work will be affected, whether they will have to relocate, and so forth. When people learn "what's in it for them," they then are more willing to listen to information about the broader organizational benefits such as more revenue or increased market share. For example, middle managers typically want to know whether they will manage the same people or report to the same boss. Shareholders want to know how changes will affect earnings. Suppliers want

Who (stakeholders)	Why (objective)	What (messages)	How (vehicles)	When (frequency)	Owner (development, delivery)
Employees	Retention, Re-engagement, Maintain productivity	Strategic rationale, implementation plans, goals, progress updates	FAQs, Email, Town Halls	Weekly, Monthly	Delivery: Executives, Managers Development: Communications department, Consultants
Customers	Maintain relationship	Strategic rationale, progress updates	Phone calls, emails, media, meetings	As required	Delivery: Executives Development: Marketing
Investors	Maintain shares	Financial and operational targets, progress updates	Analyst calls, Press releases	Monthly, quarterly	Delivery: Executives Development: Investor relations

Figure 6.3 Example communications planning matrix

to know whether their orders will be cut or whether their production efforts should be stepped up. Members of local communities may want to know whether jobs will be lost, or new jobs will be available. If stakeholders' questions are not answered by management, stakeholders will base their views on rumor and speculation, which will be less than accurate.

Determine Communication Objectives

Next, it is essential to determine the objectives of communicating with each stakeholder. For example, the objective of communications with employees may be to retain and re-engage key talent and maintain productivity across the broader workforce throughout implementation, whereas communications to investors would be geared toward them retaining or even increasing their shareholdings. Likewise, customer communications are aimed at maintaining or even strengthening the firm's relationship with them.

Decide on the Messaging

The third step of the planning matrix is to decide the messaging to various stakeholders that will best achieve the communication objectives identified in step two. Rationale for the new strategy, implementation plans and goals, and progress updates will all be messages important to deliver to middle management, front-line employees, and customers, while financial and operational targets will be of interest to investors.

Identify the Vehicles

The fourth step of the planning process is to identify the communications vehicles that will be used to communicate with each stakeholder group. For instance, intranet FAQs (frequently asked questions), group texts, emails, and face-to-face "town halls" can all be used for workforce communications. Analyst calls and press releases are appropriate vehicles for investors. Phone calls, emails, press releases, social media, and face-to-face meetings are all useful to communicate with customers.

Determine the Frequency

The fifth element of the planning matrix is to determine the frequency of communications with various stakeholders. Messaging can be done daily, weekly, monthly, and so forth, or as required when news about the transformation process is available.

Identify the Owners

Lastly, the owners of communications development and delivery should be identified. For example, members of the firm's communications department might be responsible for crafting the content of various employee messages or developing talking points for face-to-face meetings between managers and employees, while executives are responsible for delivering workforce communications.

Fair Process: Communicate Even When There Is Nothing to Tell

A "killer phrase" during strategy implementation expressed by numerous management teams is "We will only communicate when there is something to tell." However, early in an implementation process, it may not be possible to communicate definitive answers to people's questions about positions, roles, pay and rewards, and so forth because the details may not yet be settled. Although details should be provided as quickly as possible, their absence does not mean communication should be held back until detailed answers are available. Regular, frequent communication should be continued, with content centering on the "fair process" being undertaken to develop the answers that people are asking for.

Communication about the process can include information about the implementation management structure, the teams working on the implementation, membership of each implementation team, the implementation timeline, and the expected implementation deliverables. The concept of communicating a "fair process" is that people care not only about outcomes but also about the process used to produce those outcomes. Communication about a "fair process" has been found to positively influence attitudes and behaviors crucial to maintaining high workforce performance during transformation efforts (Kim and Mauborgne, 1997). Therefore, you can always communicate during strategic transformation efforts, even if "there is nothing to tell."

Training Is a Key Part of Strategic Transformation Communications

We have already seen the importance of providing extensive communication throughout strategy execution. Beyond providing information and knowledge to help reduce workforce resistance, training to equip people with new skills they will need for new procedures, systems, and the like is also essential to facilitate successful strategy implementation. In their discussion about training as a tool for managing resistance to transformation, May and Kettelhut (1996, p. 8) observe "Individuals need to feel competent and to continually develop their competence. Transformation generally involves new knowledge, skills or abilities, and this often places people in positions where they initially lack that which they need to feel competent." Unfortunately, many executives view training as an expensive luxury. However, training is a necessity during strategic transformation efforts, significantly contributing to lowering workforce resistance to implementation.

Participants and Key Activities

There can be multiple internal and external participants involved in planning and delivering strategic transformation communications who perform essential activities, including:

- *Senior executives.* Allocate resources to implementation communications, approve implementation messaging, and deliver implementation communications.
- *Internal communications and training departments.* Plan and develop the content of transformation communications and workforce training. Coordinate transformation communications and training activities. Establish feedback mechanisms to solicit employee questions and feedback throughout the transformation effort.
- *External communications and training consultants.* Assist with planning and crafting the content of transformation communications and workforce training.

Best Practices

Make communication a priority. Unfortunately, management often view transformation communications as a side issue or they delegate it to others. However, management must communicate early and often, and overtly participate in transformation communications.

Link communications to strategic goals. Ensure messages are linked to the goals of the transformation effort. For example, suppose that a goal of the transformation effort is to grow market share. Messages about this effort should include the reasons for growing market share, the specific growth strategies, and the benefits of growth to each stakeholder (employees, customers, and shareholders).

Be candid. Strategic communications should be forthright. It is best not to gloss over potential problems. People should be made aware of the realistic limits of a strategy, so they are less likely to jump to conclusions about worst-case scenarios. For example, announcing that getting a struggling business unit back to a stable financial position entails a "retrenchment strategy" with a goal of 10 percent cost reduction over the next twelve months will help prevent people from assuming that the entire unit will be shut down.

Be proactive. Strategic communications should be proactive rather than reactive. Plan communications ahead of implementation and disseminate messages early. A proactive approach helps management from having to take a defensive position when a transformation effort gets underway.

Be consistent. All messages should be consistent and repeated through various channels such as videos, emails, face-to-face "town halls," online meetings, and so forth. Because of their personal filters, people are more likely to misinterpret a one-time announcement because they often do not hear the whole message, or they may focus only on certain aspects of a message. Most of the time, people care first about how proposed changes will affect them, their "me issues." Repeated, consistent communications help people absorb and internalize the full content of messages.

Regularly solicit feedback. Throughout strategy implementation efforts, management need to establish mechanisms for two-way communications. Stakeholders should be able to provide feedback during the design and roll-out of transformation efforts. Effective feedback can include stakeholders' questions, concerns, and improvement suggestions. Gathering stakeholder feedback throughout a transformation process helps to continually enhance and adjust implementation.

Potential Pitfalls

Delegating communications. If one exists, it can be helpful to delegate some aspects of transformation messaging to a firm's communications department, who can help formulate messages, set up delivery channels, and manage the logistics of various face-to-face communication events, for example. However, final accountability for delivery of strategic transformation communications must reside with management. When senior managers delegate communications, they send a strong message that the transformation effort isn't worth their time. The workforce interprets that as a lack of senior management commitment and as a result middle management and employees become reluctant to commit their own time and energy to the transformation effort.

Unclear and incomplete communications. Sending communications with unclear or incomplete descriptions of what is required results in implementation break-downs as employees don't understand exactly what they need to do, and they begin to question management's knowledge of the details. Implementation communications don't need to be perfect, but they do need to be thorough.

One and done. Management often take the view that once they announce a strategic initiative, the goals of the effort, or provide a new skills training course, then the job of communicating is done, but one-time communications are not sufficient. Once a transformation effort is underway, it's important to keep the channels of communication open. Ongoing, repeatable communications are required to build workforce knowledge and skills throughout a transformation effort.

One-way only. As changes cascade down through the organization to all levels during roll-out, people will have questions, and they need to feel that they're being listened to. They also may have helpful suggestions about how to best implement required changes in their specific departments or locations. Therefore, ongoing, two-way communications are required to solicit input and feedback from all stakeholders throughout the process.

Key Frameworks, Tools, and Templates

The primary tool to help develop and deliver effective strategic communications is the communications planning matrix. This template is used to develop a detailed communications plan addressing all stakeholders that the strategy execution effort will impact (see Appendix B).

Best-Practice Case Example

A description of Petrochemical Inc.'s approach to managing strategic transformation communications in practice is summarized in Table 6.2.

Table 6.2 Managing strategic transformation communications at Petrochemical Inc.*

The need:
- Senior management at Petrochemical Inc. recognized that continuous communication during implementation would be crucial to the implementation success of their chosen strategies: customer service improvement, acquisitions, new geographic market entry, sourcing and purchasing efficiency, and reduction of administrative costs.

The solution:
- Management assigned the internal communications department to develop a strategic transformation communications plan.
- Using the communications planning matrix, the communications team developed a multifaceted communications plan to address all internal and external stakeholders.
- The plan consisted of "two-way" communication to both disseminate information as well as regularly gather input and feedback from various stakeholder groups throughout the strategy execution process.
- Multiple "communications vehicles" were used including regularly updated intranet FAQs, group texts, emails, and face-to-face "town halls" conducted by senior management across various company locations.
- Employee feedback about their concerns, questions, and implementation improvement suggestions was regularly solicited and responded to.

The results:
- Anxiety among the workforce was identified as a key concern, especially regarding the "reduction of administrative costs" strategy. These concerns were addressed by management early and, although some layoffs did occur, management provided and communicated to the entire organization that all impacted employees were offered generous severance packages and extensive outplacement assistance.
- The quality and usefulness of the communications content and delivery was assessed quarterly during the first year of implementation and then assessed yearly during the remainder of the 5-year implementation period through stakeholder surveys, with the firm's communications efforts receiving high ratings from all stakeholder groups throughout implementation.

---

* Because of non-disclosure considerations, a global petrochemical company is referred to throughout the illustration as Petrochemical Inc.

Chapter Summary

- Throughout strategic transformation efforts, management need to provide effective communications so that rumors are not the main source of information.
- As early as three decades ago, management research and writing identified communications as a key component of effective organizational transformation.
- The Johari Window is a well-established model of building effective one-to-one interpersonal communication that can be applied to an organizational context, helping management develop and deliver effective strategic transformation communications.

- There are four phases of a strategic transformation communication process: awareness-building, implementation action, progress status, and follow-up.
- A well-designed strategic transformation communications plan includes multiple touchpoints across various stakeholder groups.
- The communications planning matrix is a helpful tool to identify each key element (stakeholders, goals, key messages, vehicles, timing, and accountabilities) of a strategic transformation communications plan.
- A "killer phrase" during strategy implementation expressed by numerous management teams is "We will only communicate when there is something to tell."
- The concept of communicating a "fair process" is that people care not only about outcomes but also about the processes used to produce those outcomes.
- Communication about the "fair process" has been found to positively influence attitudes and behaviors crucial to maintaining high workforce performance during transformation efforts.
- You can always communicate during strategic transformation efforts, even if "there is nothing to tell."
- Training to equip people with new skills they will need for new procedures is a necessity during strategic transformation efforts, significantly contributing to lowering workforce resistance to implementation.
- There can be multiple internal and external participants involved in planning and delivering strategic transformation communications who perform essential activities, including: senior executives, internal communications and training departments, and external communications and training consultants.
- The best practices of strategic transformation communications include: making communication a priority, linking communications to strategic goals, being candid, proactive, and consistent, and regularly soliciting feedback.
- Potential pitfalls of strategic transformation communications include: delegating communications, unclear and incomplete communications, "one-and-done" announcements, and one-way-only communications.
- Implementation communications don't need to be perfect, but they do need to be thorough.
- The primary tool to help manage develop and deliver an effective strategic communications plan is the communications planning matrix.

Discussion Questions

1. What activities does your organization do well regarding strategic transformation communications? What transformation communications activities could the organization perform better?

2. For your organization, who is typically involved in developing and delivering strategic transformation communications, both from internal staff and external advisers? Who should be involved?
3. What transformation communications vehicles and methods does your organization use? What others should they use?
4. What transformation communications measurement does your organization have in place? Are the measures sufficient? If not, what other measures should the organization put in place?
5. Does your organization establish two-way transformation communications, soliciting feedback, input, and suggestions from various stakeholders? What could be done better to establish two-way transformation communications?

Organizational Self-Assessment

Completing the following self-assessment (Table 6.3) will provide a view of how effectively your organization manages strategic transformation communications.

Steps to complete the self-assessment:

1. Rate each item on a scale of 0 (poor) to 10 (excellent).
2. Make notes for each item to explain the rationale for the numerical rating.
3. Add all ten scores to get a TOTAL SCORE (maximum score = 100).

Rating scale:

   0–20 = Poor (significant improvement needed)
  21–40 = Below average (improvement needed in several areas)
  41–60 = Average (identify areas of weakness and adjust)
  61–80 = Above average (identify areas that can still be improved)
  81–100 = Excellent (continuously review and refine each component for each iteration of the organization's strategy efforts)

Table 6.3 Organizational self-assessment: strategic transformation communications

Component	Rating (0 = poor, 10 = excellent)	Notes/rationale
When it comes to strategic transformation communications …		
1. We place high importance on transformation communications		
2. We place high importance on training during strategic transformation efforts		
3. We develop a comprehensive transformation communications plan addressing all stakeholders		
4. We start transformation communications early		
5. We continue transformation communications throughout the strategy execution process		
6. We establish two-way communications to solicit feedback, input, and suggestions from all stakeholders		
7. We use multiple "communications vehicles"		
8. We communicate "even when there is nothing to tell" by letting people know about the "fair process" of our transformation efforts		
9. Senior management are visibly involved in delivering strategic transformation communications		
10. We regularly assess the effectiveness of our strategic transformation communications		
TOTAL SCORE		

7

Your Best Players Will Find a New Team First—Retain and Re-Engage Them

Today's careers are more a collection of assignments than an accumulation of years at one firm. Work, especially at managerial levels, has become more of an activity than a place. Twenty- to thirty-year careers at patriarchal corporations are becoming extinct. Consequently, there has been an erosion of employees' loyalty toward their employers. One effect of this development is the increased difficulty of retaining the organization's "key talent." Moreover, even when key personnel stay on board, they lose their commitment, especially when the work environment becomes unstable, uncertain, or shifts dramatically, as is often the case during strategy execution.

Where Key Talent Goes, So Does Value

The impact of losing key talent during strategic transformation is summarized well by Green, Barbin, and Schmidt (2007, p. 44) who observe, "The real expertise about innovative products, services, or processes tends to be carried around by employees in their heads. Unlike an assembly line, employees are portable. They can walk out the door and never return … Once talent is gone, it can't be called back. And if enough talent leaves, there goes the firm's value." The reasons key talent often cite for leaving an organization during transformation efforts include poor communications (Schweiger and DeNisi, 1991), a loss of status (Cannella and Hambrick, 1993), and uncertainty about their role in the organization (Brahma and Srivastava, 2007).

Retaining Key Talent Is Not Enough

Although retention and engagement are recognized as being related, they have been identified as separate concepts (Bhatnagar, 2007; Frank, Finnegan, and Taylor, 2004; Jacob, Bond, and Galinsky, 2008). Employee retention is related to employer efforts to keep desirable workers to meet business objectives. Engagement, on the other hand, goes beyond simply retaining employees; it fosters employee interest and enthusiasm for work so that people bring discretionary effort, which can include extra time and energy (Frank et al., 2004). Harter, Schmidt, and Hayes (2002) offer a definition of engagement as being "the individual's involvement and satisfaction with as well as enthusiasm for work" (p. 269).

The Strategist's Handbook. Timothy Galpin, Oxford University Press. © Timothy Galpin (2023).
DOI: 10.1093/oso/9780192885203.003.0008

Employee engagement has been tied to the financial performance of organizations (Little and Little, 2006), and higher levels of employee engagement provide a competitive advantage that is often difficult for other firms to match (Joo and Mclean, 2006; Wright and McMahan, 1992).

As we saw in Chapter 5, there is an inevitable productivity loss during strategic transformation efforts. Therefore, throughout strategy implementation leadership must make a concerted effort to regain the commitment of key individuals and groups to their work and to the overall success of the organization. Thus, employee engagement is vital to the success of strategy execution in that it has a significant relationship with productivity, profitability, safety, and customer satisfaction (Buckingham and Coffman, 1999; Coffman and Gonzalez-Molina, 2002).

Build a Comprehensive Key Talent Retention and Re-Engagement Plan

A well-designed key talent retention and re-engagement plan includes multiple approaches across various individuals and groups. The plan clarifies the retention and re-engagement actions, roles, responsibilities, and timing throughout a transformation effort. The retention and re-engagement planning matrix (see Figure 7.1) is a tool that can be used to develop the fundamental elements of a key talent retention and re-engagement plan, which identifies key individuals and groups, the impact of losing them, their key motivators, retention and re-engagement actions, responsibilities, timing, and back-up plans.

Identify "Key Talent"

The first step in using the matrix is to identify the organization's "key talent": those individuals or groups whose loss would have the most detrimental effect on the future of the organization. People or groups can be considered "key" for various reasons, but the business impact of losing them should be the primary factor that defines them as essential.

Key People and/or Groups	Impact of Loss (monetize where possible)	Key Motivators	Retention and Re-engagement Actions	Responsibility	Timing	Back-up Plan In Case They Do Leave	Notes
1. Sales							
2. Operations							
3. R&D							
4. IT							
5. Person A							
6. Person B							
7. Person C							

Figure 7.1 Retention and re-engagement planning matrix

Quantify Their Impact

The next step in completing the matrix is to determine the business impact of losing the individuals or groups designated as "key." For example, would their absence result in the loss of significant customers, critical skills, or essential knowledge about current or future products, services, or markets? If the answer is yes, then the person or group should be considered "key" to the desired strategy's success. Moreover, the impact of their loss should be monetized where possible. For example, will you lose large customer accounts if a key salesperson leaves? If so, how much are those accounts worth? If key R&D people leave, how much are the new products or services that they typically generate worth? Monetizing the impact of losing key talent will help justify the cost and effort of actions to keep and re-engage that talent.

Identify Their Motivators

The third element of completing the template is to identify what the fundamental motivators are for each key individual or group. Some eighty years ago, Abraham Maslow defined a hierarchy of general human needs (Maslow, 1943). Similarly, executives, managers, and employees in an organizational setting have a set of personal needs that when fulfilled promote their individual engagement. The factors that have been found to contribute most to key talent's decisions to stay and re-engage during organizational transformation fall into four categories: security, perception, interaction and involvement, and status.

Develop Actions

The fourth step is to develop the retention and re-engagement actions to take. Table 7.1 identifies example actions organizational leaders can take to address the four categories of personal needs that need to be fulfilled for key talent to re-engage with the organization during organizational transformation. Implementing more than one action for each key person or group increases the chances of retaining and re-engaging them.

Assign Responsibilities

Step five is to identify and assign who will be responsible for delivering the retention and re-engagement actions generated in step four. Often, organizational leadership will not only approve the actions to take, but also personally deliver certain actions by conducting one-to-one discussions with each key person.

Table 7.1 Key talent retention and re-engagement actions

Factor	Example actions
Security	• Competitive base compensation • Attractive benefits • Retention and performance bonuses • Profit-sharing • Perks • Revised employment agreements • Customized rewards for individual key talent preferences
Perception	• Frequent communications • Clear and honest messaging • Regular progress updates • Highlight positive effects of the transition for key talent, such as organizational and professional growth opportunities • Conduct individual meetings between senior executives and identified key talent • Communicate the "fair process" (see Chapter 6)
Interaction and involvement	• Demonstrate openness to input from key talent • Regularly solicit feedback and suggestions from key talent • Involve key talent in strategic planning and implementation efforts
Status	• Identify and communicate key talent's roles and responsibilities early in the transformation process • Determine key talent reporting relationships, roles, and responsibilities via a clear organization structure • Involve key talent in organizational decision-making

Set the Clock

Step six is to determine the timing of delivering the identified retention and re-engagement actions. Some actions should occur early in the process—the offering of retention bonuses, for example. Other actions are better taken a bit later in the transformation effort, such as identifying new roles for key people once a new organization structure is decided upon. Yet other actions should occur throughout the transformation effort, including ongoing communications about the progress of the transformation process.

Develop a Back-Up Plan

The seventh and final step of producing a comprehensive key talent retention and re-engagement plan is to develop a back-up plan in cases where key people do leave. No matter how much time and effort leadership has put into planning and delivering retention and re-engagement actions, some (but significantly less than without a plan) key talent will still decide to leave. Therefore, management must put in place contingencies should key people exit the organization. Back-up procedures include identifying people who can step into vacated roles, personal communication with important customers who had relationships with key people that may have left, and greater communication with employees who reported to key managers that have decided to leave.

Detriments of Ignoring Key Talent Retention and Re-Engagement

As previously discussed, high levels of key talent retention and re-engagement lead to higher levels of individual and group performance, better strategy implementation outcomes, and ultimately higher levels of long-term company performance. However, a corollary is also implied. Specifically, failure to address key talent retention and re-engagement during strategy execution will lead to higher turnover and lower engagement of key talent, lower levels of individual performance, poor strategy implementation outcomes, and ultimately lower levels of long-term company performance. When the retention and re-engagement of key talent during organizational transformation is ignored, the downward spiral of the "cesspool syndrome" described in Chapter 5 will accelerate. This is characterized by the firm's top talent departing during poorly conducted transformation efforts because they are the most marketable employees, leaving the short-term success of the implementation as well as the long-term success of the company to the average and below-average performers that are left behind. Therefore, investing the effort and resources to retain and re-engage key talent will ultimately improve the chances of organizational success.

Demonstrate "Organizational Justice"

Some strategies result in layoffs, and how the process is handled is important to the retention and re-engagement of the employees who remain (Clemens, 2009; Leana and Feldman, 1989). When people are let go from an organization, the employees that stay are just as attentive to how the process of separation is being handled as are the exiting employees. The people remaining in the organization, the survivors, view the handling of separations as a clear indicator of the value management places on the workforce. This has a direct effect on remaining employees' continued motivation, attitude, loyalty, and commitment to the organization and its managers (Ryan, 1989), which ultimately dictates their level of re-engagement. To combat what is known as "survivor syndrome," Dessler (1999) stresses the need for management to demonstrate "organizational justice." He contends that fair procedures regarding employee separation play a key role in fostering remaining employees' engagement.

When employee separations are conducted in a manner that demonstrates both respect for the individual and the integrity of the organization, people leave with a sense of fairness. This can be achieved by using an objective process for determining the employees who will leave and those who will stay, providing fair severance packages, and offering outplacement assistance, among other actions. Demonstrating organizational justice helps foster a sense of engagement and commitment among those employees who remain in the organization because they view the separation process as being fair.

Employees Don't Quit Companies, They Quit Managers

Certainly, the firm-wide practices identified in Table 7.1 (competitive base compensation, attractive benefits, retention and performance bonuses, profit-sharing, frequent employee communications, and so forth) provide the organizational context in which an engaged workforce can develop. However, if these organizational practices are not reinforced at the individual (manager to employee) level, key talent re-engagement will often still be lacking. Griffin (1982) observed that an employee's primary contact with an organization is through his or her direct supervisor and the job itself. This is reinforced by Buckingham and Coffman (1999) who assert that employees don't quit companies, they quit managers. Consequently, individual-level engagement practices may be even more important than the firm-wide practices described above. With that in mind, Whittington and Galpin (2010) present a framework that calls for several individual-level (manager to employee) practices that supplement firm-wide employee engagement practices. The framework emphasizes the need for managers to provide their employees with opportunities for job enrichment (such as special projects, additional responsibilities, and varied tasks) as well as setting goals that clearly specify individual performance expectations. As is the case with retention actions, no matter which re-engagement actions managers choose to pursue, they should be tailored to individual employee differences (Brittain, 2007). A summary of firm-wide and individual-level engagement practices is presented in Table 7.2.

Participants and Key Activities

There can be multiple participants involved in planning and delivering key talent retention and re-engagement actions who perform essential activities, including:

- *Senior executives.* Allocate resources to implement key talent retention and re-engagement actions, approve actions, and deliver retention and re-engagement actions.

Table 7.2 Two levels of key talent retention and re-engagement practices

Firm-wide	• Select managers who demonstrate a commitment to employee people development • Provide frequent two-way workforce communications • Provide incentive pay • Demonstrate organizational justice during organizational downsizing
Individual (manager to employee) level	• Train managers and supervisors in manager to employee-level engagement best practices • Create job enrichment (special projects, additional responsibilities, varied tasks) • Ensure effective individual goal-setting • Tailor re-engagement actions to individual preferences of key talent

- *Middle management and front-line supervisors.* Deliver retention and re-engagement actions at the individual (manager to employee) level, including job enrichment, goal-setting, and tailored retention and re-engagement actions for key personnel.
- *Human resources.* Plan and develop the content of retention and re-engagement actions. Coordinate retention and re-engagement activities. Monitor and report key talent retention rates and regularly assess key talent engagement.

Best Practices

Make key talent retention and re-engagement a priority. Unfortunately, management often overlook key talent retention and re-engagement during transformation efforts, or they delegate it to others. However, management must act early and overtly participate in key talent retention and re-engagement planning and delivery.

Address key talent retention and re-engagement early. Key talent are marketable and often it does not take them long to find other employment. Therefore, management must plan and implement key talent retention and re-engagement early in the transformation process before key talent decide to leave.

Address key talent retention and re-engagement at both levels. Firm-wide practices establish the overall environment for effective key talent retention and re-engagement, while individual-level (manager to employee) practices reinforce firm-wide practices, and often have an even greater impact on effective key talent retention and re-engagement.

Potential Pitfalls

Delegating retention and re-engagement. It can be helpful to delegate to a firm's human resources department, which can help formulate actions, set up delivery channels, and manage the logistics of various retention and re-engagement activities, for example. However, often the final accountability for delivering retention and re-engagement actions rests with management. When senior managers delegate retention and re-engagement activities, they send a strong message that retaining and re-engaging the firm's key talent isn't worth their time.

One-item action plans. Management should not assume that one conversation with the firm's key talent is sufficient to retain and re-engage them. Once a transformation effort is underway, it's important to use multiple actions to reinforce the message that key talent is important to the success of the organization today and into the future.

Key Frameworks, Tools, and Templates

The primary tool to help develop and deliver an effective retention and re-engagement plan is the retention and re-engagement planning matrix. This tool is used to develop a detailed plan addressing the needs of various key talent that the strategy execution effort will impact (see Appendix B).

Best-Practice Case Example

A description of SofTech Inc.'s approach to managing key talent retention and re-engagement in practice is summarized in Table 7.3.

Table 7.3 Managing key talent retention and re-engagement at SofTech Inc.*

The need:

- As their core consumer software business was beginning to decline, management of SofTech developed a strategy to shift the core business from consumer software to business-to-business (B2B) technology solutions over a 3-year period.
- While developing their new strategy, senior management of SofTech wanted to ensure that key talent in their current core consumer business were retained and re-engaged throughout the process of shifting the firm's strategy, and that they didn't feel "left behind" as the new strategy was implemented.

The solution:

- Using the retention and re-engagement planning matrix, senior management in combination with the human resources team developed a multifaceted plan to retain and re-engage the SofTech personnel identified as "key" to continuity of the core consumer business.
- The plan consisted of firm-wide actions including frequent two-way workforce communications, additional incentive pay to key personnel, providing fair severance packages, and offering outplacement assistance to outplaced employees.
- The plan also entailed individual-level (manager to employee) actions including creating special projects and additional responsibilities for key talent, realigning individual goals with continuity of the consumer business, and tailored re-engagement actions to individual preferences of key personnel.

Continued

Table 7.3 *Continued*

The results:

- Retention of the firm's identified key talent was regularly tracked, and retention rates exceeded management's target of 90% throughout the firm's strategic shift.
- Employee engagement scores were consistently high among the designated key personnel throughout implementation.
- Revenue of the core consumer business held steady throughout the firm's 3-year shift to the new B2B business focus.

---

* Because of non-disclosure considerations, a mid-size software technology company is referred to throughout the illustration as SofTech Inc.

Chapter Summary

- Today's careers are more a collection of assignments than an accumulation of years at one firm.
- When key talent leave, value walks out the door.
- The reasons key talent often cite for leaving an organization during transformation efforts include poor communications, a loss of status, and uncertainty about their role in the organization.
- Beyond retention, management must also focus on re-engaging key talent throughout strategic transformation efforts.
- Employee engagement has been tied to the financial performance of organizations, and higher levels of employee engagement provide a competitive advantage that is often difficult for other firms to match.
- A well-designed strategic key talent retention and re-engagement plan includes multiple approaches across various individuals and groups.
- The retention and re-engagement planning matrix is a tool to identify each fundamental element of a strategic transformation key talent retention and re-engagement plan.
- A comprehensive key talent retention and re-engagement plan entails identifying key individuals and groups, the impact of losing them, their key motivators, retention and re-engagement actions, responsibilities, timing, and back-up plans.
- People or groups can be considered "key" for various reasons, but the business impact of losing them should be the primary factor that defines them as essential.
- Monetizing the impact of losing key talent will help justify the cost and effort of actions to keep and re-engage them.
- The factors that have been found to contribute most to key talent's decisions to stay and re-engage during organizational transformation fall into four categories: security, perception, interaction and involvement, and status.
- Implementing more than one action for each key person or group increases the chances of retaining and re-engaging them.

- It is often the case that organizational leadership will not only approve the actions to take but also personally deliver on those actions by conducting one-to-one discussions with each key person.
- Some actions should occur early in the process, while other actions should occur throughout the transformation effort.
- Management must put in place contingencies should key people exit the organization.
- When the retention and re-engagement of key talent during organizational transformation is ignored, the downward spiral of the "cesspool syndrome" described in Chapter 5 will accelerate.
- Some strategies result in layoffs, and how the process is handled is important to the retention and re-engagement of the employees who remain.
- To combat what is known as "survivor syndrome," management must demonstrate "organizational justice."
- Individual-level (manager to employee) engagement practices may be even more important than firm-wide practices.
- Participants involved in planning and delivering key talent retention and re-engagement actions include senior executives, middle management, front-line supervisors, and human resources staff.
- Best practices include making key talent retention and re-engagement a priority, addressing key talent retention and re-engagement early, and addressing key talent retention and re-engagement at both the firm-wide and individual (manager to employee) levels.
- Potential pitfalls include management delegating retention and re-engagement and developing one-item action plans.
- The primary tool to help manage develop and deliver an effective retention and re-engagement plan to support organizational transformation efforts is the retention and re-engagement planning matrix.

Discussion Questions

1. What activities during transformation efforts does your organization do well to retain and re-engage key talent? What key talent retention and re-engagement activities could the organization perform better?
2. For your organization, who is typically involved in developing and delivering key talent retention and re-engagement? Who should be involved?
3. How does your organization address key talent retention and re-engagement at both the firm-wide and individual (manager to employee) level? What more could be done?
4. What key talent retention and re-engagement measures does your organization currently have in place? Are the measures sufficient? If not, what other measures should the organization put in place?

Organizational Self-Assessment

Completing the following self-assessment (Table 7.4) will provide a view of how effectively your organization manages key talent retention and re-engagement.

Steps to complete the self-assessment:

1. Rate each item on a scale of 0 (poor) to 10 (excellent).
2. Make notes for each item to explain the rationale for the numerical rating.
3. Add all ten scores to get a TOTAL SCORE (maximum score = 100).

Table 7.4 Organizational self-assessment: key talent retention and re-engagement

Component	Rating (0 = poor, 10 = excellent)	Notes/rationale
When it comes to key talent retention and re-engagement during strategic transformation …		
1. We place high importance on key talent retention and re-engagement		
2. We develop a comprehensive key talent retention and re-engagement plan		
3. We start key talent retention and re-engagement early in the transformation process		
4. We continue key talent retention and re-engagement throughout the strategy execution process		
5. We address key talent retention and re-engagement at the firm-wide level		
6. We address key talent retention and re-engagement at the individual (manager to employee) level		
7. We use multiple key talent retention and re-engagement actions		
8. Senior management are visibly involved in delivering key talent retention and re-engagement actions		
9. We train managers and supervisors in manager to employee-level engagement best practices		
10. We regularly assess the effectiveness of our key talent retention and re-engagement		
TOTAL SCORE		

Rating scale:

- 0–20 = Poor (significant improvement needed)
- 21–40 = Below average (improvement needed in several areas)
- 41–60 = Average (identify areas of weakness and adjust)
- 61–80 = Above average (identify areas that can still be improved)
- 81–100 = Excellent (continuously review and refine each component for each iteration of the organization's strategy efforts)

8

Your Strategy Needs a Nudge—Aligning Organizational Culture with Strategy

Achieving and sustaining the goals of organizational change is difficult at best and for many organizations seemingly impossible. Most transformation initiatives fall short of reaching their goals where "the rubber hits the road," during implementation and follow-up. Effective strategy execution requires that changes in operations, systems, processes, and procedures are all clearly connected to an organization's culture. Making this connection not only enables effective implementation but also embeds strategic change in the day-to-day life of the organization, reinforcing and sustaining desired outcomes such as lower costs, increased revenue, greater market share, improved service, or quicker processes. Although many managers recognize that connecting culture with strategy is important for getting desired strategic changes to "stick," most do not know how to go about it. What is required, then, is a pragmatic approach to aligning organizational culture with strategy.

Organizational Culture: The Invisible and the Visible

Although culture has been shown to have a significant impact on overall firm performance (Denison, 1984; Kotter and Heskett, 1992) and firm innovation performance (Naranjo-Valencia, Jimenez-Jimenez, and Sanz-Valle, 2017), organizational culture is not easily defined. This is evident in the myriad descriptions of organizational culture that have been offered, which fall into two basic camps of psychology: personality theory and behavioral theory.

The Invisible

Personality theory suggests that the sources of a person's behavior are characteristics of the person themselves: their values, beliefs, and attitudes (Phelps, 2015). Definitions of organizational culture underpinned by personality theory include: what a firm's management and employees consider appropriate business practices (Schein, 1990), organizational norms, values, beliefs, and attitudes (Goulet and Schweiger, 2006), and a system of shared meanings held by members distinguishing an organization from other organizations (Robbins and Judge, 2012). Although descriptive, because an individual's attitudes and beliefs are often invisible, definitions of organizational culture based on personality theory do not provide managers with a

The Strategist's Handbook. Timothy Galpin, Oxford University Press. © Timothy Galpin (2023).
DOI: 10.1093/oso/9780192885203.003.0009

pragmatic approach to shaping a firm's culture beyond attempting to recruit and hire employees who appear to hold beliefs and attitudes that "fit" the organization's values, a task that is imprecise at best.

The Visible

Contrary to personality theory, behavioral theory proposes that rather than being driven by a person's attitudes and beliefs, individual behavior is driven by a person's environment (Skinner, 1974). Definitions of organizational culture supported by behavioral theory include: culture shapes workforce behavior by providing direction, stability, and cohesion to group members (Selznick, 1957), and organizational culture influences individual behavior and organizational decisions (Boeker, 1989). Behavioral theorists point to "behavioral stability and consistency as being due to multiple sources of environmental control, all contributing to the stable behavior" (Phelps, 2015, p. 559).

Although existing since the 1950s, behavioral theory (Skinner, 1953) has seen a resurgence of popularity in shaping culture. Described in the book *Nudge* (Thaler and Sunstein, 2008), compelling research demonstrates that individual and collective behavior can be influenced through what is termed "environmental choice architecture." From purchasing more items positioned at eye level on a store shelf rather than those below or above eye level, to encouraging healthy food choices by listing calorie counts of different meal choices on restaurant menus, our behavior is continually being "nudged" by the choice architecture of our environment. Table 8.1 highlights the key differences between addressing organizational culture based on behavioral ("nudge") theory versus personality theory.

When Theory Meets Practice: An Actionable Culture Management Model

Because the elements of a firm's environment are visible, managing organizational culture based on behavioral theory offers managers an actionable approach

Table 8.1 Organizational culture based on personality theory versus behavioral theory

Personality theory	Behavioral ("nudge") theory
Attitudes	Environment
Beliefs	Processes
Values	Systems
Shared meanings	Actions
Invisible	Visible
Difficult to manage	Easier to manage
Difficult to measure	Easier to measure

Cultural Levers	Current Design	Required Design to Align Culture with Strategy	Redesign Actions (Short, Medium, Long-Term)
1. Organizational Values			
2. Staffing and Selection			
3. Communications			
4. Training			
5. Rules and Policies			
6. Goals and Measures			
7. Rewards and Recognition			
8. Decision-making			
9. Organization Structure			
10. Physical Environment			
11. Customs and Norms			
12. Ceremonies and Events			

Figure 8.1 Cultural alignment model: twelve "cultural levers" to align organizational culture with strategy*

* Based on the behavioral "nudge" concept that intentionally designing an organization's "environmental choice architecture" (cultural levers) aligns workforce behaviors (organizational culture) with strategy.

to shaping a firm's culture through the intentional design of the firm's internal "environmental choice architecture." In essence, changing the elements of a firm's internal environment leads to changes in workforce behaviors, resulting in organizational culture change. Moreover, while it is difficult to measure employee attitudes and beliefs, as is necessary with a personality-based approach, a behavioral approach to managing organizational culture enables clear measurement of progress. Desired workforce behaviors can be readily observed, evaluated, recorded, and reported (De Brentani and Kleinschmidt, 2004). The cultural alignment model (Figure 8.1), composed of twelve "cultural levers," was designed based on the behavioral theory view that individual and collective workforce behaviors are "nudged" by the organization's environment.

Origins of the Model

Underpinned by behavioral theory, an early version of the cultural alignment model originated over twenty-five years ago as a framework to improve strategy implementation at several UK firms (Galpin, 1996a). In the ensuing decades, following the principles of action-based research (French, 2009), the model has been applied and refined across various industries and geographies.

1+1=3: The Multiplier Effect

A typical reaction from various executives who have not addressed cultural alignment using the twelve levers identified in Figure 8.1 is that the approach appears to be overly bureaucratic. It is a natural tendency of executives to want simple answers to complex issues such as managing culture, frequently asking, "Can't we just replace a few people who don't match the culture we want?" Or "Can we just put everyone through a culture training program?" What has become evident through multiple iterations of applying the cultural alignment model in numerous organizations across industries and geographies and supported by the findings of the Oxford Innovation Insights Project (summarized below) is that applying only one, or even a few, of the twelve cultural levers is generally ineffective.

A cultural training program, for example, may provide some awareness of the desired organizational culture, along with a brief "boost" toward instilling desired workforce behaviors. However, when everyone returns from the cultural training to their daily jobs, the rest of the organizational environment hasn't changed at all, reinforcing the disparities in the culture that existed previously. Thus, the time and resources to provide cultural training as the sole source of cultural alignment are wasted.

In contrast, implementing most, or all, of the twelve levers is much more effective at aligning culture with strategy because of the "multiplier effect," with the sum effect of applying multiple levers being greater than the whole. In essence, when it comes to the impact of applying the cultural levers, 1+1=3. To make applying multiple levers within the model manageable, a phased approach should be taken including short- (within thirty to sixty days), medium- (within six months), and longer-term implementation actions (six to twenty-four months or more).

Applying all twelve levers simultaneously to compare and integrate combining firms' cultures can seem like an intimidating task to most managers. However, changing everything at once sends "a mobilizing jolt of energy through the company ... and we imagine it would also send a chill through the spine of most CEOs" (Boyett and Boyett, 1998). Consequently, addressing all twelve levers over the short, medium, and long term during strategy execution will effectively create cultural alignment, but it requires determined and persistent leadership.

Applying the Cultural Alignment Model

Table 8.2 identifies five key steps for applying the cultural alignment model to align culture with strategy.

Table 8.2 Five-steps for applying the cultural alignment model

Step	Key activities
1. Form a cross-functional cultural alignment team	• Identify both line and human resources management representatives from across the organization to serve as a cultural alignment team.
2. Conduct a "cultural audit"	• Using the cultural alignment model as a template, identify the current content and alignment of the firm's twelve cultural levers in relation to the firm's desired strategy implementation efforts. • Does each element overtly identify aspects of the desired strategy as an organizational priority? • Is each element aligned with the others? • Identify and record potential short-, medium-, and long-term actions for incorporating the desired strategy into the firm's culture across all twelve cultural levers.
3. Create a detailed cultural alignment plan	• Develop a cultural alignment plan that includes timelines, budgets, milestones, and accountabilities for implementation across each of the twelve cultural levers. • Gain senior leadership approval for the plan.
4. Implement and build momentum	• Begin by implementing the short-term actions for the various "cultural levers" (i.e., "quick wins" that can be implemented within 30–60 days to demonstrate progress and build momentum). • Then, progress to implementing the medium- and long-term actions. • Involve senior leaders in the implementation across the twelve levers.
5. Track progress, collect evidence, and adjust	• Conduct regular reviews (weekly to begin, then monthly, then quarterly) regarding progress of the organization's cultural alignment plan (i.e., what is working well, what needs to be adjusted). • Gather data (i.e., workforce feedback via surveys and focus groups) about the firm's culture/strategy alignment (e.g., visibility of actions, views of success, suggestions for improvement). • Adjust as required, based on the data gathered.

Testing the Cultural Alignment Model: The Oxford Innovation Insights Project

According to the McKinsey Global Innovation Survey, 84 percent of executives identified innovation as a strategic priority crucial to firm growth, but only 6 percent are satisfied with their organization's innovation performance (McKinsey & Company, 2020). It comes as no surprise that innovation is a top strategic priority for many firms, as innovation has been found to have a significant positive impact on firm performance. For example, an analysis of 600 firms found that the most innovative organizations in the sample achieved 11 percent higher average annual revenue growth and 22 percent higher average annual earnings before interest, taxes, depreciation, and amortization (EBITDA) than the firms identified as less innovative (Groth, 2011). Moreover, while innovation is vital for the performance of organizations of all sizes, it's particularly essential for large companies looking to grow (or simply to maintain their present market position), with half of the S&P 500 forecasted to be replaced in the next ten years (Nieminen, 2018).

The Oxford Innovation Insights Project was established to test the cultural alignment model presented in Figure 8.1, by answering the question: how and to what extent are firms using "environmental choice architecture" to "nudge" their innovation strategy across the organization? To address this question, the twelve organizational processes ("cultural levers") identified in the cultural alignment model were used to define the components that comprise an organization's environmental choice architecture.

Semi-structured interviews were conducted with sixty "C-Suite" executives from sixty different companies, representing fifteen different industries (see Figure 8.2). Thirteen percent of the respondents have titles of chief executive officer or managing director, while 87 percent have other "C-Suite" titles: chief financial officer, chief operating officer, chief information officer, chief marketing officer, senior vice president, or vice president. Each executive was asked to respond to the same four items:

1. To what extent do you agree or disagree with the following statement? Innovation is a strategic priority for our firm.
2. On a scale of 1 (low innovation) to 10 (high innovation), please rate your firm's organization-wide level of innovation.
3. Which of the following processes does your firm use to encourage innovation across the organization? (Please choose all that apply.)

   - Organizational values
   - Staffing and selection
   - Communications
   - Training
   - Rules and policies
   - Goals and measures
   - Rewards and recognition
   - Decision-making
   - Organization structure
   - Physical environment
   - Customs and norms
   - Ceremonies and events

4. For the processes that your firm utilizes, please provide examples of how each is designed to encourage innovation behaviors across your workforce.

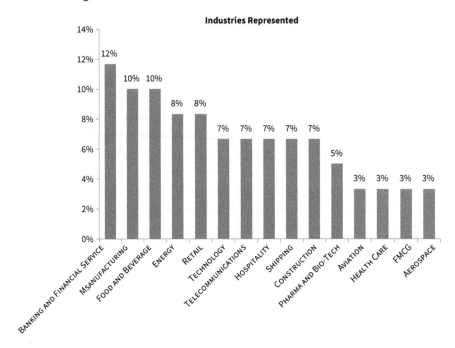

Figure 8.2 Oxford Innovation Insights Project: industries represented

Key Findings

Q1: Eighty-six percent of respondents to the Oxford Innovation Insights Project "strongly agreed" (63 percent) or "agreed" (23 percent) with the statement "Innovation is a strategic priority for our firm," while just 14 percent disagreed with the statement. This finding is slightly more than but consistent with previous innovation survey results, which found that 84 percent of participants identified innovation as a strategic priority (Nieminen, 2018).

Q2: Most respondents (92 percent) rated their companies as having either a "moderate" (55 percent) or "low" (37 percent) level of firm-wide innovation, while just 8 percent rated their companies as having a "high" level of firm-wide innovation.

Q3: The environmental choice architecture components (cultural levers) most frequently used by firms to encourage innovation behaviors across the workforce were communication (92 percent), organizational values (58 percent), and training (55 percent) (see Figure 8.3). The high usage of these three processes may be due to their ease of implementation and they are often seen as the least controversial to apply. Meanwhile, the low utilization of levers such as rules and policies (5 percent), organization structure (8 percent), ceremonies and events (7 percent), and goals and measures (13 percent) may be due to these levers (except for ceremonies and events) often being more controversial to implement and their use can create more resistance among management and employees. Additionally, a strong positive relationship (0.82) was found between "high-innovation" firms and the number of environmental choice architecture components (cultural levers) they use to encourage innovation (see Figure 8.4). While from a limited sample, this finding supports the notion that the more culture levers used, the greater the alignment created between an organization's culture and its strategy.

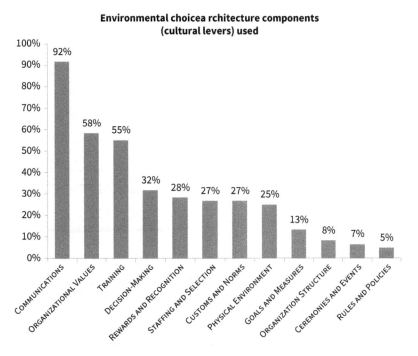

Figure 8.3 Oxford Innovation Insights Project: cultural levers used

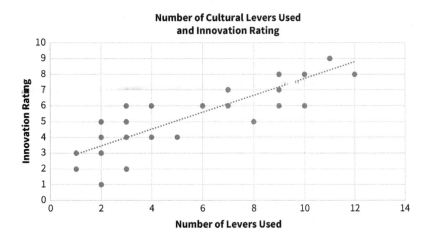

Figure 8.4 Oxford Innovation Insights Project: relationship between the number of cultural levers used and innovation rating

Q4: Examples provided by the study participants illustrating how each cultural lever is used in their organization to "nudge" innovation are included in Figure 8.5. Of note is the simplicity of many of the "nudges" within each lever, as well as the limited time, effort, and cost involved in implementing many of the example nudges.

"Cultural Levers" (elements comprising an organization's "environmental choice architecture")	Percent of companies using	Example Innovation "Nudges"
Organizational Values	58%	• Innovation is included in our corporate values. • We identify innovation behaviors that describe what "innovation" means to the firm (e.g. "share ideas to make tasks quicker, safer, or easier for the customer, then test the ideas to see how they work").
Staffing and Selection	27%	• We have made innovation a key requirement for hiring and promotion of all staff, not just R&D. • We use case interviews to assess a candidate's ideation and lateral thinking. • During interviews, we ask candidates to "tell us about a time when you implemented an improvement idea (small or large) at work and describe how you measured the results."
Communications	92%	• We regularly communicate the importance of innovation to all areas and levels of the company. • We use multiple methods to communicate our innovation messages to all employees (e.g., email, face-to-face, newsletters, etc.). • We emphasize that innovation is not limited to new product or service ideas, but also includes coming up with and implementing ideas for new business processes.
Training	55%	• We hold innovation training sessions for most areas of our business. • Our innovation training includes where to look for new ideas, how best to share ideas, and how to implement and measure ideas.
Rules and Policies	5%	• We have established a set protocol for submitting innovation ideas.
Goals and Measures	13%	• We have established "innovation metrics" (e.g., the number of new ideas submitted by department and across the firm, number of ideas implemented, and return on investment of ideas implemented). • We have established formal innovation goals across departments (e.g., cycle-time reduction, services improvement, and cost savings).
Rewards and Recognition	28%	• We provide rewards to employees whose ideas have resulted in business or service improvements (e.g., cash rewards, time off, or gift cards). • We recognize employees for coming up with and implementing business or service improvements (e.g., writeup and photo in the company newsletter, "employee of the month" linked to innovation).
Decision-making	32%	• We have pushed service and business model innovation implementation decisions down to front-line managers and employees. • We have established an "innovation gating" process to approve significant innovation proposals (e.g., proposals above a certain spending threshold). • Our innovation gating process involves a set protocol for reviewing and deciding which innovation ideas move forward to pilot-testing and rollout.
Organization Structure	8%	• We have flattened our organization structure to reduce layers of approval for innovation implementation. • We have organized our firm's structure around processes, rather than functional silos to facilitate more business model innovation.
Physical Environment	25%	• We have co-located departmental teams in the same work areas to encourage interaction and innovation. • We have a lot of wall-hangings in our common areas that list our company values, including innovation.
Customs and Norms	27%	• We hold regular "idea-sharing" lunches to facilitate innovation across project teams. • We have established "innovation ambassadors" whose role is to seek out and share ideas across departments and functions.
Ceremonies and Events	7%	• We hold quarterly two-day "innovation hackathons," which include different teams, departments, and functions. • We conduct an annual "innovation awards" ceremony.

Figure 8.5 Oxford Innovation Insights Project: example innovation "nudges" used within each cultural lever

Nudging Innovation across the Firm Leads to Better Market Performance

Forty-eight of the sixty firms represented in the Oxford Innovation Insights Project were publicly traded firms. A comparison of these firms' average annual share price performance over a five-year period (2015–19) against the S&P Global 1200 Index (ticker symbol SPG1200) for the same period found that the eighteen firms rated as having a low level of firm-wide innovation returned 3.2 percent lower average annual returns than the benchmark. The twenty-six firms rated as having a moderate level of firm-wide innovation returned 2.1 percent higher average annual returns than the benchmark, while the four firms rated as having a high level of firm-wide innovation achieved 4.6 percent better average annual returns than the benchmark. Although from a narrow sample size, these market returns, combined with the strong relationship identified between the number of cultural levers used and higher levels of firm-wide innovation, support the concept that applying more cultural levers to "nudge" innovation across a firm leads to higher levels of firm-wide innovation, resulting in superior firm market performance. This finding is in line with previous research into the market performance of innovative firms versus benchmark stock indexes. The "Innovation Alpha Index," consisting of 120 global and 100 public US highly innovative companies, generated 4.1 percent higher annual shareholder returns than their peers "because they invest in intangible assets" (van Ark, 2019).

Participants and Key Activities

There can be multiple participants involved in aligning organizational culture with strategy who perform essential activities, including:

- *Senior executives.* Allocate resources to plan and implement cultural alignment actions, approve actions, provide "go/no go" decisions on proposed cultural integration actions, and participate in the delivery of various cultural alignment actions.
- *Cultural alignment team members.* Conduct a "cultural audit," develop a cultural alignment plan, oversee implementation actions, and measure and adjust cultural alignment actions throughout the strategy implementation effort.
- *Human resources.* Assist the cultural alignment team with implementing cultural alignment actions.

Best Practices

Leverage the "multiplier effect." Make the whole cultural alignment effort greater than the sum of its parts (1+1=3) by implementing half or more of the twelve cultural levers.

Implement "quick wins." To build early momentum, identify high-visibility, high-impact cultural "quick wins" that can be implemented within thirty to sixty days.

Out with the old, in with the new. Eliminate legacy "organizational choice architecture" by doing away with old aspects of each cultural lever that supported the old strategy, and replace legacy aspects with new "choice architecture" that supports the new strategy.

Align culture where you can. If you lead a division, department, or even a small team, you can still use the cultural alignment model to change the culture that is in your sphere of influence.

Potential Pitfalls

Delegating cultural alignment. It can be helpful for senior management to delegate planning to the cultural alignment team. However, often the final accountability for delivering cultural alignment actions rests with management. When senior managers delegate alignment activities, they send a strong message that cultural alignment isn't worth their time.

One and done. Only implementing one or two "easy" levers such as communication and/or training will raise awareness but is insufficient to align organizational culture with strategy.

Delaying the start. Waiting to address cultural alignment until after operational and technical implementation will marginalize the impact of the strategy execution effort.

Key Frameworks, Tools, and Templates

The primary tool to plan and deliver cultural alignment with strategy is the cultural alignment model. This tool is used to develop a detailed plan addressing each of the twelve cultural levers (see Appendix B).

Best-Practice Case Example

A description of EuroBank's approach to aligning organizational culture with strategy in practice is summarized in Table 8.3.

Chapter Summary

- Effective strategy execution requires that changes in operations, systems, processes, and procedures are all clearly connected to an organization's culture.

Table 8.3 Aligning organizational culture with strategy at EuroBank*

The need:

- With the rapid rise of fintech combined with changing customer preferences about how to access and use financial services, innovation had become a top strategic priority for the leadership team of a large European bank.
- As a result of the shifting financial services market, the CEO of EuroBank wanted to establish a "culture of innovation" (his words) across the organization, composed of over 50,000 employees across 37 countries.
- Although the bank had already established relationships with and invested in several fintech startups, the CEO knew that this would not be enough to create the culture of innovation that would enable the bank to identify and implement the new products, services, processes, technologies, and business models required to compete in the future.
- Ideas needed to come from, and projects had to be pursued, not only within the IT department where much of the bank's R&D had been occurring but also across the firm.
- The CEO needed a clear and actionable approach to align the bank's culture with the innovation strategy, which would have a tangible and measurable impact.

The solution:

- The cultural alignment process began with the "C-level" leadership team of EuroBank overtly identifying innovation as one of the bank's five core values.
- Then, a twelve-person cultural alignment team representing a cross-section of managers and employees across the bank's regional locations, along with three human resources representatives, was established to tackle the task of aligning EuroBank's culture with the innovation strategy.
- The team applied the culture alignment model to conduct a "cultural audit," assessing the gaps that existed between the current design of each of the twelve "cultural levers" and the desired future design of each lever required to "nudge" innovative behaviors across EuroBank's workforce.
- After current and future design gaps were identified, the cultural alignment team began a detailed design of EuroBank's "organizational choice architecture" by redesigning the content and delivery of the twelve cultural levers.
- The team identified a timeline of short-, medium-, and long-term "nudges" for each lever.
- The team also developed a detailed budget required for implementation and gained approval for their plans from EuroBank's executive team.
- Once the cultural alignment plans were approved, implementation began with "quick-win" actions (implemented within 30 days), including regular "innovation-themed" communication and events displaying EuroBank's latest innovations to all employees.
- Next, medium-term actions (30 days to 6 months) were implemented, such as innovation training for all managers and employees, establishing an idea submission and vetting process for the bank, recognition and rewards for submitting new product, process, technology, or service ideas, and the formation of innovation teams to implement approved ideas.
- Then, long-term actions (6–24 months) were installed that included flattening the bank's organization structure by removing two layers of management, accelerating the decision-making process for newly proposed innovation efforts, and aligning the bank's goals, measures, and rewards to encourage innovation.

The results:

- Measurement involving survey and focus group feedback across EuroBank's employees was collected monthly for the first 6 months, then quarterly.
- For all rating periods during the first 2 years after implementation began, well over three quarters of EuroBank's workforce rated the "innovation culture" efforts as "highly effective" or "extremely effective."
- Regular adjustments were made throughout the implementation based on the feedback collected.
- Beyond the employee feedback collected, idea submissions and participation in idea development and implementation across EuroBank "increased significantly."
- EuroBank's employee engagement, measured annually, showed increased engagement at both 1 year and 2 years post-implementation launch.

---

* Because of non-disclosure considerations, a large European bank is referred to throughout the illustration as EuroBank.

- Although many managers recognize that connecting culture with strategy is important for getting desired strategic changes to "stick," most do not know how to go about it.
- Although culture has been shown to have a significant impact on overall firm performance and firm innovation performance, organizational culture is not easily defined.
- The various descriptions of organizational culture that have been offered fall into two basic camps of psychology: personality theory and behavioral theory.
- Personality theory suggests that the sources of a person's behavior are characteristics of the person themselves: their values, beliefs, and attitudes.
- Contrary to personality theory, behavioral theory proposes that rather than being driven by a person's attitudes and beliefs, individual behavior is driven by a person's environment.
- Although existing since the 1950s, behavioral theory has seen a resurgence of popularity in shaping culture, as described in the book *Nudge*.
- Because the elements of a firm's environment are visible, managing organizational culture based on behavioral theory offers managers an actionable approach to shaping a firm's culture through the intentional design of the firm's internal environment.
- In essence, changing the elements of a firm's internal environment leads to changes in workforce behaviors, resulting in organizational culture change.
- The cultural alignment model, composed of twelve "cultural levers," was designed based on the behavioral theory view that individual and collective workforce behaviors are "nudged" by an organization's environment.
- It is a natural tendency of executives to want simple answers to complex issues such as managing culture, wanting to only implement one or two "easy" cultural levers.
- What has become evident through multiple iterations of applying the cultural alignment model in numerous organizations across industries and geographies and supported by the findings of the Oxford Innovation Insights Project is that applying only one, or even a few, of the twelve cultural levers is generally ineffective.
- In contrast, implementing most, or all, of the twelve levers is much more effective at aligning culture with strategy because of the "multiplier effect," with the impact of applying multiple levers being greater than the whole (1+1=3).
- To make applying multiple levers within the model manageable, a phased approach should be taken including short-, medium-, and long-term implementation actions.
- Addressing all twelve levers over the short, medium, and long term during strategy execution will effectively create cultural alignment, but it requires determined and persistent leadership.
- There are five key steps for applying the cultural alignment model to align culture with strategy: (1) form a cross-functional cultural alignment team,

(2) conduct a "cultural audit," (3) create a detailed cultural alignment plan, (4) implement and build momentum, and (5) track progress, collect evidence, and adjust.

- The Oxford Innovation Insights Project was established to test the Cultural Alignment Model by answering the question: how and to what extent are firms using "environmental choice architecture" to "nudge" their innovation strategy across the organization?
- A key finding of the Oxford Innovation Insights Project is that a strong positive relationship (0.82) was identified between "high-innovation" firms and the number of environmental choice architecture components (cultural levers) they use to encourage innovation.
- Multiple participants are involved in aligning organizational culture with strategy who perform essential activities, including senior executives, cultural alignment team members, and human resources staff.
- The best practices of aligning organizational culture with strategy include leveraging the "multiplier effect," implementing "quick wins," eliminating legacy "organizational choice architecture," and changing culture in your sphere of influence.
- Potential pitfalls include delegating cultural alignment, only implementing one or two "easy" levers, and waiting to address cultural alignment until after operational and technical implementation.
- The primary tool to develop and deliver cultural alignment with strategy is the cultural alignment model.

Discussion Questions

1. What activities does your organization do well to align culture with strategy? What cultural alignment activities could the organization perform better?
2. For your organization, who is typically involved in developing and delivering cultural alignment with strategy? Who should be involved?
3. Which "cultural levers" does your organization currently use to align culture with strategy? Which additional levers should they use?
4. How does your organization currently measure cultural alignment with strategy? Are the measures sufficient? If not, what other measures should the organization put in place?

Organizational Self-Assessment

Completing the following self-assessment (Table 8.4) will provide a view of how effectively your organization aligns culture with strategy.

Steps to complete the self-assessment:

1. Rate each item on a scale of 0 (poor) to 10 (excellent).
2. Make notes for each item to explain the rationale for the numerical rating.
3. Add all ten scores to get a TOTAL SCORE (maximum score = 100).

Rating scale:

0–20 = Poor (significant improvement needed)
21–40 = Below average (improvement needed in several areas)
41–60 = Average (identify areas of weakness and adjust)
61–80 = Above average (identify areas that can still be improved)
81–100 = Excellent (continuously review and refine each component for each iteration of the organization's strategy efforts)

Table 8.4 Organizational self-assessment: aligning organizational culture with strategy

Component	Rating (0 = poor, 10 = excellent)	Notes/rationale
When it comes to aligning culture with strategy …		
1. We place high importance on aligning culture with strategy		
2. We establish a "cultural alignment team" to plan and implement required culture/strategy alignment		
3. We develop a comprehensive cultural alignment plan		
4. We start cultural alignment early in the change process		
5. We implement high-impact, high-visibility cultural alignment "quick wins"		
6. We continue cultural alignment throughout the strategy execution process		
7. We redesign the organization's "choice architecture" by realigning at least half of the twelve "cultural levers"		
8. We eliminate legacy organizational "choice architecture"		
9. Senior management are visibly involved in aligning culture with strategy		
10. We regularly assess the effectiveness of our culture/strategy alignment efforts		
TOTAL SCORE		

PART III
BEYOND BUSINESS STRATEGY

9

Nonmarket Strategy

Nonmarket strategy is a term applied to the aspects of business strategy that address relationships that do not unfold within commercial markets but still affect the company's ability to reach its strategic goals. A company's nonmarket environment is composed of various entities including regulators, governments, citizens, non-governmental organizations (NGOs), activists, and the media. The nonmarket environment has grown in complexity and importance, including, for example, intellectual property, health and safety, emissions and fuel standards, trade policy, consumer protection, competition policy, and diversity and inclusion. Consequently, "regulatory risk" and "reputational risk" have been ranked as top strategic risks by executives (Deloitte, 2007). Moreover, the World 50 (a C-suite executive networking group) reported that 95 percent of its members felt that the pressure to take positions on contentious issues ranging from immigration to vaccination has become normalized (Edgecliffe-Johnson, 2022).

The Importance of the Nonmarket to Firm Performance

The nonmarket is important because it can limit or enhance a firm's strategic advantages. In fact, a study of over 1,000 executives representing a wide range of industries, regions, and functional specialties found that government is more likely to impact a firm's financial value than any other stakeholder group, except customers (Dua, Heil, and Wilkins, 2010). Examples of strategic advantages that can be either limited or enhanced by the company's nonmarket operating environment include:

- *Cost:* cost-saving mergers and acquisitions (M&As) can be blocked or approved by competition or national security regulators.
- *Growth:* growth-creating M&As can be blocked or approved by competition or national security regulators.
- *First mover:* approved patents allow firms to be first to market.
- *Sole provider:* approved patents allow firms to be the only provider in the market.
- *Demand:* products made of rare or endangered species are banned by regulators.
- *Complement:* software firms are not allowed to bundle operating systems and browsers.

The Strategist's Handbook. Timothy Galpin, Oxford University Press. © Timothy Galpin (2023).
DOI: 10.1093/oso/9780192885203.003.0010

The Nonmarket Issue Lifecycle

The development of nonmarket issues can be understood in terms of a lifecycle, which creates a trade-off between where in the lifecycle a nonmarket issue is and managerial control over the issue (see Figure 9.1). Early in the lifecycle, key participants in issue formation and awareness include the media and private activists. Later in the issue lifecycle, political and legal institutions become primary participants who shape control of an issue. The trade-offs between issue development and control move through a logical progression:

Issue identification. The issue lifecycle commences when awareness of an issue begins, and the issues is put "on the radar" of society and firms. At this stage, management have a great deal of control over the information and narrative surrounding the issue (for example, the early messaging about tobacco was that smoking hasn't been proven to be harmful). The impact on the firm is also negligible at this stage, with limited impact on sales and costs (tobacco companies still sold a lot of cigarettes).

Interest formation. Next, more knowledge of the issue is developed and disseminated in the form of research reports and news articles. At this stage, management begin losing control of the information available and messaging about the issue (a preponderance of research and news articles began to demonstrate and communicate the harmful effects of smoking to smokers and those around them via

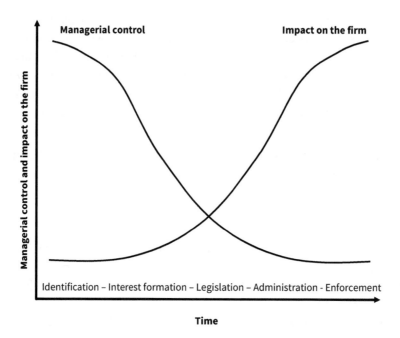

Figure 9.1 Nonmarket issue lifecycle, management control, and impact on the firm

"second-hand smoke"). The impact on the firm starts to increase (tobacco firms found it necessary to defend their products in the news, as sales started to dip).

Legislation. Government regulation comes into play. Managerial control in this stage is greatly diminished, as firms are compelled to comply (or face significant financial or criminal penalties) with rules put in place by governments to manage the issue on behalf of "the public interest" (tobacco companies must put warning labels on their packaging). The impact on the firm's costs and revenue increases (tobacco firms face fines for breach of regulations and revenue decrease starts to accelerate).

Administration. Governments refine the regulation. Loss of managerial control accelerates as new or stricter rules are put into place (indoor smoking is banned in many jurisdictions). The impact on the firm's costs and revenue accelerates (tobacco firms must pay fines for breach of additional regulations and revenue decreases significantly).

Enforcement. Governments levy penalties for breaches of regulation. At this stage, management has essentially lost control of the issue as fines and other penalties are imposed (tobacco firms pay fines for breaches). The impact on the firms' costs and revenue is significant (tobacco firms' revenue is significantly lower).

Why Companies Need a Nonmarket Strategy

Various reasons exist for why companies need to pursue a nonmarket strategy as part of their business strategy (Bach and Allen, 2010). First, companies face both financial and reputational risk in the nonmarket, from government regulations, social campaigns, and political movements. Second, a nonmarket strategy allows a company to shape the environment in which it operates, creating opportunities for lowering costs or increasing revenue. Third, managing key issues and actors across the issue lifecycle discussed above is crucial to firm success. Finally, because of limited resources, a company cannot and should not have a position on everything.

Developing a Multifaceted Nonmarket Strategy

Nonmarket strategy is multifaceted and includes decisions about three aspects: (1) the firm's approach (relational or transactional), (2) the level of participation (collective or individual), and (3) nonmarket strategy (informational, financial incentives, or constituency-building) (Hillman and Hitt, 1999). It should be noted that these options are not mutually exclusive, with more than one choice being viable if a firm has the resources to pursue more than one option under each category. Let's look at what each of these decisions and options entail.

Nonmarket Approaches

The nonmarket approach a firm takes will differ in terms of length and scope. Transactional approaches to nonmarket strategy are characterized by a short-term focus on an issue-by-issue basis, whereas a relational approach is longer term and cross-issue. The nonmarket approach a firm chooses should be based on several factors, including:

- the degree to which government policy impacts the firm
- the level of the firm's product diversification
- the degree of "corporatism" (where large corporations have considerable influence on government policy) or "pluralism" (when a wider variety of interest groups influence government policy) in the country the firm is operating in.

Nonmarket Participation

A firm's nonmarket participation will be to act either individually or as part of a collective effort. Individual participation are solitary efforts by single firms, while collective participation is characterized by collaboration and cooperation between firms, such as trade associations. The level of nonmarket participation a firm chooses should be based on resource availability (money, people, time) and knowledge of the political process in the country or region the firm is operating in. Firms with a low level of knowledge in a region are likely better off participating in a collective approach, whereas firms with a high level of regional knowledge can "go it alone" when it comes to their nonmarket participation.

Nonmarket Strategy

Several options exist for the type of nonmarket strategy a firm can choose. An "informational nonmarket strategy" can entail lobbying, conducting and publishing research projects, providing expert witness testimony about the issue, and releasing position papers and technical reports that address the issue. A "financial nonmarket strategy" can include political contributions, providing speaking honorariums for government officials, and making political hiring and appointments to the firm's staff. A "constituency-building" strategy can involve advocacy advertising, public relations campaigns, and the mobilization of employees, suppliers, and customers.

The nonmarket strategy a firm chooses should be based on several factors including the stage of the lifecycle an issue is in. For example, if the issue is in the awareness or interest formation stage, the appropriate nonmarket strategy would be informational, whereas if the issue has moved to the legislation or enforcement stage, a financial or constituency-building strategy may be required. Beyond the lifecycle stage the issue is in, management should also consider their firm's resource availability (people, time, money) and the level of perceived public credibility the firm has if wanting to pursue an informational strategy, for example.

Example Nonmarket Strategy Decisions

Examples of firms that made and applied the various nonmarket decisions described above include Toyota, who lobbied for individual Prius drivers to gain access to California carpool lanes, which previously forbid vehicles with solitary occupants to use the lanes (Bach and Allen, 2010). The choices for this nonmarket effort were a transactional (short-term) approach, individual (go-it-alone) firm participation, and an informational (lobbying) nonmarket strategy. Another example is the US sugar industry benefiting from import quotas (SICE, 1990), which entailed a relational (long-term) approach, collective (trade organization) participation, and financial (political funding) nonmarket strategies.

Integrating Market and Nonmarket Strategy

Nonmarket strategy should support and integrate with the firm's market (business) strategy. Both the market and nonmarket strategy processes entail analyzing the external environment for trends and developments that can present either opportunities or threats to the firm. Moreover, these analyses overlap. Figure 9.2 illustrates the overlap and integration of market and nonmarket strategy.

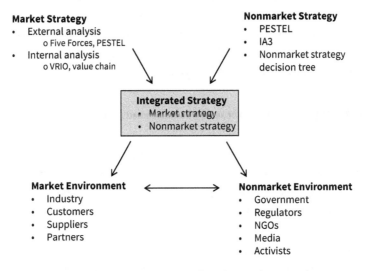

Figure 9.2 Overlap and integration of market and nonmarket strategy

Participants and Key Activities

The main participants in developing and implementing a firm's nonmarket strategy are:

- *Senior executives.* Identify potential and priority nonmarket issues and preferred nonmarket strategies. Participate in relation-building, information dissemination, and constituency-building nonmarket activities. Approve budgets for financial nonmarket strategies.
- *Internal government relations team.* Assist senior management with identifying potential and priority nonmarket issues and preferred nonmarket strategies. Participate in implementing individual and collective nonmarket approaches, relation-building, information dissemination, and constituency-building nonmarket activities.

Best Practices

Prioritize. Some nonmarket issues will be more important to the firm than others. Management must decide which nonmarket issues will create the greatest cost or revenue advantages or will most reduce the firm's financial or reputational risk.

Integrate nonmarket with business strategy. Nonmarket strategy should not stand alone; rather, nonmarket strategy should be a part of the firm's business strategy, helping the firm achieve competitive advantage where possible.

Continually monitor the nonmarket environment. As the nonmarket environment becomes ever more complex and priority issues often change, firms must regularly monitor developments and "hot issues" in the nonmarket to help management determine which issues the firm should participate in.

Be proactive. Starting early in the issue lifecycle to shape the direction and narrative helps the firm "get out in front" of important issues, rather than having to react to rules and regulations later in the lifecycle.

Potential Pitfalls

Ignoring the nonmarket. Large firms have found that because of their market power and visibility, they cannot ignore nonmarket issues. However, even small firms with limited resources can choose and implement a nonmarket strategy, by joining industry groups or releasing position papers and marketing campaigns relating to nonmarket issues.

Getting embroiled in contentious issues. Many nonmarket issues can seem like "no-win" situations, and what may seem like a reasonable stance for the firm to promote may backfire. Therefore, management must consider all the ramifications of taking a position on contentious issues.

Trying to delay the inevitable. Momentum around some nonmarket issues can build quickly and require early, rapid shifts in a firm's business strategy. Although it is tempting for management to try to counter the direction of an issue to preserve their current business model, the more prudent solution would be to shift business strategy to take advantage of changing societal views.

Key Frameworks, Tools, and Templates

The key tools that can help management formulate a firm's nonmarket strategy (see Appendix B) are as follows.

PESTEL (Aguilar, 1967). A PESTEL analysis (see Chapter 1) identifies nonmarket issues that can impact the organization's future performance. The PESTEL framework consists of six categories: political, economic, social, technological, environmental, and legal.

IA3 framework (Bach and Allen, 2010). The IA3 framework can help understand and analyze firm-specific nonmarket issues. The IA3 framework consists of six questions:

- *What is the issue?* Various issues include intellectual property, health and safety, emissions and fuel standards, trade policy, consumer protection, competition policy, diversity and inclusion, and so forth.
- *Who are the actors?* Nonmarket actors include governments, NGOs, activists, and the media.
- *What are the actors' interests?* Various actors may be interested in equality, safety, sustainability, financial gain, and so on.
- *In what arena to the actors meet?* Nonmarket arenas can include the press, online forums, rallies, elections, and so forth.
- *What information moves the issue?* Nonmarket information can include research, position papers, expert opinion, emotion, and so on.
- *What assets do the actors need to prevail?* Nonmarket assets can include political power, funding, band equity, networks, and so forth.

Nonmarket decision tree (Hillman and Hitt, 1999). A nonmarket decision tree helps management design a nonmarket strategy for each priority issue. As identified above, three aspects that require management decisions are the firm's: (1) nonmarket approach, (2) participation level, and (3) nonmarket strategy.

Best-Practice Case Example

A description of BigTech Inc.'s approach to nonmarket strategy in practice is summarized in Table 9.1.

Table 9.1 Nonmarket strategy at BigTech Inc.*

The need:

- A global technology firm wanted to test their autonomous driving technology under "live" city driving conditions.
- The firm needed a nonmarket approach to obtain approval from local city and state authorities to conduct driverless car trials.

The solution:

- Management worked with the firm's government relations group to develop a nonmarket strategy approach to obtain the required approvals.
- The firm's approach was transactional (short term, one issue) as it was focused on the immediate need for governmental approvals to test their driverless cars.
- Although a member of a collective industry group promoting the benefits of and safety data about driverless technology, the firm's participation in this case was individual (go it alone) to secure the approvals needed for their specific testing needs.
- The firm employed both informational (lobbying) and financial (political funding through campaign donations, as well as expanding their operations in the local city) nonmarket strategies.

The results:

- The firm secured approval for multi-year testing of their autonomous driving technology from both city and state government.

---

* Because of non-disclosure considerations, a global technology firm is referred to throughout the illustration as BigTech Inc.

Chapter Summary

- Nonmarket strategy is a term applied to the aspects of business strategy that address relationships that do not unfold within commercial markets but still affect the company's ability to reach its strategic goals.
- A company's nonmarket environment is composed of various entities including regulators, governments, citizens, NGOs, activists, and the media.
- "Regulatory risk" and "reputational risk" have been ranked as top strategic risks by executives.
- The nonmarket is important because it can limit or enhance a firm's strategic advantages.
- A study of over 1,000 executives representing a wide range of industries, regions, and functional specialties found that government is more likely to impact a firm's financial value than any other stakeholder group, except customers.
- The development of nonmarket issues can be understood in terms of a lifecycle, which creates a trade-off between where in the lifecycle a nonmarket issue is and managerial control over the issue.
- The issue lifecycle consists of: issue identification, interest formation, legislation, administration, and enforcement.
- Early in the lifecycle, key participants in issue formulation and awareness include the media and private activists.

- Later in the issue lifecycle, political and legal institutions become primary participants who shape control of an issue.
- Various reasons exist for why companies need to pursue a nonmarket strategy as part of their business strategy, including mitigating financial and reputational risk, shaping the environment in which the firm operates, and managing key issues and actors across the lifecycle.
- Nonmarket strategy is multifaceted and includes decisions about three aspects: (1) the firm's approach (relational or transactional), (2) the level of participation (collective or individual), and (3) nonmarket strategy (informational, financial incentives, or constituency-building).
- Nonmarket strategy should support and integrate with the firm's market (business) strategy.
- The main participants in developing and implementing a firm's nonmarket strategy are senior executives and the internal government relations team.
- Best practices in nonmarket strategy include prioritizing nonmarket issues, integrating nonmarket with business strategy, and continually monitoring the nonmarket environment to identify "hot issues."
- Potential pitfalls in nonmarket strategy include ignoring the nonmarket, getting embroiled in contentious issues, and trying to delay the inevitable impact of nonmarket issues on the firm.
- Key nonmarket frameworks are PESTEL, IA3, and the nonmarket decision tree.

Discussion Questions

1. What activities does your organization do well regarding its nonmarket strategy? What aspects of nonmarket strategy could your organization perform better?
2. Who is typically involved in developing and implementing your organization's nonmarket strategy? Who should be involved?
3. Which approach does your organization typically take to nonmarket strategy: transactional (issue by issue) or relational (long term)? Which approach should they use?
4. Which form of participation does your organization typically take to nonmarket strategy: individual (go it alone) or collective (working with other firms or participation in industry groups)? Which approach should they use?
5. Which type of nonmarket strategy does your firm typically use: informational, financial, or constituency-building? Which should they use?
6. How often does your organization review its nonmarket strategy? Should the frequency of nonmarket strategy reviews change and, if so, why?
7. How does your organization monitor nonmarket strategy success? What aspects should be monitored?

Organizational Self-Assessment

Completing the following self-assessment (Table 9.2) will provide a view of how effectively your organization addresses nonmarket strategy.

Steps to complete the self-assessment:

1. Rate each item on a scale of 0 (poor) to 10 (excellent).
2. Make notes for each item to explain the rationale for the numerical rating.
3. Add all ten scores to get a TOTAL SCORE (maximum score = 100).

Table 9.2 Organizational self-assessment: nonmarket strategy

Component	Rating (0 = poor, 10 = excellent)	Notes/rationale
When it comes to nonmarket strategy …		
1. We place importance on nonmarket strategy		
2. We apply a clear method to develop our nonmarket strategy		
3. We use a defined set of tools to develop our nonmarket strategy		
4. We have the right people involved in developing our nonmarket strategy		
5. We integrate our nonmarket strategy with our business strategy		
6. We are proactive about nonmarket strategy rather than reactive		
7. We have sufficient resources to implement our nonmarket strategy		
8. We monitor the success of our nonmarket strategy		
9. We regularly review and update our nonmarket strategy in line with our business strategy		
10. We would be considered "best practice" in how we develop and implement our nonmarket strategy		
TOTAL SCORE		

Rating scale:

> 0–20 = Poor (significant improvement needed)
>
> 21–40 = Below average (improvement needed in several areas)
>
> 41–60 = Average (identify areas of weakness and adjust)
>
> 61–80 = Above average (identify areas that can still be improved)
>
> 81–100 = Excellent (continuously review and refine each component for each iteration of the organization's strategy efforts)

10
How Corporate Parents Add Strategic Value

There is often confusion between "business strategy" and "corporate strategy." The fundamental differences between business and corporate strategy are in the level of organizational focus and in the primary questions management must answer.

Business Strategy

Business strategy resides at the business unit level and requires business unit-level management to answer the question "How do we compete?" It requires deciding whether low costs, better and more varied products, and/or high levels of customer service and responsiveness are most likely to yield the best results.

Corporate Strategy

Corporate strategy resides at the multi-business unit level and answers two key questions. First, corporate-level management must decide "Which businesses should we be in?", requiring them to analyze and select the markets and industries in which to operate. Once the decision has been made to diversify, management must then determine "How will the corporate office manage the array of businesses?", requiring management to make decisions about their corporate parenting approach.

The Growth Gap

Sustaining growth is hard to do. Known as the "growth gap," there is often a substantial difference between the growth markets expect of firms based on their past performance and the growth they deliver (see Figure 10.1). Based on an analysis of the growth of ninety-three firms before and after entering the Fortune 50 between 1955 and 2006, firms enter the Fortune 50 by growing quickly, with average annual growth rates for each of the five years prior to entering the Fortune 50 ranging from 9 to 20 percent. They continue to grow for the first year after entering the Fortune 50 at an astounding 28.6 percent. Then, their performance falls off drastically one year after entry into the Fortune 50, with average annual growth rates for years two through fifteen after entering the Fortune 50 ranging from a high of 5.1 to a low of −3.9 percent (Laurie et al., 2006).

The Strategist's Handbook. Timothy Galpin, Oxford University Press. © Timothy Galpin (2023).
DOI: 10.1093/oso/9780192885203.003.0011

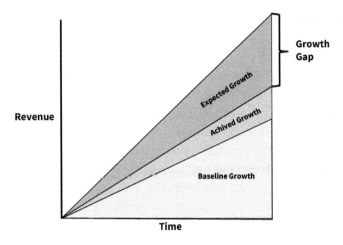

Figure 10.1 The growth gap

Closing the Growth Gap

To close the growth gap, Ansoff (1957) offers four basic alternatives available to firms based on their selection of market and product offering. When faced with a growth gap, firms typically follow a logical progression through the areas of Ansoff's matrix (see Figure 10.2), from market penetration first, then to related diversification, and finally to conglomerate diversification.

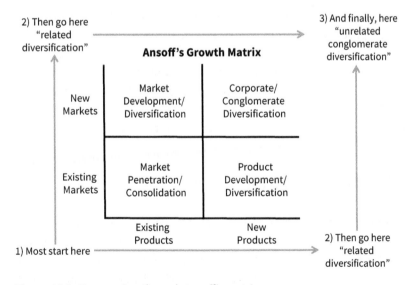

Figure 10.2 Progression through Ansoff's matrix

Market Penetration

A market penetration strategy is characterized by a firm's attempt to grow using its existing products and services in existing markets. Market penetration involves increasing market share within existing markets. This can be achieved by selling more products or services to established customers or by finding new customers within existing markets. The company pursues increased sales for its existing products in its current markets by lowering prices, increased promotion and distribution support, market consolidation through merging with or acquiring rivals in the same market, and/or modest product refinements. Examples of a market penetration growth strategy include heavy promotion campaigns by Coca-Cola (Oakley, 2015).

Related Diversification

Related diversification occurs when a business attempts to grow by offering the same product to new markets or offering new products to existing markets. Tesla's expansion globally with the same products it sells in the US market (Models S and X) is an example of same product, new market growth. Likewise, an example of the new product, same market growth strategy is Tesla's introduction of the lower-priced Model 3 in the US market.

Unrelated Diversification

Finally, unrelated conglomerate diversification happens when a firm moves into offering new products in new markets. General Electric (example businesses include consumer electronics, aviation, real estate, financial services, energy, water, and lighting), The Tune Group (example business units include aviation, sports, education, lodging, insurance, telecommunications, and entertainment), and Tata (example businesses include manufacturing, realty, aerospace, retail, financial services, hotels, and aviation) are all examples of conglomerate diversification.

Diversification and Performance

While corporate diversification is commonplace (Nippa et al., 2011), evidence demonstrates that diversified firms encounter significant performance issues (Palich et al., 2000). Figure 10.3 illustrates how firms perform along a spectrum of diversification. The curvilinear relationship, or inverted U, between diversification and performance illustrates that firms pursuing related diversification outperform undiversified firms. However, performance falls off significantly for conglomerates consisting of unrelated businesses (Johnson et al., 2017). The poor performance of

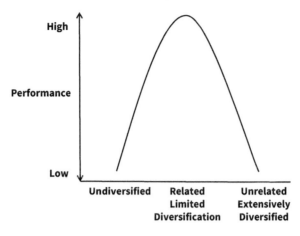

Figure 10.3 Diversification and performance: research findings

highly diversified firms has been attributed to a variety of problems, including the high cost of a corporate infrastructure, added bureaucratic complexity, obscured financial performance of weak portfolio companies, and a lack of discipline (i.e., unfocused corporate parenting) in managing a diversified portfolio of businesses.

Managing the Portfolio

Not all businesses in a corporate portfolio will perform equally. Therefore, a portfolio analysis will help determine which businesses to maintain at the current level of investment, those to invest in for growth, others to divest out of, or business units to add to the portfolio. A key portfolio analysis tool is the BCG matrix (Henderson, 1970). The matrix plots businesses in a corporate portfolio on two axes, the current market share of each business unit, and the rate of market growth of each business unit. Positioning each business unit on the matrix identifies four categories of businesses in a corporate portfolio:

Dogs. Business units with low market share and low growth rates are candidates for divestment.

Cash cows. Business units in the portfolio with high market share but low growth are ideal to maintain and harvest the cash flows, which can be used to fund investment in other portfolio businesses.

Question marks. Portfolio businesses with high growth rates but low market share. Corporate management must decide whether to invest in these business units to grow their market share.

Stars. Businesses in the portfolio with high market share and high growth. These are business units that corporate management will continue to invest in to become even more dominant in their industries.

Focused Corporate Parenting Is a Core Competency

The value-adding effect of the corporate head office on individual business units comprising the firm's portfolio is termed the "parenting advantage" (Campbell et al., 1995). Corporate parents can add or destroy value in their portfolio companies in numerous ways. For example, value-destroying activities include increasing costs, adding bureaucratic complexity, or obscuring poor business unit performance, while value-adding activities involve coaching business unit management, facilitating synergies between business units, providing efficient and effective central administrative services, and helping manage external relations. Three fundamental types of corporate parents exist: portfolio manager, synergizer, and capability developer.

The Portfolio Manager

Portfolio manager corporate offices act as strategic investors and are not concerned with the relatedness of the business units in their portfolio or interfering in the management decisions of the business units. Instead, portfolio managers perform the role of knowledgeable investors, informed board members, and an in-house bank, funding investments in various business units (Vermeulen, 2013). Berkshire Hathaway is a clear example of a corporate parent that has focused on a portfolio management parenting approach (Thorndike, 2012). The integrated bundle of capabilities forming the core competency of portfolio management includes financial analysis, capital budgeting, fiscal management, acquisition and divestiture transaction experience, and strategic investment savvy.

The Synergizer

The synergizer corporate office seeks to share business practices across business units. Synergy managers do not strive to bring business practices into various units from the corporate center. Rather, they establish mechanisms for sharing processes, people, and systems across business units, with the aim of improving efficiency and effectiveness among the units (Porter, 1987). General Electric under former CEO Jack Welch, who persistently advocated the "shameless stealing of good ideas" between business units, implemented a corporate parenting approach focused on facilitating cross-unit synergies such as management training, human resources (HR) practices, and business process improvements (Knoll, 2008; Slater, 1999). The cohesive set of capabilities forming the core competency of synergy management includes core knowledge identification and capture, business process analysis, meeting facilitation, communication, technology-based learning systems implementation and training design and delivery.

The Capability Developer

The capability developer applies its own central capabilities to add value to business units. Capability developers are not concerned with pursuing collaboration across business units or transferring capabilities between business units, as is the case for synergy managers. Rather, capability developers focus on the resources they as corporate parents can transfer downwards to improve the performance of business units (Johnson et al., 2017). Unilever has been highlighted as a corporate parent that focuses on capability development within their business units, such as imparting fiscal management expertise, HR management processes, and marketing practices (Caligiuri, 2012; Campbell et al., 1995). The corporate-level core competency of business unit capability development includes corporate-to-business-unit communication, talent identification, specific business process expertise such as marketing or global supply chain management, and training design and delivery.

Focused Parenting Creates Strategic Value

Unfocused corporate parenting is common, while focused corporate parenting is rare. Both the academic and practice literature suggest that focusing on one of the three principal corporate parenting approaches provides several benefits. First, discipline on the part of the corporate parent prevents its drifting into inappropriate activities or taking on unnecessary costs (Johnson et al., 2017). Second, the ability to adopt and maintain a strong strategic focus is necessary to realize the potential of the core competency approach (Clark, 2000). Third, each of the three firms identified above as examples of focused corporate parenting (General Electric, Unilever, and Berkshire Hathaway) experienced stock prices that significantly outperformed the S&P 500 index for the twenty-year period between 1988 and 2008.

Just as individual firms "cannot succeed by trying to be all things to all people" (Treacy and Wiersema, 1995, p. 12), it follows that corporate parents cannot succeed by trying to be all things to their business units. Because of the specialized bundle of capabilities involved in each parenting role, it is virtually impossible for a corporate office to be competent at two or all three roles at the same time. Likewise, a corporate parent attempting to fulfill each role concurrently will only serve to confuse business unit management.

As diversification is commonplace (Nippa et al., 2011), simply diversifying without a focused corporate parenting approach does not fulfill the valuable, rare, inimitable, organizational (VRIO) criteria for competitive advantage discussed previously in Chapter 2. However, firms that can implement a focused corporate parenting approach do realize each of the VRIO criteria (see Table 10.1). Therefore, simply diversifying does not provide firms with a competitive advantage, but diversifying combined with a focused corporate parenting approach does.

Table 10.1 Unfocused corporate parenting versus focused corporate parenting

VRIO criteria	Fulfills VRIO?	Rationale
Unfocused corporate parenting		
Value: Does the resource/capability enable the firm to improve its efficiency or effectiveness?	NO	• Unfocused corporate parenting creates confusion, unnecessary costs, and inefficiencies, destroying value.
Rarity: Is control of the resource/capability in the hands of a relative few?	NO	• Unfocused corporate parenting is common among diversified firms.
Inimitability: Is it difficult to imitate, and will there be significant cost and/or time disadvantage to a firm trying to obtain, develop, or duplicate the resource/capability?	NO	• It is easy for many firms to become unfocused in their corporate parenting approach, trying to be all things to all business units.
Organization: Is the firm organized in such a way that it is ready and able to exploit the resource/capability?	NO	• Many corporate offices are not organized to effectively implement a focused parenting approach as new businesses are added to their portfolio.
Focused corporate parenting		
Value: Does the resource/capability enable the firm to improve its efficiency or effectiveness?	YES	• A focused corporate parenting approach creates value through the implementation of proven value-creating activities.
Rarity: Is control of the resource/capability in the hands of a relative few?	YES	• Focused corporate parenting is uncommon among diversified firms.
Inimitability: Is it difficult to imitate, and will there be significant cost and/or time disadvantage to a firm trying to obtain, develop, or duplicate the resource/capability?	YES	• An integrated focused corporate parenting competency is hard to duplicate because of the effort, time, and cost involved.
Organization: Is the firm organized in such a way that it is ready and able to exploit the resource/capability?	YES	• A focused corporate parenting approach requires a firm to organize around an integrated bundle of capabilities, applying all the relevant skills, knowledge, tools, and talent required for value creation.

Building a Focused Corporate Parenting Core Competency

Building a focused corporate parenting approach includes seven key steps (see Table 10.2). The process begins by conducting a corporate parenting performance review to establish an understanding of the corporate office's current approach. This review involves identifying what works well and what could be done better regarding

Table 10.2 Building a focused corporate parenting approach

Component	Key activities
1. **Conduct a current corporate parenting performance review**	• Identify what works well and what could be done better regarding the firm's current corporate parenting activities. • Determine how focused or unfocused the firm's current parenting activities are. • Identify and catalog the firm's current corporate parenting practices, talent, and tools. • Record key learnings to apply to the firm's future corporate parenting activities.
2. **Decide which parenting approach to focus on**	• Based on the current parenting performance review, decide which corporate parenting approach to focus on in the future: - Portfolio manager - Synergy manager - Capability developer
3. **Identify needed corporate parenting practices, talent, and tools**	• Identify corporate-level practices required for the chosen parenting approach. • Identify key corporate-level talent and skills necessary for the chosen parenting approach. • Identify corporate-level tools and templates necessary for the chosen parenting approach.
4. **Identify gaps**	• Identify gaps between the firm's current and future corporate parenting practices, talent, and tools.
5. **Conduct corporate parenting training**	• Develop training content for the desired parenting approach. • Identify training participants based on the corporate parenting talent inventory above. • Schedule and conduct corporate parenting training.
6. **Establish a corporate parenting knowledge repository**	• Establish a corporate parenting knowledge repository, housed on the firm's intranet, for the chosen parenting approach. • Populate the repository with firm-specific tools, templates, and best-practice information for the chosen parenting approach.
7. **Conduct regular maintenance**	• Conduct regular reviews of the firm's corporate parenting performance, practices, talent, and tools. • Update practices, talent, and tools in the firm's corporate parenting repository as needed

the corporate office's current business unit parenting activities; for example, determining how focused or unfocused the firm's parenting activities are, identifying and cataloging the firm's corporate parenting practices, talent, and tools, and recording key learnings to apply to the firm's future corporate parenting activities.

Based on the parenting performance review, management must then decide which corporate parenting approach to focus on in the future: portfolio manager, synergy manager, or capability developer. Once management decides upon its desired parenting approach, the next step is to identify the corporate parenting practices, talent, and tools required to build the chosen parenting approach into a core competency. Examples of the integrated bundle of capabilities forming the core competency of each parenting approach are identified above. Then, the gaps between the firm's current and future corporate parenting practices, talent, and tools should be identified.

To begin closing the identified gaps between the firm's current and desired future parenting needs, the next step is to implement training, which includes developing training content for the desired parenting approach, identifying training participants based on the corporate parenting talent inventory above (i.e., those who will be responsible for implementing the desired parenting approach), and scheduling and conducting training sessions for the identified participants. In addition to the training sessions, as part of the firm's knowledge capture efforts, a corporate parenting knowledge repository should be established. The repository can be housed on the firm's intranet and should contain tools, templates, and best-practice information for the chosen parenting approach. As the selected parenting approach is implemented, the final step is maintenance. Maintenance efforts include conducting regular reviews of the firm's corporate parenting performance, practices, talent, and tools, and updating the firm's corporate parenting repository as needed.

Participants and Key Activities

The main participants in developing and implementing corporate strategy are:

- *Corporate-level executives.* Executives at the corporate level of a conglomerate decide which businesses to include in their corporate portfolio and how the corporate office will "parent" their portfolio businesses.
- *Business unit executives.* Plan and implement the business unit strategy. Work with corporate executives regarding optimizing the parenting approach from the corporate office.

Best Practices

Determine the type of parent. Corporate executives must decide which type of corporate parent the corporate office will be: portfolio manager, synergizer, or capability developer.

Focus. Evidence demonstrates that a focused corporate parent adds value to the business in the corporate portfolio.

Manage the portfolio. Conduct a regular portfolio analysis to identify business units that should be maintained, invested in, divested, or added.

Potential Pitfalls

Trying to be all things to all business units. Corporate management trying to be all three types of corporate parent only serves to confuse business unit management about the role of the corporate office.

Over-diversification. Research has found that some diversification is good for overall corporate performance, but too much diversification ultimately diminishes corporate performance.

Poor portfolio management. Waiting too long to invest in "question marks" (businesses with high growth but low market share) enables competitors in that industry to forge ahead of the business unit. Likewise, not divesting out of poor-performing businesses ("dogs") will drag down overall corporate performance.

Key Frameworks, Tools, and Templates

The primary corporate strategy tools include (see Appendix B):

Ansoff's matrix. Used by business unit management to identify growth opportunities (market penetration, new products, new services) and corporate management to identify opportunities to add businesses to the corporate portfolio.

BCG matrix. Used to assess the business unit portfolio of a corporate conglomerate to identify opportunities for investment, divestments, maintenance, or additions to the portfolio.

The value chain. Used by the "synergizer" corporate parent to identify overlaps between business units that provide opportunities for cross-pollination of operating methods or the possible establishment of shared services for back-office functions (e.g., HR, information technology, procurement, and so forth).

Best-Practice Case Example

A description of Conglomerate Inc.'s approach to corporate strategy in practice is summarized in Table 10.3.

Chapter Summary

- The fundamental differences between business and corporate strategy are in the level of organizational focus and the primary questions management must answer.

Table 10.3 Corporate strategy at Conglomerate Inc.*

The need:

- Corporate management of Conglomerate Inc. realized that as their portfolio of businesses grew, they did not have a clear approach to "corporate parenting," which was confusing the various business units' management teams.
- The corporate office needed to define and implement a clear corporate parenting approach.

The solution:

- Corporate management tasked a team to conduct a corporate parenting performance review to identify what works well and what could be done better regarding the firm's current corporate parenting activities.
- The team conducted interviews with the management teams in each business unit, as well as corporate staff, about the roles the corporate office has typically fulfilled regarding setting business unit strategy, financial investment, and operational decisions within each business unit.
- The team identified that the most positive impact on business unit performance the corporate office made was when it helped identify synergy opportunities across the various portfolio business units, including operational efficiencies and go-to-market methods.
- The team then identified best practices for focusing the corporate office on being a superior "synergizer parent."
- The team established a knowledge repository to house and disseminate key learnings for synergy opportunities identified across the business units.
- A training program was developed to provide corporate and business unit management with awareness of and skills in cross-business knowledge-sharing best practices.

The results:

- Quarterly reviews were conducted of the firm's corporate parenting performance, practices, talent, and tools.
- Cost reduction associated with the business process cross-pollination between business units was tracked, identifying significant savings across business units.

---

* Because of non-disclosure considerations, a globally diversified corporation is referred to throughout the illustration as Conglomerate Inc.

- Business strategy resides at the business unit level and requires business unit managers to answer the question "How do we compete?"
- Corporate strategy resides at the multi-business unit, corporate office level and answers two key questions: (1) "Which businesses should we be in?" and (2) "How will the corporate office manage the array of businesses?"
- Known as the "growth gap," there is often a substantial difference between the growth markets expect of firms based on their past performance and the growth they deliver.
- Four basic growth alternatives are available to firms based on their selection of market and product offering.
- When faced with a growth gap, firms typically follow a logical progression through the areas of Ansoff's matrix, from market penetration to related diversification, and finally to conglomerate diversification.
- While corporate diversification is commonplace, evidence demonstrates that diversified firms encounter significant performance issues.

- A portfolio analysis will help a corporate office determine which businesses to maintain at the current level of investment, invest in for further growth, divest out of, or add to the corporate portfolio.
- A key portfolio analysis tool is the BCG matrix, segmenting business units into: dogs, stars, cash cows, and question marks.
- The value-adding effect of the corporate head office on individual business units comprising the firm's portfolio is termed the "parenting advantage."
- Three fundamental types of corporate parents exist: portfolio manager, synergizer, and capability developer.
- Unfocused corporate parenting is common, while focused corporate parenting is rare.
- Just as individual firms "cannot succeed by trying to be all things to all people," it follows that corporate parents cannot succeed by trying to be all things to their business units.
- Firms that can implement a focused corporate parenting approach realize each of the VRIO criteria.
- Building a focused corporate parenting approach includes seven key steps.
- The main participants in developing and implementing corporate strategy are: corporate-level executives and business unit executives.
- The best practices of corporate-level strategy include: determining the type of parent, focus, and managing the corporate portfolio.
- Potential pitfalls of corporate-level strategy include: trying to be all things to all business units, over-diversification, and poor portfolio management.
- The key tools to assist with corporate strategy are Ansoff's matrix, the BCG matrix, and the value chain.

Discussion Questions

1. What activities does your organization do well regarding corporate strategy? What corporate strategy activities could the organization perform better?
2. Does your organization have a corporate parenting approach? How well does it execute its parenting approach? What could your organization do better when it comes to executing its corporate parenting approach?
3. Does your organization have the appropriate business units in its corporate portfolio? Which businesses should it have?
4. Does your organization conduct a regular corporate portfolio analysis? If so, what businesses are stars, dogs, cash cows, and question marks?
5. Are there synergy opportunities between the business units in your organization's corporate portfolio? What are those potential synergies?

Organizational Self-Assessment

Completing the following self-assessment (Table 10.4) will provide a view of how effectively your organization addresses corporate strategy.

Steps to complete the self-assessment:

1. Rate each item on a scale of 0 (poor) to 10 (excellent).
2. Make notes for each item to explain the rationale for the numerical rating.
3. Add all ten scores to get a TOTAL SCORE (maximum score = 100).

Rating scale:

   0–20 = Poor (significant improvement needed)
   21–40 = Below average (improvement needed in several areas)
   41–60 = Average (identify areas of weakness and adjust)
   61–80 = Above average (identify areas that can still be improved)
   81–100 = Excellent (continuously review and refine each component for each iteration of the organization's strategy efforts)

Table 10.4 Organizational self-assessment: corporate strategy

Component	Rating (0 = poor, 10 = excellent)	Notes/rationale
When it comes to corporate strategy …		
1. We regularly review our corporate portfolio of businesses		
2. We apply a clear method and tools to review our corporate portfolio of businesses		
3. We know which businesses in our corporate portfolio are stars, dogs, cash cows, and question marks		
4. We have identified our "corporate parenting" focus		
5. The leaders of our business units clearly understand our chosen corporate parenting approach		
6. We identify and "cross-pollinate" cost reduction synergies across our various business units		
7. We identify and "cross-pollinate" revenue improvement synergies across our various business units		
8. We regularly review and refine our corporate parenting approach		
9. Regarding our corporate parenting approach, we avoid trying to be "all things to all business units"		
10. We regularly assess the effectiveness of our corporate parenting approach		
TOTAL SCORE		

11

Pursuing Alliances, Joint Ventures, Mergers, and Acquisitions

Mergers and acquisitions (M&As) are ubiquitous terms that include a spectrum of arrangements including non-equity alliances and partnerships, equity alliances, joint ventures, and M&As, each with increasing ownership. As ownership increases, control increases, but so does risk (see Figure 11.1). If done well, M&As, in their various forms, can create value. However, ample evidence demonstrates that M&As create significant post-deal performance issues for acquiring, "buy-side" firms. For example, a broad analysis of 2,500 deals found that more than 60 percent destroyed shareholder value (Lewis and McKone, 2016). The poor results from M&As have been attributed to a variety of management missteps across the process, in M&A strategy, target identification, due diligence, negotiation, integration, and measurement (Cartwright and Schoenberg, 2006; Faelten et al., 2016). In the current era of transient competitive advantage, digital transformation, and disruptive innovation, M&As are certain to be increasingly challenging.

While M&As are a multi-staged and cross-disciplinary process, too often corporate leaders approach them as a financial exercise to facilitate their growth strategy. This increases the likelihood that confounding implementation problems will arise in the subsequent post-transaction stages. Although analyzing, planning, and assessing value prior to transaction close is important, any seasoned CEO who has been through at least one M&A will recognize, and has likely learned the hard way, that value is only realized after the deal closes, through effective implementation. What is needed then is a management-oriented model providing an integrated and actionable end-to-end view of the M&A process.

The Foundation of an M&A Core Competency: A Comprehensive Deal Flow Model

Combining M&A experience with a systemized and documented M&A process has been found to improve success. An analysis of 228 bank mergers found that combining two key factors, experience and a clear M&A methodology, enhances deal performance. The first factor, which the researchers call "tacit knowledge," consists of M&A experience and exists largely in the minds of executives, managers, and employees. The second factor, which they term "codified knowledge," consists of written procedures that a company articulates in an "M&A playbook," which guides actions and decision-making throughout the M&A process, both pre- and

The Strategist's Handbook. Timothy Galpin, Oxford University Press. © Timothy Galpin (2023).
DOI: 10.1093/oso/9780192885203.003.0012

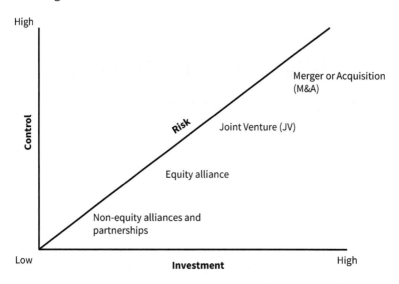

Figure 11.1 Ownership options: investment, risk, and control

post-transaction close (Zollo and Singh, 2007). Despite evidence that a systematized M&A process improves deal success, other research has found that almost two thirds (60 percent) of surveyed executives indicated their firms do not have a documented comprehensive end-to-end M&A process (Galpin and Herndon, 2014).

A Tested M&A Model for Managers: The Deal Flow Model

The deal flow model offers a cross-disciplinary, end-to-end view of the M&A process consisting of ten stages across three phases (see Figure 11.2).

The Deal Flow Model Is Linear; M&As Are Not

As veteran dealmakers know, M&As are not a simple sequential process. For the sake of clarity, the deal flow model is arranged as ten distinct stages across three phases. M&A language ("pre-deal," "deal" and "post-deal"), as used among M&A professionals and researchers, also implies a chronological approach to M&As. In practice, however, there are no clear lines between many of the stages identified in the model. The stages involve multiple overlapping activities. While each deal may be sequenced a bit differently, firms building their M&A competency can use the model to record and catalog their M&A process tools, templates, and talent across the ten stages to create an M&A playbook.

Core Activities across the Ten M&A Stages

Key objectives and core activities of the ten stages of the deal flow model are identified in Figure 11.3. The objectives and activities were developed and refined through

Three Phases   **Ten Stages**

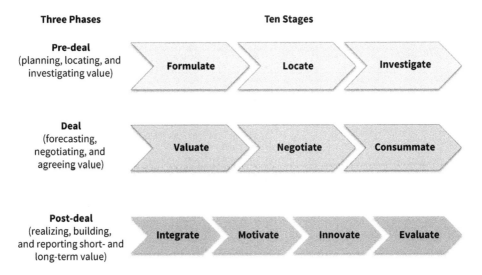

Figure 11.2 Deal flow model

a combination of experience gained by applying the model and by incorporating best practices found throughout empirical and practice M&A literature. Over the past several decades, both M&A researchers and professionals have written much about the various pitfalls and best practices during each of the ten stages. Several comprehensive reviews of M&A research exist, summarizing empirical findings regarding "pre- and post-deal" success factors (Barkema and Schijven, 2008; Caiazza and Volpe, 2015; Steigenberger, 2017; Vazirani, 2012). The M&A practice literature has also identified pitfalls and best practices within various stages of the deal flow model (Cascio, 2010; Kullman, 2012.

Lessons Learned in Industry and Private Equity

Lessons can be learned from companies that have built an integrated end-to-end M&A expertise. Best practices applied by General Electric, for instance, include assessing cultural fit early in the deal process during the "Investigate" stage, selecting an integration manager before deals are closed during the "Negotiate" stage, providing necessary resources and assigning accountabilities for implementation during the "Integrate" stage, and continual updating of M&A tools and templates for application on future deals (Ashkenas et al., 1998). Another experienced dealmaker, Cisco, develops a well-defined acquisition strategy for their transactions during the "Formulate" stage, implements clear retention plans during the "Motivate" stage, visibly measures success of each deal during the "Evaluate" stage, and, like General Electric, refines the firm's M&A tools and process for use on subsequent transactions (Toppenberg et al., 2015).

Stage	Key Objective	Core Activities
Formulate	Clear M&A strategy	• Define the business strategy. • Define an M&A strategy to support the business strategy.
Locate	Targets that fit the M&A strategy	• Identify potential targets. • Assess strategic and organizational "fit" of potential targets.
Investigate	No surprises after deal close	• Conduct financial, operational, legal, technological, and organizational due diligence. • Draft operational and cultural integration plans. • Draft communications plans. • Draft key talent retention plan. • Draft key customer retention plan.
Valuate	Realistic price range	• Determine cost and revenue assumptions. • Develop valuation models using multiple techniques.
Negotiate	Agreed deal terms	• Meet with target's negotiating team. • Discuss and agree deal terms. • Submit bid (in an auction transaction).
Consummate	Transaction completion	• Draft transaction documentation. • Sign documentation. • Gain regulatory approval. • Transfer transaction funding.
Integrate	Synergy capture	• Execute integration plans. • Adjust implementation as needed. • Implement key customer retention and re-engagement plan.
Motivate	Maximum workforce productivity	• Implement communications plan. • Implement key talent retention and re-engagement plan. • Implement cultual integration plan.
Innovate	Additional revenue growth	• Transfer knowledge between firms. • Develop and implement new or enhanced products, services, and/or processes.
Evaluate	Measured and reported deal success	• Track and report operational intcgration activities and milestones. • Track and report cultural integration activities and milestones. • Track and report key talent retention activities and milestones. • Track and report synergy capture (cost reduction and revenue enhancement).

Figure 11.3 Key objectives and core activities across the ten stages of the deal flow model

In addition to these high-profile industry examples, even in the financially focused domain of private equity a shift from approaching M&As solely as a financial exercise to conducting M&As instead as an integrated process of value creation, spanning transaction through implementation, is occurring (Gilligan and Galpin, 2022). When borrowing costs are low and M&A activity is booming; hedge funds, sovereign wealth funds, and pension funds compete for deals, thus elevating the importance of creating long-term value over short-term financial victories or losses. During an interview with the *Financial Times*, the managing director of private equity firm Carlyle Europe Partners, Marco De Benedetti, noted that he believes the industry can counter that threat by having "superior" value-creation plans for the companies they buy, stressing, "Private equity is no longer able to generate returns by simply relying on financial engineering. Today it is about hard work and building something" (Espinoza, 2017). Table 11.1 identifies seven key steps that companies can work through to build their M&A competency.

Table 11.1 Seven steps to build a firm's M&A competency

Component	key activities
1. **M&A performance assessment**	• Identify recent M&A transactions. • Identify what went well and what could have been done better across the entire M&A process—the ten stages of the deal flow model. • Catalog key learnings to apply to future M&As during each M&A stage.
2. **M&A internal talent inventory**	• Identify key M&A talent across functions. • Identify roles each person has performed during past M&A efforts and will be able to perform during future efforts throughout each stage of the deal flow model. • Catalog key M&A talent identified.
3. **M&A external talent inventory**	• Identify key service providers used in prior M&As—legal, financial, tax. • Identify potential other service providers and determine how each could support talent on future M&As. • Conduct analysis of current and potential M&A service providers to determine "best fit" with the company. • Select future M&A service providers.
4. **M&A tools and templates inventory**	• Conduct M&A tools and templates inventory across functions and M&A stages—due diligence checklists, valuation templates, communications planning matrix, cultural analysis and integration matrix, integration project management tools. • Identify M&A tools' overlaps and gaps. • Rationalize tools' overlaps and gaps. • Catalog future M&A tools and templates.
5. **M&A training**	• Identify M&A training needs/objectives based on the recent M&A performance and key M&A talent capabilities assessments above. • Develop training content for each stage of the deal flow model, designed to achieve each training objective identified. • Identify training participants based on the M&A talent inventory above. • Schedule and conduct cross-functional M&A training.
6. **M&A knowledge repository**	• Establish an M&A knowledge repository, housed on the firm's intranet, for each stage of the deal flow model. • Populate the repository with M&A tools and templates across each of the ten M&A stages.
7. **M&A competency maintenance**	• Conduct regular reviews of M&A tools, templates, and talent. • Update tools, templates, and talent in the M&A repository as needed.

Addressing M&As as an Integrated Core Competency Provides Competitive Advantage

As M&As have become ubiquitous globally, firms that can execute only the transactional elements of deals well (sourcing, financially analyzing, valuing and closing deals) do not satisfy the valuable, rare, inimitable, organizational (VRIO) criteria (discussed previously in Chapter 2) for M&A competency as a competitive advantage. Meanwhile, firms that can skillfully execute an integrated M&A competency, across the full process from transaction through implementation, do realize each of the VRIO criteria (see Table 11.2). Therefore, simply "doing deals" does not provide firms with competitive advantage but doing and implementing deals strategically through a value-enhancing M&A process does.

Developing M&As as an integrated set of capabilities across the process, a core competency that meets the criteria of the VRIO framework, provides four key advantages for firms. First, establishing an M&A process within a firm makes the practice repeatable. Second, management can identify and build M&A talent strength across each process stage. Third, a set of M&A tools and templates can be applied during each stage. Fourth, once a high level of integrated M&A competence is established in the firm, other firms will find it difficult to match the same combination of M&A talent, tools, and execution.

Now that M&As have become the preferred growth strategy for many executive teams, success depends on doing and implementing deals well. Only focusing on M&As as a financial transaction is too narrow an approach. Instead, using an actionable, end-to-end process model, mobilizing diverse talent across the organization, and integrating capabilities across the entire M&A process will provide a valuable, rare, and inimitable advantage for firms, enabling them to "win at the acquisition game."

Participants and Key Activities

M&As are a team sport. At various points throughout the process, internal and external resources of both the buyer and the seller are engaged to work on pre-transaction, transaction, and post-transaction activities. For example, external advisers such as attorneys assist both the buyer and the seller with negotiating deal terms, legal documentation of the transaction, and fulfillment of regulatory requirements. Banks assist both the buyer and seller with valuation analyses and assist buyers with transaction financing. Public relations firms assist with crafting and delivering messaging to various external stakeholders including shareholders, the media, and communities. Internally, functions such as strategy, legal, human resources, information technology, operations, sales, and others assist with transaction planning, completion, and post-transaction implementation.

Table 11.2 M&As as a transaction versus an integrated process

M&As as a transaction		
VRIO criteria	Fulfills VRIO?	Rationale
Value: Does the resource/capability enable the firm to improve its efficiency or effectiveness?	NO	• Completing a transaction only provides the firm with an opportunity to improve its efficiency or effectiveness, while value is realized through implementation.
Rarity: Is control of the resource/capability in the hands of a relative few?	NO	• Numerous companies possess transaction capabilities.
Inimitability: Is it difficult to imitate, and will there be significant cost and/or time disadvantage to a firm trying to obtain, develop, or duplicate the resource/capability?	NO	• Firms can easily source—through hiring or contracting—financial and legal transaction capability on a full- or part-time basis.
Organization: Is the firm organized in such a way that it is ready and able to exploit the resource/capability?	YES	• Many companies employ in-house teams able to source, analyze, value, and consummate the financial and legal elements of their M&A transactions.

M&As as an integrated process of activities from transaction through implementation		
VRIO criteria	Fulfills VRIO?	Rationale
Value: Does the resource/capability enable the firm to improve its efficiency or effectiveness?	YES	• Projected deal synergies—improved firm efficiency and effectiveness—are realized through effective implementation.
Rarity: Is control of the resource/capability in the hands of a relative few?	YES	• Most firms only focus on the transaction rather than an integrated M&A approach spanning pre- and post-transaction capabilities.
Inimitability: Is it difficult to imitate, and will there be significant cost and/or time disadvantage to a firm trying to obtain, develop, or duplicate the resource/capability?	YES	• An integrated M&A competency is hard to duplicate because of the effort, time, and cost involved.
Organization: Is the firm organized in such a way that it is ready and able to exploit the resource/capability?	YES	• An integrated approach to M&As requires a firm to organize around an integrated end-to-end process, applying all the relevant skills, knowledge, tools, and talent required for transaction completion and post-transaction value creation.

Best Practices

Build an "M&A playbook." A key aspect of building M&As as an organizational core competency is to codify the firm's transaction knowledge (tools, templates, and checklists) across the three phases and ten stages of the deal flow model.

Combine codified and tacit knowledge. Identify M&A talent across the organization who possess the knowledge and skills to work on different aspects of pre- and post-deal activities, and skillfully apply the firm's M&A playbook.

Continually upgrade M&A capability. Conduct systematic assessments of the firm's M&A successes and mistakes to regularly improve the firm's M&A processes, tools, and talent.

Potential Pitfalls

Treating M&As as "the deal" only. The activities and deliverables of the pre-deal and deal phases of the deal flow model are important to assess, forecast, and agree deal value. However, a common pitfall is to ignore the post-deal phase, as that is where deal value is realized.

Muddling through. M&As are a complex activity, with many simultaneous "moving parts." Poor coordination of the various transaction participants and activities leads to poor M&A outcomes.

Limited tracking and measurement. No M&A goes exactly according to plan. Therefore, regular measurement and tracking is required to adjust as the process progresses, both pre- and post-transaction.

Key Frameworks, Tools, and Templates

Numerous M&A tools, templates, and checklists exist to assist firms with pre-deal, deal, and post-deal activities. For a broad set of M&A tools and templates across the three phases and ten stages of the deal flow model, in the form of an "M&A workbook," see Galpin (2020).

Best-Practice Case Example

A description of Aerospace Inc.'s approach to building a repeatable M&A capability in practice is summarized in Table 11.3.

Chapter Summary

- Mergers and acquisitions (M&As) are ubiquitous terms that include a spectrum of arrangements including non-equity alliances and partnerships, equity alliances, joint ventures, and M&As, each with increasing ownership.
- As ownership increases, control increases, but so does risk.

Table 11.3 Building an M&A core competency at Aerospace Inc.*

The need:

- Aerospace Inc. is a publicly traded designer, manufacturer, and service provider of control solutions for the aerospace and industrial markets, with annual revenue of more than $2 billion US.
- Over the previous decade the firm completed more than ten transactions of various sizes, representing more than $1 billion US in aggregate transaction value.
- As the firm's strategy combines organic growth supplemented by potential acquisitions, the executive team at Aerospace Inc. wanted to be sure any future transactions they may undertake would result in maximum value creation for the firm and its shareholders.
- To that end, the head of the firm's strategy function initiated a multifaceted effort to strengthen the company's M&A competency.

The solution:

- To begin the process, the strategy team examined the company's approach to several recent deals they had conducted, explaining, "When we assessed the performance of our past acquisitions, we found a lot of things we did well, but as with any complex activity such as M&A transactions, we found opportunities for improvement."
- The team concluded that future deals should be approached as an integrated, end-to-end process, from transaction through implementation.
- After reviewing recent transactions, the team then identified company-specific M&A tools and templates throughout the entire M&A process. For example, potential target analysis and prioritization tools (Locate), functional due diligence checklists and a cultural comparison and integration template (Investigate), project tracking and management tools (Integrate), communications planning and key talent retention matrices (Motivate), and transaction success measurement tools (Evaluate), among others, were identified or developed and stored on the firm's intranet.
- The tools and templates analysis was designed to ensure the company possesses an optimal "M&A playbook" across the various organizational functions and deal stages for any future transactions (codified knowledge).
- The next task was to identify M&A talent across the organization that possess the knowledge and skills to work on different aspects of future pre- and post-deal activities (tacit knowledge). These staff members comprised a cross-functional representation of the company from finance, accounting and tax, human resources, information technology, legal, operations, communications, and marketing.
- Concurrently, external advisers with specialized M&A capabilities were also identified that would partner with the firm to assist internal talent on tasks such as legal and transaction documentation, financial analysis, and tax treatment.
- Once various tools, templates, and talent (both internal and external) were identified, the team arranged for a two-day training session to be conducted by internal company and external experts for key M&A talent from across all organizational functions.
- The purpose of the training was to facilitate both awareness and future application of an integrated M&A competency across the deal stages.
- The training agenda was organized and delivered based on the various components of the deal flow model, with session topics including the firm's approach to and tools for M&A: strategy (Formulate), potential target identification and "deal pipeline" management (Locate), due diligence (Investigate), valuation (Valuate), negotiations (Negotiate), deal close (Consummate), integration management and coordination (Integrate), communication and organizational culture (Motivate), product and service enhancement (Innovate), and deal success measurement and reporting (Evaluate).

Continued

Table 11.3 *Continued*

The results:

- In his remarks to the participants during the close of the training session, the head of the firm's strategy team noted, "We know we did a lot of good things during our previous deals. After this session, the firm is now even better positioned for future deals with an integrated, cross-functional approach across the entire M&A process."
- Since the training, the strategy team has updated and refined key tools and templates that form the company's M&A playbook for each stage of the process.
- Moving forward, the team will conduct regular reviews of the firm's M&A tools, templates, and talent and revise the playbook as needed.

---

* Because of non-disclosure considerations, a diversified aerospace company is referred to throughout the illustration as Aerospace Inc.

- Ample evidence demonstrates that M&As create significant post-deal performance issues for acquiring, "buy-side" firms.
- While M&As are a multi-staged and cross-disciplinary process, too often corporate leaders approach them as a financial exercise to facilitate their growth strategy.
- Combining M&A experience (tacit knowledge) with a systemized and documented M&A process (codified knowledge) has been found to improve success.
- Despite evidence that a systematized M&A process improves deal success, other research has found that almost two thirds (60 percent) of surveyed executives indicated their firms do not have a documented comprehensive end-to-end M&A process.
- The deal flow model offers a cross-disciplinary, end-to-end view of the M&A process, consisting of ten stages across three phases.
- The stages of the deal flow model involve multiple overlapping activities.
- Firms building their M&A competency can use the model to record and catalog their M&A process tools, templates, and talent across the ten stages to create an "M&A playbook."
- Several comprehensive reviews of M&A research exist, summarizing empirical findings regarding "pre- and post-deal" success factors.
- The M&A practice literature has also reported the pitfalls and best practices within various stages of the deal flow model.
- Lessons can be learned from companies that have built integrated end-to-end M&A expertise.
- Even in the financially focused domain of private equity, a shift from approaching M&A solely as a financial exercise to conducting M&A instead as an integrated process of value creation, spanning transaction through implementation, is occurring.
- There are seven key steps that companies can work through to build their M&A competency.
- Firms that can skillfully execute an integrated M&A competency, across the full process from transaction through implementation, realize each of the VRIO criteria, creating competitive advantage.

- M&As are a team sport. At various points throughout the process, internal and external resources of both the buyer and seller are engaged to work on pre-transaction, transaction, and post-transaction activities.
- Best practices of creating M&As as a core competency include building an M&A playbook, combining codified and tacit knowledge, and continually upgrading the firm's M&A capability.
- Potential pitfalls include treating M&As as "the deal" only, muddling through the process, and conducting limited tracking and measurement.
- Numerous M&A tools, templates, and checklists exist to assist firms with pre-deal, deal, and post-deal activities.

Discussion Questions

1. What activities does your company do well across the M&A process? What activities could the company perform better?
2. Have the results of your company's past M&A efforts met expectations? Why or why not?
3. Does your organization view its M&A efforts as an integrated process, from strategy through implementation and evaluation?
4. Does your firm use a comprehensive M&A process framework and "playbook" to organize its integration activities (codified knowledge)?
5. Has your firm identified both internal and external talent (tacit knowledge) to work on M&A efforts?
6. Does your company view M&As as a core competency? What more could your firm do to build M&As as a core competency?
7. How might the deal flow model help your company build its M&A capability?

Organizational Self-Assessment

Completing the following self-assessment (Table 11.4) will provide a view of how effectively your organization addresses the M&A process.

Steps to complete the self-assessment:

1. Rate each item on a scale of 0 (poor) to 10 (excellent).
2. Make notes for each item to explain the rationale for the numerical rating.
3. Add all ten scores to get a TOTAL SCORE (maximum score = 100).

Rating scale:

0–20 = Poor (significant improvement needed)
21–40 = Below average (improvement needed in several areas)
41–60 = Average (identify areas of weakness and adjust)

61–80 = Above average (identify areas that can still be improved)

81–100 = Excellent (continuously review and refine each component for each iteration of the organization's strategy efforts)

Table 11.4 Organizational self-assessment: M&As

Component	Rating (0 = poor, 10 = excellent)	Notes/rationale
When it comes to M&As …		
1. We view M&As as a comprehensive process from strategy through implementation		
2. We clearly understand the complexities involved across the M&A process		
3. We are clear about the stages of the M&A process we do well		
4. We are clear about the stages of the M&A process we need to improve		
5. We have skilled and experienced M&A talent across all stages of the M&A process (tacit knowledge)		
6. We have built a comprehensive "M&A playbook" by cataloging tools and templates across all stages of the M&A process (codified knowledge)		
7. We take an integrated and coordinated cross-functional approach to our M&A efforts during all pre- and post-deal stages		
8. M&As are a core competency of our company		
9. We have had clearly measured success in our past M&A efforts		
10. We would be considered "best practice" in how we conduct M&As across the entire process		
TOTAL SCORE		

12
Shareholder Activism and Restructuring

When it comes to activists influencing the management agendas of companies, there are generally two types. "Social activists" are primarily concerned with influencing a firm's ESG (environmental, social, and governance) agenda, whereas "financial activists" principally focus on creating greater returns to a firm's shareholders. This chapter addresses the approaches and impacts of financial activists and offers a process for management to effectively address shareholder activism should a financial activist take a stake in their company.

Financial activists are most often hedge funds that take small but relatively significant stakes in firms, typically around 5 percent of outstanding shares (The Economist, 2015). Upon buying a small but relatively significant portion of a firm's shares, an activist then tries to influence management's agenda by gaining other shareholders' support for their demands, which often include representation on the company's board, cost-cutting, selling of underperforming assets, and returning cash to shareholders.

Activism and Its Impact Are Growing across the Globe

The rise of shareholder activism in recent decades started in the United States, but activists now also see opportunities outside of the US and are committing more money to activism in search of good returns and greater accountability from companies in many regions (Deloitte, 2018). In little more than a decade, from 2009 to 2021 activist hedge funds' assets under management rose from approximately $39 billion to $130 billion US (Hunker, 2021).

The Pros and Cons of Activist Investors

While they have been called "capitalism's unlikely heroes" (The Economist, 2015), there are both pros and cons of activist investors (see Table 12.1).

Company Factors That Attract Financial Activists

Several factors make firms attractive to activist investors (Hunker, 2021), including:

- *Total shareholder return (TSR).* Even firms with a positive TSR track record can draw an activist's attention to a company, especially when compared with a set

The Strategist's Handbook. Timothy Galpin, Oxford University Press. © Timothy Galpin (2023).
DOI: 10.1093/oso/9780192885203.003.0013

Table 12.1 Pros and cons of activist investors

Pros	Cons
• Drive corporate renewal	• Not always right
• Discourage management complacency	• Look out for themselves
• Bring new ideas to the company	• Can lower the stock price when exiting large holdings
• Improve company performance	• Short-term focus (but not always)
• Benefit other shareholders	• May advocate draconian cost-cutting
• Benefit other stakeholders	• Firms choose to go private because they feel under siege

of peer companies' or the market's TSR, illuminating underperformance on a relative basis.

- *Organizational complexity.* Firms with conglomerate structures of multiple diverse business units frequently find themselves targets of activists because businesses with dedicated management teams and balance sheets have been found to perform better when they are not part of a larger conglomerate organization. Moreover, investors often value a conglomerate company when low-performing portfolio businesses are sold off and high-performing business units are retained.
- *An inefficient balance sheet.* Capital structure-oriented activism advocates for excess cash being returned to shareholders when the company has no near-term opportunities to deploy the capital, such as funding growth through M&As.
- *Problematic corporate governance.* Corporate governance problems, such as slow decision-making or board in-fighting, enhance an activist's storyline to a company's other large investors around the causes for firm underperformance. Activists know that large investors will withhold votes from incumbent directors and vote to elect activist board nominees if they feel there are governance concerns.

Activist Investor Aims, Tactics, and Returns

Aims

Activist shareholders typically seek to achieve one or more of three main objectives in companies they invest in: change the strategy and governance, change the company's capital structure, and/or redeploy the asset base. Activists use various approaches to achieve these objectives (see Table 12.2). Of the approaches that activists pursue, gaining board seats is the most prevalent, occurring 38 percent of the time, followed by M&A-related demands such as selling underperforming assets or stopping an ill-considered acquisition (35 percent) and changing the business strategy (25 percent) (Deloitte, 2018).

Table 12.2 Objectives and approaches of activist investors

Objective	Approach	Description
Change the strategy and governance	• Amend the existing strategy	• Make simple adjustments to the existing strategy, which can create value (e.g., entering new geographic regions)
	• Intensify the existing strategy's execution	• Accelerate strategy implementation, and set new, more aggressive performance targets
	• Change the governance structure	• Gain board seats, change senior management
Change the capital structure	• Change debt levels (increase or decrease)	• Increase leverage to release capital to shareholders (e.g., share buy-backs or special dividends)
	• Replace equity capital	• Find other investors who will demand higher returns and further delineate equity risk (e.g., issue preferred shares with a higher claim to dividends)
	• Change the payout	• Change dividend policy, pay special dividend • Sources of new payout levels can include increased cash flow from improved operational performance or increased leverage
Redeploy the asset base	• Break up the company	• Sum of the parts is greater than the whole • Sell underperforming assets (reinvest in core business or distribute proceeds to shareholders)
	• Merge with another company	• "Stronger together" (e.g., greater market share, reduce overlaps and gain cost synergies, achieve cross-selling revenue synergies)
	• Sell the company	• Realize control premium

Tactics

The tactics activist investors employ can be collaborative, confrontational, or a mix of the two. Collaborative tactics involve sending a letter to management proposing fundamental strategic changes, working with the company's leadership through regular meetings with management, participation in board meetings, and ongoing communication with management and the board to achieve their aims. A common confrontational tactic is for the activist to initiate a media campaign calling for a change of firm strategy, the selling of underperforming assets or the sale of the entire company, or a change of the firm's senior leadership. Another confrontational tactic is for the activist to initiate a "proxy fight" where the activist attempts to assemble a group of likeminded shareholders to join forces and attempt to gather enough support to win a shareholder vote to, for example, replace the firm's senior leadership or gain a board seat for the activist. The most extreme confrontational tactic is for an activist shareholder to engage the firm's leadership in a legal battle to stop an ill-considered acquisition, for example.

Returns

In general, shareholder activism creates returns above benchmarks. For example, the average activist hedge fund gained 8.76 percent in the first quarter of 2021 versus the average hedge-fund industry gain of 6 percent and the S&P 500 index gain of 5.8 percent (Herbst-Bayliss, 2021). Moreover, the average return following the public announcement of activist intent is 6.34 percent versus the average return following announcements of passive investment intent of just 0.59 percent (Albuquerque et al., 2021).

In addition to the general performance of activist funds cited above, an in-depth field study of the tactics and returns of the Hermes Focus Fund (a financial activist fund) found that over a six-year period the fund was "actively engaged" in thirty of the forty-one investments it held in its portfolio, holding an average 4.8 percent stake in each of the fund's investments. The fund advocated for and achieved various objectives including changing board members in seventeen of the companies in its portfolio, replacing the CEO in fifteen of its portfolio companies, increasing dividends in seventeen companies, a more focused strategy in twenty-eight companies, assets sales in ten companies, and stopping acquisitions in nine companies. During the six-year period of the study, the fund achieved an average annual return of 8.2 percent versus an all-FTSE annual return of 3.3 percent (Becht et al., 2009).

Example Activist Investor Campaigns

- *Dan Loeb's Third Point and Disney.* Agitating for sweeping changes at Disney, including a shake-up of its board, a spin-off of the sports television network ESPN and aggressive cost-cutting (Grimes et al., 2022).

- *Ping An and HSBC.* The bank's largest shareholder, Chinese insurer Ping An, escalates its calls for what would be the biggest shake-up in the bank's 157-year history, a split of its Asian and Western operations (Due Diligence, 2022).
- *ValueAct and New York Times.* ValueAct Capital, the activist hedge fund, acquired a 7 percent stake in The New York Times Company and is putting pressure on the media group to boost digital sales by pushing subscribers toward a higher-priced bundle of its products (Barker and Fontanella-Khan, 2022).
- *Nelson Peltz's Trian Partners and Unilever.* Having secured a seat on Unilever's board, Nelson Peltz is ready to draw on his well-used playbook for reviving sluggish consumer product companies. The activist investor spent four years fixing Procter & Gamble's "suffocating bureaucracy" and wants to do the same at Unilever. Analysts are predicting actions including better execution by refocusing resources on where the firm has a competitive advantage, a reallocation of capital from the existing businesses to pursuing external growth through M&As, and meticulous portfolio management to release additional revenue (Elder, 2022).

Dealing with Activist Investors

When dealing with activist investors it is crucial for the firm's management to take control of the agenda and frame the debate by working through three key tasks: (1) assessing the activist's position, (2) deciding whether to engage with the activist, and (3) choosing and implementing an engagement strategy (Bentley, 2021). Figure 12.1 presents a shareholder activism decision tree that walks management through the options for these three tasks.

Assess the Activist's Position

First, when confronted with an activist campaign, management must endeavor to understand exactly what the activist is seeking by clearly evaluating the activist's position using both quantitative analysis and a qualitative evaluation of the activist's previous behavior in other firms. Upon doing their own analysis of the activist's position, management can then determine whether the activist may be correct about the unrealized performance opportunities of the firm. This analysis can also help management determine the general attitude and typical approach of the activist as being primarily cooperative or confrontational and reveal the potential impact of the activist's campaign on other shareholders.

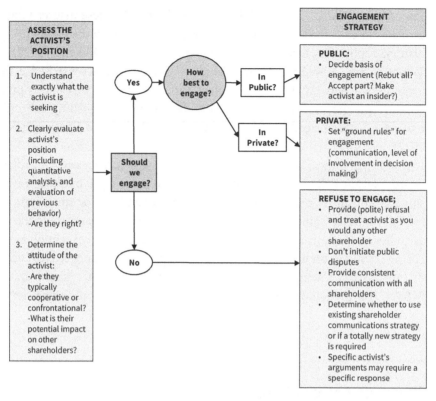

Figure 12.1 Shareholder activism decision tree

Decide Whether to Engage

The next task is for management to decide whether to engage with the activist. Should management decide that, yes, they will engage with the activist, they then must determine how best to engage with the activist, either in public or in private. If management decides that, no, they will not engage, then they should implement a series of steps to keep the activist at "arm's length."

Choose and Implement an Engagement Strategy

Based upon their choice in task two of either to engage or not, the final task is for management to choose and implement an engagement strategy. If management has chosen to engage with the activist in public, then management must choose to either rebut all the activist's proposals or accept some of their proposals. Public engagement will also require management to develop and implement a savvy media campaign to counter the public statements of the activist about the company, its board, and its management team. If management chooses to engage the investor in private, they need to establish "ground rules" for engagement including the format and frequency of communications between management and the activist, and the activist's level of involvement in strategic decision-making.

If management decides not to engage with the activist, they should respectfully refuse engagement and treat the activist as they would any other shareholder. Management should provide consistent communication with all shareholders and avoid initiating public disputes with the activist. In doing so, management need to determine whether to use their existing shareholder communications strategy or if a new strategy is required. Finally, particular arguments put forth by the activist may require a specific response from management.

Participants and Key Activities

The main participants in developing and implementing a firm's approach to addressing shareholder activism are as follows.

Activist investors. Identify companies to target for activism. Develop specific activism objectives and approaches for each company in their portfolio. Work in a collaborative or confrontational manner to achieve their aims in each company in their portfolio. Solicit participation from other shareholders in their activism campaigns.

Other shareholders. Participate in actions initiated by activist shareholders such as proxy fights and letters to management.

Senior executives. When confronted with shareholder activism, work through the shareholder activism decision tree to assess the activist's position, decide whether to engage with the activist, and choose and implement an engagement strategy.

Board members. Assist senior management with working through the shareholder activism decision tree and implementing an engagement strategy.

Investor relations. The firm's investor relations department assists senior management and the board with working through the shareholder activism decision tree and implementing an engagement strategy.

Best Practices

Prepare. As investor activism is on the rise, rather than waiting for an activist investor to wage a campaign, management should proactively prepare for an activist approach. To ready themselves, management can work through the shareholder activism decision tree for a hypothetical activist approach.

Address performance issues before an activist does. Management can make their firm much less attractive to activist investors by addressing what might make the company appealing to an activist. For example, working to at least achieve TSR parity with peers, reduce organizational complexity, readjust the company's capital structure, and address problematic corporate governance will all help keep activist investors at bay.

Collaboration is better than confrontation. The adage "keep your friends close and your enemies closer" is a good rule to follow when it comes to dealing with activist investors. Numerous management teams have found it prudent to consider and implement at least some of the suggestions put forth by an activist investor. Collaboration helps management avoid the difficult and stressful confrontational campaigns activists can wage.

Potential Pitfalls

Ignoring the issue. With the continued expansion of investor activism globally, management who assume they will indefinitely avoid activist investors do so at their peril.

No plan. Realizing that activist investors may be interested in their company, management should run through various scenarios in anticipation of what an activist may demand from the company. Doing so will help management put a plan in place should they face an activist campaign.

Not even considering collaboration. Management hubris is powerful. Therefore, when confronted by shareholder activism, management will often not even consider collaborating with the activist. This approach inevitably results in a high-profile public confrontation between management and the activist.

Key Frameworks, Tools, and Templates

The primary tool to assist management in addressing shareholder activism is the shareholder activism decision tree. This tool is used to help the firm's management take control of the activism agenda and frame the debate by working through three key tasks: (1) assessing the activist's position, (2) deciding whether to engage with the activist, and (3) choosing and implementing an engagement strategy (see Appendix B).

Best-Practice Case Example

A description of Consumer Goods Inc.'s approach to addressing shareholder activism in practice is summarized in Table 12.3.

Table 12.3 Addressing shareholder activism at Consumer Goods Inc.*

The need:

- An activist investment fund purchased 6% of the outstanding shares of a large diversified packaged goods company, Consumer Goods Inc.
- Via a letter to management, the activist fund requested to meet with the CEO and chairman of the board to discuss their suggestions and requests.
- The activist called for management to accelerate strategic and operational decision-making by simplifying the organization structure.
- The activist also advocated for management to sell underperforming business units, invest in more marketing of high-performing core products to increase revenue, and pay a special dividend to shareholders.
- The activist also requested a board seat.

The solution:

- Upon receiving the letter from the activist investor, the senior team of Consumer Goods Inc., along with their firm's investor relations department, worked through the considerations of the shareholder activism decision tree.
- First, management determined that several of the activist's suggestions and requests were useful and likely should be implemented.
- Next, management decided to privately engage with the activist fund.
- Management worked with the activist fund's team to establish collaborative arrangements including regular meetings between the fund's team and company leadership, and regular reporting from management to the activist about implementation progress of the activist's suggestions for strategic, operational, and governance changes.
- Management and the board also decided to accept the activist's request for a board seat.

The results:

- Immediately upon the market learning of the activist's share purchase, shares of Consumer Goods Inc. increased over 6%, as other investors welcomed the prospect of a company overhaul.
- Consumer Goods Inc. stock increased almost 90% during the subsequent four years.

* Because of non-disclosure considerations, a large consumer packaged goods firm is referred to throughout the illustration as Consumer Goods Inc.

Chapter Summary

- When it comes to influencing the management agendas of companies, there are generally two types of activists: "social activists" and "financial activists."
- Financial activists are most often hedge funds that take small but relatively significant stakes in firms, typically around 5 percent of outstanding shares.
- The rise of shareholder activism in recent decades started in the United States but activists now also see opportunities outside of the US.
- From 2009 to 2021 activist hedge funds' assets under management rose from approximately $39 billion to $130 billion US.
- There are both pros and cons to activist investors.
- The advantages of shareholder activism include driving corporate renewal, discouraging management complacency, bringing new ideas to a company, and improving company performance, which benefits all shareholders.

- The downsides of activist investors include a short-term focus, they may advocate draconian cost-cutting, and a firm's stock price can drop when an activist exits their shareholding.
- Several factors attract financial activists to invest in a company including poor relative TSR, organizational complexity, an inefficient balance sheet, and problematic corporate governance.
- Activist shareholders typically seek to achieve one or more of three main objectives in companies they invest in: change the strategy and governance, change the company's capital structure, and/or redeploy the asset base.
- Of the approaches that activists pursue, gaining board seats is the most prevalent, occurring 38 percent of the time, followed by M&A-related demands such as selling underperforming assets or stopping an ill-considered acquisition (35 percent) and changing the business strategy (25 percent).
- The tactics activist investors employ can be collaborative, confrontational, or a mix of the two.
- In general, shareholder activism creates returns above benchmarks.
- Example activist investor campaigns are Dan Loeb's Third Point and Disney, Ping An and HSBC, ValueAct and The New York Times, and Nelson Peltz's Trian Partners and Unilever.
- When dealing with activist investors it is crucial for the firm's management to take control of the agenda and frame the debate by working through three key tasks: (1) assessing the activist's position, (2) deciding whether to engage with the activist, and (3) choosing and implementing an engagement strategy.
- The main participants in developing and implementing a firm's approach to dealing with shareholder activism are activist investors, other shareholders, senior executives, board members, and a firm's investor relations department.
- The best practices for firms to deal with shareholder activism include preparation, addressing performance issues before an activist does, and collaboration rather than confrontation.
- The potential pitfalls encountered regarding shareholder activism include ignoring the issue, not having a plan in place, and not even considering a collaborative approach.
- The primary tool to assist management in addressing shareholder activism is the shareholder activism decision tree.

Discussion Questions

1. Has your organization been subjected to an activist campaign? How did management respond?
2. What activities does your organization do well to prepare for or deal with activist investors?

3. What activities to prepare for or deal with activist investors could your organization perform better?

4. Who is typically involved in developing and implementing your organization's activist investor approach? Who should be involved?

5. Which approach does your organization typically take to activist investors: collaborative or confrontational? Which approach should they use?

6. How often does your organization review its approach to investor activism? Should the frequency of reviews change and, if so, why?

7. How does your organization monitor the success of their approach to investor activism? What aspects should be monitored?

Organizational Self-Assessment

Completing the following self-assessment (Table 12.4) will provide a view of how effectively your organization addresses investor activism.

Table 12.4 Organizational self-assessment: investor activism

Component	Rating (0 = poor, 10 = excellent)	Notes/rationale
When it comes to investor activism …		
1. We place importance on investor activism		
2. We apply a clear method to develop our approach to investor activism		
3. We use a defined tool to develop our approach to investor activism		
4. We have the right people involved in developing our approach to investor activism		
5. We are proactive about investor activism rather than reactive		
6. We take a collaborative rather than confrontational approach to investor activism		
7. Our company has benefited from working with activist investors		
8. We monitor the success of our approach to investor activism		
9. We regularly review and update our approach to investor activism		
10. We would be considered "best practice" in how we address investor activism		
TOTAL SCORE		

Steps to complete the self-assessment:

1. Rate each item on a scale of 0 (poor) to 10 (excellent).
2. Make notes for each item to explain the rationale for the numerical rating.
3. Add all ten scores to get a TOTAL SCORE (maximum score = 100).

Rating scale:

0–20 = Poor (significant improvement needed)
21–40 = Below average (improvement needed in several areas)
41–60 = Average (identify areas of weakness and adjust)
61–80 = Above average (identify areas that can still be improved)
81–100 = Excellent (continuously review and refine each component for each iteration of the organization's strategy efforts)

The Oxford Strategy Insights Project

The Oxford Strategy Insights Project received input from 167 executives and managers across 26 industries, spanning over 30 countries, regarding their firm's strategy process.

Profile of the Respondents

Senior Executives

The 167 respondents represented seven different title categories (see Figure A.1). Most respondents (27 percent) identified themselves as senior manager or manager, followed by executive vice president (VP), senior VP or VP (23 percent), "other C-suite" executives holding such titles as chief information officer, chief financial officer, chief operating officer, and so forth (17 percent), consultant (12 percent), analyst (10 percent), chief executive officer (CEO) or managing director (MD) (8 percent), and board member (4 percent). Over half (51 percent) of the respondents' titles are considered "senior executives."

Multiple Industries

Twenty-six different industries are represented (see Figure A.2), with seven of the twenty-six industries comprising over half (58 percent) of the industries in the study: banking (commercial and retail) (12 percent), technology (software, hardware, services) (11 percent), financial services (10 percent), consulting (7 percent), energy (6 percent), pharmaceuticals (6 percent), and insurance (5 percent).

Traditional Strategic Planning Still Dominates

Planning Process

Traditional, "top-down" planning is by far the most prevalent approach. When asked "How would you characterize your organization's strategic planning process?", over two thirds of respondents (69 percent) indicated "formal/top-down planning," with only 11 percent of firms employing a "dynamic/democratized" approach and 20 percent using both "formal/top-down and dynamic/democratized" (see Figure A.3).

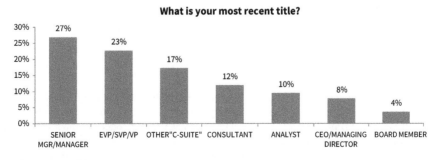

Figure A.1 Titles

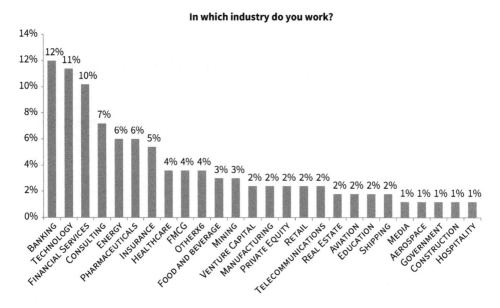

Figure A.2   Industries

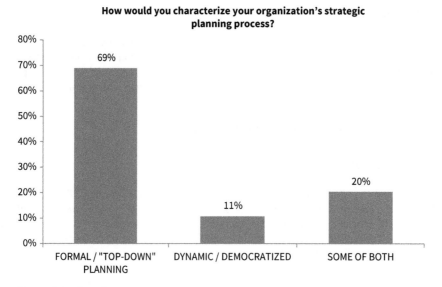

Figure A.3   Planning process

Planning Frequency

Firms appear to use as much short-term planning cycles as long-term cycles. When asked "What is the frequency of your organization's strategic planning process?", on the short-term end of the spectrum almost half (46 percent) of respondents indicated that their firm's strategic planning cycle is either "yearly" (39 percent) or "every two years" (7 percent). Meanwhile, on the longer-term side, over one third (36 percent) indicated either "every four to five years" (34 percent) or "more than every five years" (2 percent), with 18 percent indicating "every three years" (see Figure A.4).

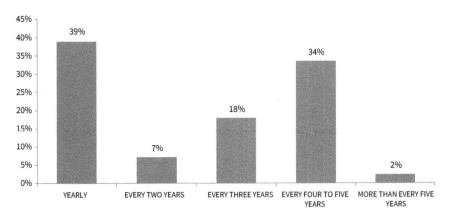

Figure A.4 Planning frequency

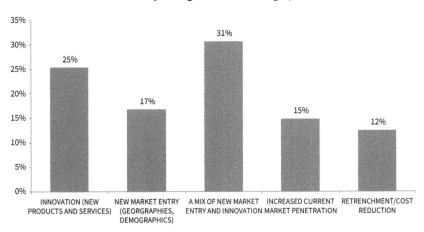

Figure A.5 Strategic priorities

Entering New Markets and Innovation Are Strategic Priorities

Most companies plan to grow through a combination of entering new markets (geographies and demographics) and through innovation (offering new products and services). When asked "What are your organization's strategic priorities?", about one third of respondents (31 percent) indicated "a mix of new market entry and innovation," followed by "innovation (new products and services)" (25 percent), "new market entry (geographies, demographics)" (17 percent), "increased current market penetration" (15 percent), and "retrenchment/cost reduction" (12 percent) (see Figure A.5).

Execution Is the Biggest Gap

Effective Execution Is Lacking

As planning entails forecasting and setting targets for future value creation while implementation is where value creation actually occurs, it is concerning that the biggest gap in the strategy process is in execution. When asked "How would you rate your organization's strategy execution?", a vast majority of respondents (82 percent) answered "very ineffective" (19 percent), "ineffective" (36 percent), or average (28 percent), with only 18 percent of respondents indicating "effective" (14 percent) or "very effective" (4 percent) (see Figure A.6).

Little Use of an Implementation Infrastructure

A best practice of effective strategy execution efforts, which are often cross-functional undertakings, is to establish an implementation management infrastructure, including a program manager who manages and coordinates the implementation effort. However, when asked "Does your organization use an effective strategy execution infrastructure, including a dedicated implementation program manager?", most respondents (83 percent) indicated "infrequently" (47 percent) or "never" (36 percent), with just 17 percent of respondents indicating "always" (5 percent), "frequently" (6 percent), and "about half the time" (7 percent) (see Figure A.7).

Figure A.6   Strategy execution

Figure A.7   Implementation infrastructure

Time Is Not of the Essence

Logic suggests that firms would strive to accelerate their strategy execution efforts to diminish the inevitable productivity drop organizations experience during strategic transformation efforts. Yet, when asked to respond to the question, "The average time it takes for my organization to implement a new strategy is …," over two thirds of respondents (67 percent) indicated "more than 24 months," with the remaining 33 percent indicating a timeframe less than twenty-four months (see Figure A.8).

Measurement Is the Bright Spot

A key component of many firms' strategy process is measurement. When asked "How would you rate your organization's strategic measurement and reporting?", almost half of respondents (46 percent) answered "effective" (30 percent) or "very effective" (16 percent), with just under one third (32 percent) indicating "very ineffective" (13 percent) or "ineffective" (19 percent) (see Figure A.9). However, it is unclear whether respondents were considering both main categories of strategic measurement: process measures (progress against key implementation milestones such as tasks, budgets, and timelines) and outcome measures (achievement of projected outcomes including financial, customer, business process, and organization learning).

Figure A.8 Implementation timeframe

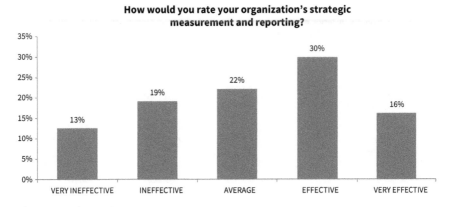

Figure A.9 Strategic measurement

Some Corporate Offices Influence Business Unit Strategy, While Others Do Not

When considering multi-business unit organizations, it appears that some corporate offices have a significant influence on business unit strategy, whereas others allow business unit management more strategic freedom. Almost two thirds (63 percent) of respondents are part of a multi-business unit organization. When asked "If your organization has a corporate and multi-business unit (conglomerate) structure, how much autonomy do the business units have when it comes to strategy formulation?", just under half (47 percent) of respondents indicated that the business units have "no autonomy" (22 percent) or "little autonomy" (25 percent), while just over half (53 percent) of respondents indicated "some autonomy" (30 percent) or "high autonomy" (23 percent) (see Figure A.10).

Summary and Implications

The Oxford Strategy Insights Project gathered the views of 167 executives and managers across various industries and geographies about their strategy process. Traditional, "top-down" planning is by far the most prevalent approach, with firms using as much short-term planning cycles (e.g., yearly) as long-term cycles (e.g., every four to five years). Most companies plan to grow through a combination of entering new markets (geographies and demographics) and innovation (offering new products and services). However, strategic priorities may change as economies around the globe are anticipated to go into recession when retrenchment and cost reduction often becomes the primary focus for many firms.

Implementation Needs to Be Managed, Coordinated, and Accelerated

The biggest gap highlighted by the Oxford Strategy Insights Project is effective strategy execution. An overwhelming majority of respondents indicated that their organization's strategy execution efforts are ineffective and slow, with accelerated implementation being the exception rather than the norm. In line with these findings, few firms appear to be applying the best practice of establishing an implementation management infrastructure, including a program manager tasked with managing and coordinating the firm's strategy implementation effort. The one positive element related to strategy execution is that most firms seem to have an effective strategic measurement and reporting process. Open-ended comments provided by respondents support these findings, with one respondent declaring, "The biggest area for improvement in our strategy process by far is execution," and another commenting, "Strategy is nothing without implementation, that is where we are lacking the most."

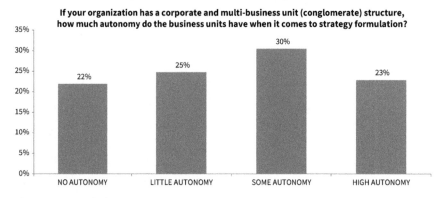

Figure A.10 Multi-business unit organizations

Strategy Workbook

- This workbook contains processes, tools, and templates that can be used to facilitate effective strategy formulation and execution efforts across industries (including for-profit, not-for-profit, and government entities), various geographies, and all sizes and stages of organizations.
- The processes and tools presented can be used comprehensively or selectively.
- While the processes and tools included in this workbook present an end-to-end perspective of strategy formulation and execution, they are by no means exhaustive.

By the end of this workbook you should have a good picture of your organization's strategic direction and implementation plan.

  I. Strategy Formulation
 II. Strategy Execution
III. Beyond Business Strategy

Strategy Formulation

Conduct a strategic performance analysis for your organization …

Exercise: Current strategic performance analysis and evaluation

Strategic Initiatives	KPIs	Performance relative to each KPI	Notes – Small changes? – Large improvements? – No change, but better implementation? – Eliminate? – Add an entirely new strategic initiative?
Strategic Initiative:			
Strategic Initiative:			
Strategic Initiative:			

… To determine if your firm requires a shift of strategy or needs to better implement the current strategy.

Determine which is the best strategy process for your organization—traditional or dynamic.

Two variations of the strategy process

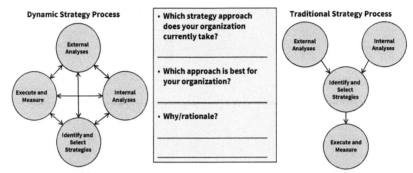

Dynamic Strategy Process	
Focus	Opportunity Capture
Who	Cross-functional and cross-level
When	On-going
How	Customer and market contact
Where	Organizational and functional boundaries

Traditional Strategy Process	
Focus	Planning
Who	Strategy team (BD, CD) and/or consultants
When	Annual cycle
How	Detailed research
Where	Centralized/HQ

An external analysis identifies opportunities and threats …

Two variations of the strategy process

Dynamic Strategy Process

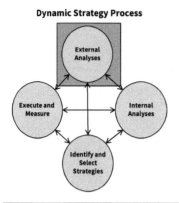

Traditional Strategy Process

Dynamic Strategy Process	
Focus	Opportunity Capture
Who	Cross-functional and cross-level
When	On-going
How	Customer and market contact
Where	Organizational and functional boundaries

Traditional Strategy Process	
Focus	Planning
Who	Strategy team (BD, CD) and/or consultants
When	Annual cycle
How	Detailed research
Where	Centralized/HQ

… Conduct a Five Forces analysis for your organization …

Five Forces: Your Industry

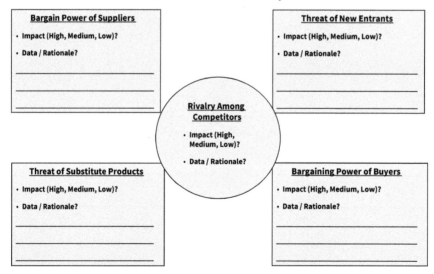

... And a PESTEL analysis to identify organization specific opportunities and threats ...

PESTEL Analysis: Your Organization

Political	Economic	Social	Technological	Environmental	Legal

... A PESTEL analysis can be combined with scenario planning ...

Probability-Weighted Scenario Planning: Example

	Key Elements/ Characteristics (from PESTEL analysis)	Probability of occurrence (%)	Impact on the Business (1=low, 10=high)	Probability-weighted Impact*
Scenario 1: Increased environmental regulation	• New environmental regulation introduced in the next 24 months	80%	4	3.2
Scenario 2: Economic downturn	• Global economic downturn the next 12 months	50%	10	5.0
Scenario 3: New industry entrants with new technology	• Disruptive technology introduced in the next 36 months	100%	8	8

*Multiply the impact on the business by the probability percentage.

… Conduct a scenario analysis for your organization …

Probability-Weighted Scenario Planning: Your Organization

	Key Elements/ Characteristics (from PESTEL analysis)	Probability of occurrence (%)	Impact on the Business (1=low, 10=high)	Probability-weighted Impact
Scenario 1:	•			
Scenario 2:	•			
Scenario 3:	•			

*Multiply the impact on the business by the probability percentage.

… Summarize the key external factors for your organization in an "EFAS Table."

External Factors Analysis Summary (EFAS) Table

External Strategic Factors	Rationale/Data
Opportunities* (Five Forces, PESTEL, Scenarios) 1. 2. 3. 4. 5.	
Threats (Five Forces, PESTEL, Scenarios) 1. 2. 3. 4. 5.	

*Opportunities should be identified as trends, rather than recommendations

NOTE: Rank factors from 1 = 'highest' to 5 = 'lowest' potential importance/impact on the company's future

An internal analysis identifies opportunities and threats …

Two variations of the strategy process

Dynamic Strategy Process

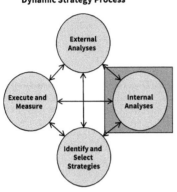

Traditional Strategy Process

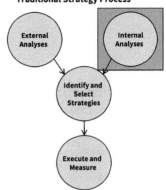

Dynamic Strategy Process	
Focus	Opportunity Capture
Who	Cross-functional and cross-level
When	On-going
How	Customer and market contact
Where	Organizational and functional boundaries

Traditional Strategy Process	
Focus	Planning
Who	Strategy team (BD, CD) and/or consultants
When	Annual cycle
How	Detailed research
Where	Centralized/HQ

… Some resources create competitive advantage, while others do not …

RBV: Core Competencies: VRIO

Resource-Based View (RBV)
(Wernerfelt, 1984)

Relies on resources

Tangible Assets
(easily purchased on the open market)

Intangible Assets
(not easily purchased on the open market)

In an integrated and unique combination which become

Core Competencies
(Prahalad and Hamel, 1990)

That are valuable, rare, inimitable, and organizational

VRIO – Strategically Valuable Resources
(Valuable, Rare, Inimitable, Organizational)
(Barney, 1995)

Providing

Competitive Advantage

… Conduct a VRIO analysis to identify "strategically valuable resources" within your organization …

VRIO Analysis

Resource:		
VRIO Criteria	**Fulfills VRIO?**	**Rationale/Data**
Value: Does the resource/capability enable the firm to improve its efficiency or effectiveness?	YES / NO	
Rarity: Is control of the resource/capability in the hands of a relative few?	YES / NO	
Inimitability: Is it difficult to imitate, and will there be significant cost and/or time disadvantage to a firm trying to obtain, develop, or duplicate the resource/capability?	YES / NO	
Organization: Is the firm organized in such a way that it is ready and able to exploit the resource/capability?	YES / NO	

… The VRIO analysis can be used in combination with the value chain …

Value Chain[i] / VRIO Analysis[ii]: Your Organization

Value Chain

Support Activities (HR, IT, Finance, Accounting, Purchasing, etc.)

Inbound Logistics | Operations | Outbound Logistics | Marketing and Sales | Service

Margin

VRIO Analysis

Resource:		
VRIO Criteria	**Fulfills VRIO?**	**Rationale/Data**
Value: Does the resource/capability enable the firm to improve its efficiency or effectiveness?	YES / NO	
Rarity: Is control of the resource/capability in the hands of a relative few?	YES / NO	
Inimitability: Is it difficult to imitate, and will there be significant cost and/or time disadvantage to a firm trying to obtain, develop, or duplicate the resource/capability?	YES / NO	
Organization: Is the firm organized in such a way that it is ready and able to exploit the resource/capability?	YES / NO	

Exercise

- Which resources along your firm's value chain are strengths or weaknesses? What data can be collected to support the categorization? • Which resources along your firm's value chain are core competencies that fulfill the VRIO or Five Forces criteria? Are they tangible or intangible resources, or a combination of both?

---

[i] Porter, M. E. (1985). *Competitive Advantage: Creating and Sustaining Superior Performance*. New York.: Simon and Schuster.

[ii] Barney, J. B. (1995), "Looking inside for competitive advantage," *Academy Of Management Executive*, (9)4, 49–61

... Summarize the key internal factors for your organization in an "IFAS Table."

Internal Factors Analysis Summary (IFAS) Table

Internal Strategic Factors	Rationale/Data
Strengths (Value Chain, VRIO, Five-Tests) 1. 2. 3. 4. 5.	
Weaknesses (Value Chain, VRIO, Five-Tests) 1. 2. 3. 4. 5.	

NOTE: Rank factors from 1 = 'highest' to 5 = 'lowest' potential importance/impact on the company's future

Incorporate the external and internal analyses to identify and select high-impact strategies ...

Two variations of the strategy process

Dynamic Strategy Process

Traditional Strategy Process

Dynamic Strategy Process	
Focus	Opportunity Capture
Who	Cross-functional and cross-level
When	On-going
How	Customer and market contact
Where	Organizational and functional boundaries

Traditional Strategy Process	
Focus	Planning
Who	Strategy team (BD, CD) and/or consultants
When	Annual cycle
How	Detailed research
Where	Centralized/HQ

... Use Ansoff's matrix[iii] to identify potential growth strategies for your organization ...

Growth Matrix

	Existing Products/Services	New Products/Services
New Markets	Market Development/Diversification	Corporate/Conglomerate Diversification
Existing Markets	Market Penetration/Consolidation	Product/Services Development/ Diversification

---

iii Ansoff, H. I. "Strategies for diversification." *Harvard Business Review*, 1957, 35(5), pp. 113–124.

... Control, investment, and risk should all be considered when entering new markets.

Exercise - Market entry options and key considerations - Which can your organization pursue?

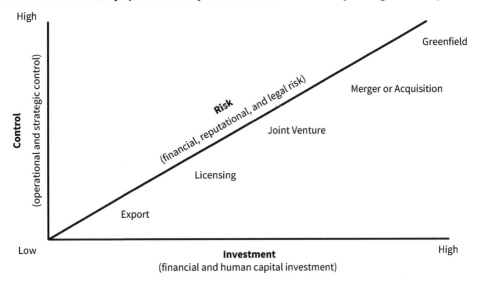

... A systematic market entry profile begins with a "business environment assessment" ...

Example: Business Environment Assessment

Business Environment Factors	Potential Markets				
	A	B	C	D	E
Ease of doing business	2	5	4	3	1
Regulations	1	5	3	4	4
Rule of law (e.g., contract enforcement)	3	4	2	2	1
Corruption	3	5	4	1	2
Competition	2	5	3	2	3
Human capital / local talent	3	5	2	4	2
Total Business Environment Score	14	29	18	16	13

1 = Low market attractiveness 5 = High market attractiveness

… Produce a "business environment assessment" for markets your organization might enter …

Business Environment Assessment: Your Organization

Business Environment Factors	Potential Markets				
	A	B	C	D	E
Ease of doing business					
Regulations					
Rule of law (e.g., contract enforcement)					
Corruption					
Competition					
Human capital / local talent					
Total Business Environment Score					

1 = Low market attractiveness 5 = High market attractiveness

… A systematic market entry profile should also include a "market access assessment" …

Example: Market Access Assessment

Market Access Factors	Potential Markets				
	A	B	C	D	E
Partners	2	4	4	1	1
Proximity	4	3	5	2	5
E-commerce	3	2	3	2	1
Distribution channels	4	4	5	3	2
Retail landscape	4	3	5	2	3
Infrastructure (ports, roads, internet, etc.)	4	4	5	2	2
Total Market Access Score	21	20	27	12	14

1 = Low market attractiveness 5 = High market attractiveness

... Produce a "market access assessment" for markets your organization might enter ...

Market Access Assessment: Your Organization

Market Access Factors	Potential Markets				
	A	B	C	D	E
Partners					
Proximity					
E-commerce					
Distribution channels					
Retail landscape					
Infrastructure (ports, roads, internet, etc.)					
Total Market Access Score					

1 = Low market attractiveness   5 = High market attractiveness

... Combining the business environment and market access assessment completes ...

Example: Market Entry Profile Map

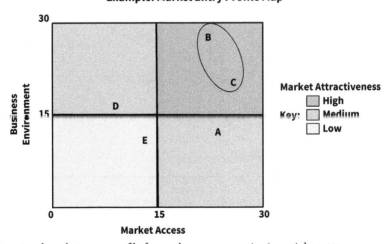

... A structured market entry profile for markets your organization might enter ...

... Combine the business environment and market access assessments to complete ...

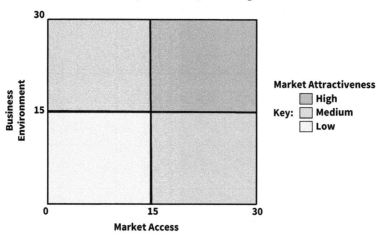

Market Entry Profile Map: Your Organization

... A structured market entry profile for your organization ...

... Control, investment, and risk also apply when identifying options to launch new products or services ...

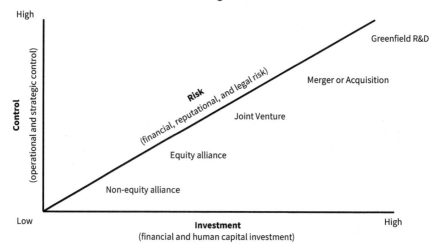

Exercise: New Products and Services Options and Key Considerations—Which Will Your Organization Pursue?

… Use an innovation landscape map to generate strategies for technical and business model innovation …

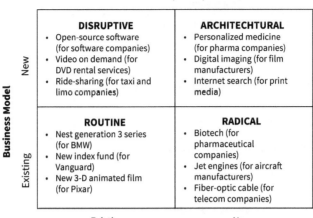

…Create an Innovation Landscape Map for your organization …

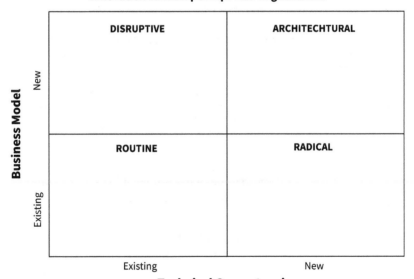

iv Pisano, G. P. (2015). "You need an innovation strategy." *Harvard Business Review*, 93, 44–54.

… Technological innovation can occur at several levels …

Four levels of innovation[v]

Level	Description	Innovations
One	• **New features on existing products or services** o Investment: Low o Risk: Low o Payoff: Low	
Two	• **Advancement of existing products and services** o Investment: Medium o Risk: Medium o Payoff: Medium	
Three	• **Evolutionary products and services** o Investment: Large o Risk: Medium o Payoff: Large	
Four	• **Revolutionary products and services** o Investment: Large o Risk: High o Payoff: Large to limitless	

Exercise:

… What levels of innovation can/should your organization pursue? …

… Conduct a platform ecosystem[vi] analysis for your organization …

Platform Ecosystem: Your Organization

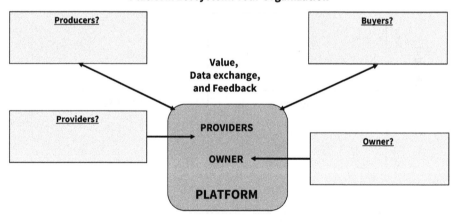

[v] Miner, K. 2010. "The four levels of innovation." *Graziadio Business Review*, 13(4): 15.

[vi] Alstyne, M. W. V., Parker, G. G., Choudary, S. P. (2016). "Pipelines, Platforms, and the New Rules of Strategy." *Harvard Business Review*, 94(4), 54–62.

... Conduct a value net[vii] analysis for your organization ...

Value Net:Your Organization

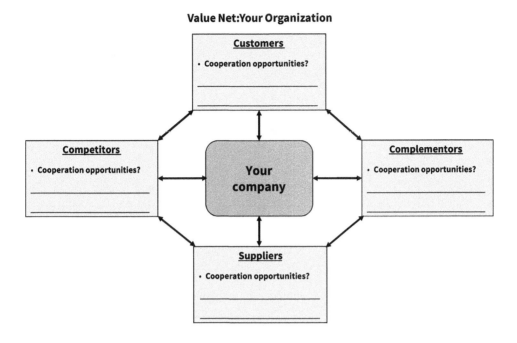

... Use a strategy canvas to determine optimal competitive positioning within an industry ...

Strategy canvas example: Southwest Airlines

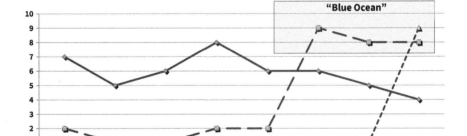

*Southwest Airlines has used a "car travel" model to create strategic differentiation.[viii]

... And identify "blue ocean" opportunities ...

[vii] Brandenburger, A. M. and Nalebuff, B. J. (1996). *Co-opetition*. Doubleday, New York.
[viii] Kim, W. C., and Mauborgne, R. 2005. *Blue Ocean Strategy*. Boston: Harvard Business School Publishing Corporation.

… Develop a strategy canvas for your organization to identify "blue ocean" opportunities …

Strategy Canvas: Your Organization

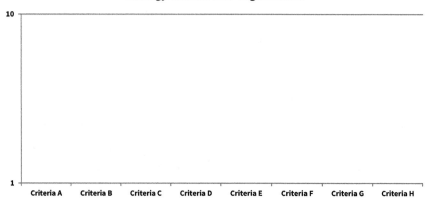

… Apply at least one framework to identify several strategies your organization might pursue …

Exercise: Identifying Strategies

1..	11..
2..	12..
3..	13..
4..	14..
5..	15..
6..	16..
7..	17..
8..	18..
9..	19..
10..	20.. 'Wild Idea' – Here

… Along with a "wild idea" (e.g., a lodging company establishing hotels in outer space) …

… However, because of limited resources (capital, time, and people), firms cannot do everything …

Strategic Priorities Map

Impact
(e.g., revenue
growth, cost
reduction,
service
improvement,
IRR, NPV)

High

| Highest Priority | High Priority |
| Medium Priority | Low Priority |

Low

Low   **Level of Effort / Investment Required**   High

Key: Circle size indicates level of risk (service, operational, financial, reputational, etc.)

High Risk   **Medium Risk**   **Low Risk**

… Identify three to five priority strategies for your organization

Strategy Execution

Once you select priority strategies, effective execution becomes paramount …

Two variations of the strategy process

Dynamic Strategy Process

Traditional Strategy Process

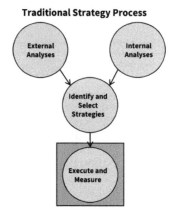

Dynamic Strategy Process	
Focus	Opportunity Capture
Who	Cross-functional and cross-level
When	On-going
How	Customer and market contact
Where	Organizational and functional boundaries

Traditional Strategy Process	
Focus	Planning
Who	Strategy team (BD, CD) and/or consultants
When	Annual cycle
How	Detailed research
Where	Centralized/HQ

… Effective strategy execution begins with establishing an "implementation infrastructure" …

Implementation Program Management Infrastructure

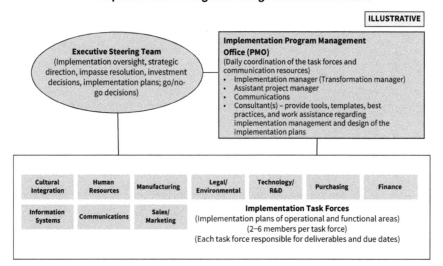

... Identify an "implementation infrastructure" for your organization ...

Exercise: Implementation Program Management Infrastructure for Your Organization

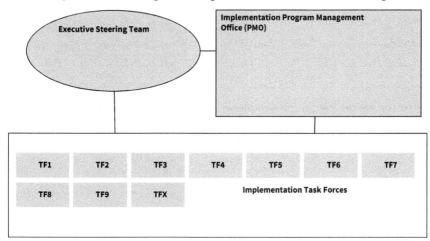

... Which applies a rapid implementation issues identification and decision-making process ...

Example Weekly Implementation Issues Identification and Decision-Making

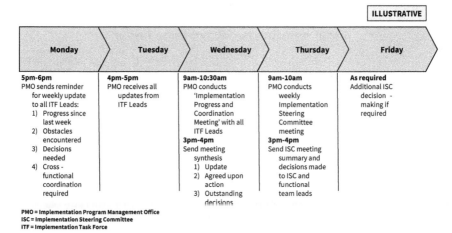

... Develop and apply a weekly implementation management "cadence" for your organization ...

… Effective strategy execution is facilitated by sound project planning …

Priority Strategy: Implementation Plan

Item Description	Responsibility	Duration	Units (days, weeks, or months)	Start Date	End Date	Estimated Cost
Task1						$0
Task2						$0
Task3						$0
						$0
						$0
						$0
						$0
						$0
						$0
						$0
						$0
						$0
						$0
						$0
						$0
						$0
						$0
						$0
						$0
						$0
						$0
					Total	$0

… For each priority strategy you have identified …

… Ongoing workstream status tracking is essential to keeping implementation on track …

Implementation Workstream Status Tracker

ILLUSTRATIVE

	Project	Workstream	Owner	Current Week Status	Prior Week Status
1.	Infrastructure	Technology	David S	Behind Schedule	Behind Schedule
2.	Benefits Analysis - HR	People	Susan T	At Risk	Behind Schedule
3.	Operating Contract Review	Operations	James L	At Risk	At Risk
4.	Vision, Mission, Culture	Culture	Amit U	At Risk	At Risk
5.	Business Intelligence	Technology	Maria P	At Risk	At Risk
6.	Aligning Employee Handbook/Policy	People	Mark S	At Risk	On Schedule
7.	Site Management System	Technology	David S	On Schedule	On Schedule
8.	Communication Plans	Operations	James L	On Schedule	On Schedule
9.	HRIS System	People	Susan T	On Schedule	On Schedule
10.	Website	Technology	James L	On Schedule	On Schedule
11.	Custom Applications	Technology	David S	On Schedule	On Schedule
12.	Service Desk	Technology	Amit U	On Schedule	On Schedule
13.	Process / SOP	Operations	Susan T	On Schedule	On Schedule
14.	Customer Management	Operations	Susan T	On Schedule	On Schedule
15.	Insurance	Operations	Bill S	On Schedule	On Schedule
16.	Disposals	Corp. Dev.	Jill M	On Schedule	On Schedule
17.	Distribution	Operations	David S	On Schedule	On Schedule
18.	Debt	Financing	David S	On Schedule	On Schedule
19.	401k Analysis	People	James L	On Schedule	On Schedule
20.	Rebranding	Marketing	James L	On Schedule	On Schedule
21.	Marketing Software	Marketing	Lisa T	On Schedule	On Schedule

… Identify balanced measures to track and report success …

Priority Strategies: Balanced Measures[ix]

Measurement Areas	Baseline	Targets
Financial		
Customer		
Business Process		
Innovation and Learning		

… For each priority strategy.

[ix] Kaplan, R. S., and Norton, D. R. 2005. "The balanced scorecard: measures that drive performance." *Harvard Business Review*, 83(7/8): 172–180 .

Manage resistance to change at each level

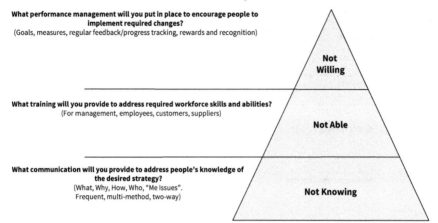

The Resistance Pyramid

What performance management will you put in place to encourage people to implement required changes?
(Goals, measures, regular feedback/progress tracking, rewards and recognition)

Not Willing

What training will you provide to address required workforce skills and abilities?
(For management, employees, customers, suppliers)

Not Able

What communication will you provide to address people's knowledge of the desired strategy?
(What, Why, How, Who, "Me Issues".
Frequent, multi-method, two-way)

Not Knowing

Communicate even when there is "nothing to tell" …

Strategic Communications Planning Matrix

Who (stakeholders)	Why (objective)	What (messages)	How (vehicles)	When (frequency)	Owner (development, delivery)

… Because people want to know that there is a "fair process"

Develop a "Retention and Re-Engagement Matrix" to provide a clear, business-driven analysis of …

Retention and Re-Engagement Matrix

Key People and/or Groups	Impact of Loss (monetize where possible)	Key Motivators	Retention and Rerecruitment Actions	Responsibility	Timing	Back-up Plan In Case They Do Leave	Notes
1. Sales							
2. Operations							
3. R&D							
4. IT							
5. Person A							
6. Person B							
7. Person C							

… Your top talent, and how to keep and "re-engage" them during strategy implementation

"Culture eats strategy for breakfast," so aligning culture with strategy is critical to success …

Personality Theory[x] versus Behavioral Theory[xi]

Personality Theory	Behavioral Theory
• Attitudes	• Environment
• Beliefs	• Processes
• Values	• Systems
• Shared meanings	• Actions
• Invisible	• Visible
• Difficult to compare	• Easier to compare
• Difficult to manage/integrate	• Easier to manage/integrate
• Difficult to measure	• Easier to measure

Based on behavioral theory, individual and collective behavior (company culture) can be "nudged" by arranging an organization's environmental "choice architecture" differently.[xii]

… Which is achieved by aligning twelve "cultural levers" with strategy.

Cultural Alignment: Twelve Cultural Levers

Cultural Lever	Description: – Content – Process – People – Other	Metrics: – Frequency – Cycle-time – Cost – Other	Current Design	Required Design	Redesign Actions (short, medim, long-term)
1. Staffing and Selection					
2. Communications					
3. Training					
4. Rules and Policies					
5. Goals and Measures					
6. Rewards and Recognition					
7. Decision-making					
8. Organization Structure					
9. Physical Environment					
10. Leadership Behaviors					
11. Customs and Norms					
12. Ceremonies and Events					

[x] Phelps, B. 2015. "Behavioral perspectives on personality and self." *Psychological Record*, 65(3): 557–565.
[xi] Skinner, B. F. 1953. *Science and Human Behavior*. New York: Free Press.
[xii] Thaler, R. H., and Sunstein, C. R. 2008. *Nudge: Improving Decisions about Health, Wealth, and Happiness*. New York: Penguin.

Beyond Business Strategy

A PESTEL analysis identifies nonmarket issues that can impact the organization's future performance …

PESTEL[xiii] Analysis: Your Organization

Political	Economic	Social	Technological	Environmental	Legal

… The IA3 framework helps understand and analyze firm specific nonmarket issues …

Nonmarket: IA3 Framework[xiv]

- What is the **Issue**?

- Who are the **Actors**?

- What are the actors' **Interests**?

- In what **Arena** to the actors meet?

- What **Information** moves the issue?

- What **Assets** do the actors need to prevail?

[xiii] Aguilar F. J. (1967). *Scanning the Business Environment*. New York: Macmillan
[xiv] Aguilar F. J. (1967). *Scanning the Business Environment*. New York: Macmillan

… And a nonmarket decision tree helps you design your nonmarket strategy for each priority issue.

Nonmarket: Decision Tree[xv]

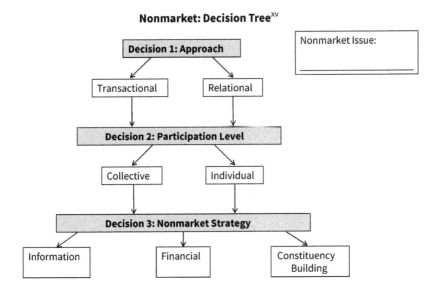

[xv] Hillman, A.J., Hitt, M.A. 1999. "Corporate political strategy formulation: a model of approach, participation, and strategy decisions." *The Academy of Management Review*, 24(4): 825–842.

There is a key difference between business and corporate strategy ...

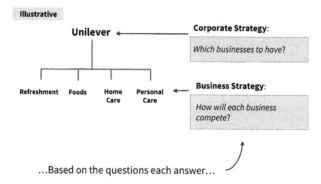

Corporate versus Business Strategy: Example

...Based on the questions each answer...

... Ansoff's matrix[xvi] identifies corporate/conglomerate diversification opportunities ...

Growth Matrix: Your Organization

... For your organization ...

[xvi] Ansoff, H.I. "Strategies for diversification." *Harvard Business Review*, 1957, 35(5), pp. 113–124.

... Analyzing a conglomerate's current portfolio of businesses ...

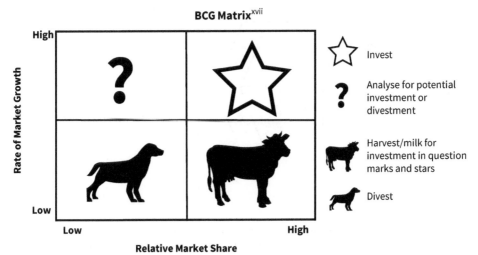

... Helps determine future strategic choices ...

... Perform a portfolio analysis for your business units ...

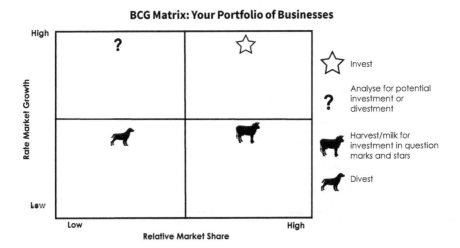

... The value of corporate diversification can be analyzed using the value chain ...

Star Image by rawpixel.com on Freepik; Dog Image by Freepik; Cow Image by ilonitta on Freepik

xvii Henderson, B. 1970. "The product portfolio." *BCG*, https://www.bcg.com/publications/1970/strategy-the-product-portfolio

Value Chain:[xviii] Your Portfolio of Businesses

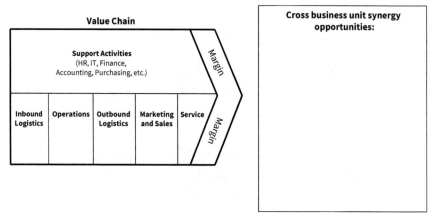

Exercise:

For your firm's portfolio of businesses, identify which parts of the business units' value chains possess synergy potential across business units to *lower costs* or *generate additional revenue.*

... There are three types of "corporate parents," and you should choose one to focus on.

Three Key Types of Corporate Parents: Your Corporate Office

Level	Description	Your Organization
Competency Builder	• Focus on the resources or capabilities they as corporate parents can transfer downwards to improve the performance of business units (e.g., fiscal management expertise, HR management management processes, and marketing practices)	**Current?** **Future?**
Synergiser	• Establish mechanisms for sharing processes, people, and systems across business units, with the aim of improving efficiency and effectiveness among the units	**Current?** **Future?**
Strategic Investor	• Perform the role of knowledgeable investors, informed board members, and an in-house bank, funding investments in various business units	**Current?** **Future?**

[xviii] Porter, M.E. 1985. *Competitive Advantage: Creating and Sustaining Superior Performance.* New York: Simon and Schuster.

This self-assessment provides a view of how your company applies a comprehensive M&A process.

M&A Process Self-Assessment

Component	Rating (0 = poor, 10 = excellent)	Notes/Rationale
1. We view M&A as a comprehensive process from strategy through implementation		
1. We clearly understand the complexities involved across the M&A process		
1. We are clear about the stages of the M&A process we do well		
1. We are clear about the stages of the M&A process we need to improve		
1. We have skilled and experienced M&A talent across all stages of the M&A process (tacit knowledge)		
1. We have cataloged and use effective tools and templates across all stages of the M&A process (codified knowledge)		
1. We take an integrated and coordinated cross functional approach to our M&A efforts during all pre- and post-deal stages		
1. We would be considered "best practice" in how we conduct M&A across the entire process		
1. M&A is a core competence of our organization		
1. We have clearly measured success in our past M&A efforts		
TOTAL SCORE		

Steps to complete the self-assessment:
1. Rate each item on a scale of 0 (poor) to 10 (excellent).
2. Make notes for each item to explain the rationale for the numerical rating.
3. Add all ten scores to get a TOTAL SCORE (maximum score = 100).

Rating scale:
0-20 = Poor (significant improvement needed)
21-40 = Below Average (improvement needed in several areas)
41-60 = Average (identify areas of weakness and adjust)
61-80 = Above Average (identify areas that can still be improved)
81-100 = Excellent (continuously review and refine each component for each iteration of the firm's M&A efforts)

Activists target various types of companies, with various objectives they seek to achieve …

… When dealing with activist investors it is crucial to take control of the agenda and frame the debate …

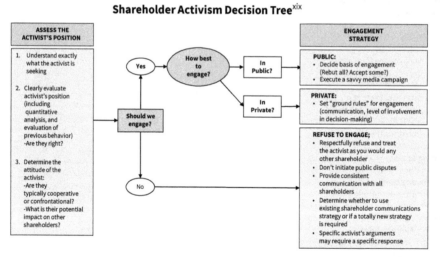

---

xix Adapted from Bentley, M. 2021. "When the wolf finally came: shareholder activism." Presentation, *Saïd Business School*: Oxford UK.

… What would you do if (when) an activist shareholder targets you and your firm?

Exercise: As an Executive, How Would You Respond to Activist Shareholders That Target You and Your Firm?

Your response to activist shareholders	Reasons / Rationale for your response

References

Aguilar, F.J. 1967. *Scanning the Business Environment*. New York: Macmillan.

Albuquerque, R., Fos, V., and Schroth, E.A. 2021. "Value creation in shareholder activism." *Journal of Financial Economics*, 145(2): 153–178.

Alstyne, M.W.V., Parker, G.G., and Choudary, S.P. 2016. "Pipelines, platforms, and the new rules of strategy." *Harvard Business Review*, 94(4): 54–62.

Altmayer, C. 2006. "Moving to performance-based management." *Government Finance Review*, 22(3): 8–14.

Andrews, H.I. 1971. *The Concept of Corporate Strategy*. Homewood, IL: Dow Jones-Irwin.

Ansoff, H.I. 1957. "Strategies for diversification." *Harvard Business Review*, 35(5): 113–124.

Ashkenas, R.N., DeMonaco, L.J., and Francis, S.C. 1998. "Making the deal real: how GE Capital integrates acquisitions." *Harvard Business Review*, 76(1): 165–178.

Bach, D. and Allen, D.B. 2010. "What every CEO needs to know about nonmarket strategy." *MIT Sloan Management Review*, 51(3): 41–48.

Barkema, H.G. and Schijven, M. 2008. "How do firms learn to make acquisitions? A review of past research and an agenda for the future." *Journal of Management*, 34(3): 594–634.

Barker, A. and Fontanella-Kahn, J. 2022. "ValueAct takes 7% stake in New York Times with call for new approach." *Financial Times*, accessed September 4, 2022, www.ft.com/content/b69100bf-c857-4992-894a-af85ad0e164b.

Barnard, C.I. 1938. *The Functions of the Executive*. Cambridge, MA: Harvard University Press.

Barney, J.B. 1995. "Looking inside for competitive advantage." *Academy of Management Executive*, 9(4): 49–61.

Bateh, J., Castaneda, M.E., and Farah, J.E. 2013. "Employee resistance to organizational change." *International Journal of Management & Information Systems*, 17(2): 113–116.

Becht, M., Franks, J., Mayer, C., and Rossi, S. 2009. "Returns to shareholder activism: evidence from a clinical study of the Hermes UK Focus Fund." *The Review of Financial Studies*, 22(8): 3093–3129.

Bedeian, A.G. and Armenakis, A.A. 1998. "The cesspool syndrome: how dreck floats to the top of declining organizations." *The Academy of Management Executive*, 12(1): 58–67.

Behn, R.D. 2003. "Why measure performance?" *Public Administration Review*, 63(5): 586–606.

Bentley, M. 2021. "When the wolf finally came: shareholder activism." In-person presentation, Senior Managing Director, Europe Guggenheim Partners (Institutional Affiliation). Oxford, UK: Saïd Business School, 1–28.

Betsch, C. and Kunz, J.J. 2008. "Individual strategy preferences and decisional fit." *Journal of Behavioral Decision Making*, 21(5): 532–555.

Bhatnagar, J. 2007. "Talent management strategy of employee engagement in Indian ITES employees: key to retention." *Employee Relations*, 29(6): 640–663.

Boeker, W. 1989. "Strategic change: the effects of founding and history." *The Academy of Management Journal*, 32(3): 489–515.

Bonn, I. 2001. "Developing strategic thinking as a core competency." *Management Decision*, 39(1): 63–76.

Booz Allen & Hamilton. 2022. "Our heritage." *Booz Allen & Hamilton*, accessed May 4, 2022, www.boozallen.com/about/our-heritage.html.

Borchardt, J. 2011. "Making mid-course corrections to improve project management." *Contract Management*, 51(7): 52–61.

Bossidy, L. and Charan, R. 2002. *Execution: The Discipline of Getting Things Done*. New York: Crown Business.

Boston Consulting Group. 2022. "The history of Boston Consulting Group." *Boston Consulting Group*, accessed May 4, 2022, www.bcg.com/about/overview/our-history.

Boyd, B.K. 1996. "Strategic planning and financial performance: a meta-analytic review." *Journal of Management Studies*, 28(4): 353–374.

Boyett, J.H. and Boyett, J.T. 1998. *The Guru Guide: The Best Ideas of the Top Management Thinkers*. New York: John Wiley & Sons.

Brahma, S.S. and Srivastava, K.B. 2007. "Communication, executive retention, and employee stress as predictors of acquisition performance: an empirical evidence." *ICFAI Journal of Mergers & Acquisitions*, 4(4): 7–26.

Brandenburger, A.M. and Nalebuff, B.J. 1996. *Co-opetition*. New York: Doubleday.

Brittain, S. 2007. "How to … manage key talent." *People Management*, 13(12): 46–47.

Buckingham, M. and Coffman, C. 1999. *First, Break All the Rules: What the World's Greatest Managers Do Differently*. New York: Simon & Shuster.

Caiazza, R. and Volpe, T. 2015. "M&A process: a literature review and research agenda." *Business Process Management Journal*, 21(1): 205–220.

Caligiuri, P. 2012. "When Unilever bought Ben and Jerry's: a story of CEO adaptability." *Fast Company*, accessed August 26, 2022, www.fastcompany.com/3000398/when-unilever-bought-ben-jerrys-story-ceo-adaptability.

Campbell, A., Goold, M., and Alexander, M. 1995. "Corporate strategy: the quest for parenting advantage." *Harvard Business Review*, 73(2): 120–132.

Canales, J. and Caldart A. 2017. "Encouraging emergence of cross-business strategic initiatives." *European Management Journal*, 35(3): 300–313.

Cannella, A.A. Jr., and Hambrick, D.C. 1993. "Effects of executive departures on the performance of acquired firms." *Strategic Management Journal*, 14(special issue): 137–152.

Cartwright, S. and Schoenberg, R. 2006. "Thirty years of mergers and acquisitions research: recent advances and future opportunities." *British Journal of Management*, 17(S1): S1–S5.

Cascio, W.F. 2010. "Done deal: now manage post-merger integration." *HR Magazine*, 55(10): 42–46.

Chandler, A.D. 1962. *Strategy and Structure*. Cambridge, MA: MIT Press.

Chandler, A.D. Jr. 1977. *The Visible Hand: The Managerial Revolution in American Business*. Cambridge, MA: Harvard University Press.

Clark, D.N. 2000. "Implementation issues in core competence strategy making." *Strategic Change*, 9(2): 115–127.

Cleary M., Hartnett K., and Dubuque K. 2011. "Road map to efficient merger integration." *American Banker*, 176(44): 9.

Clemens, N. 2009. "The impact of financial crisis." *Applied Clinical Trials*, 18(7): 74.

Clemons, E.K., Thatcher, M.E., and Row, M.C. 1995. "Identifying sources of reengineering failure: a study of the behavioral factors contributing to reengineering risks." *Journal of Management Information Systems*, 12(2): 9–36.

Coffman, C. and Gonzalez-Molina, G. 2002. *Follow This Path: How the World's Greatest Organizations Drive Growth by Unleashing Human Potential*. New York: Warner Books, Inc.

Companies History. 2022. "Bain & Co.," *Companies History*, accessed May 4, 2022, www.companieshistory.com/bain-co.

Copenhagen Institute for Future Studies. 2022. "Megatrends," accessed June 5, 2022, https://cifs.dk.

De Brentani, U. and Kleinschmidt, E.J. 2004. "Corporate culture and commitment: impact on performance of international new product development programs." *Journal of Product Innovation Management*, 21(5): 309–333.

Deloitte. 2007. "300 executives around the world say their view of strategic risk is changing." *Exploring Strategic Risk*, accessed August 29, 2022, www2.deloitte.com/content/dam/Deloitte/global/Documents/Governance-Risk-Compliance/dttl-grc-exploring-strategic-risk.pdf.

Deloitte. 2018. "Be your own activist." *Developing an Activist Mindset*, accessed September 4, 2022, www2.deloitte.com/content/dam/Deloitte/de/Documents/finance/Deloitte%5FBe%20your%20own%20activist.pdf.

Denison, D.R. 1984. "Bringing corporate culture to the bottom line." *Organizational Dynamics*, 13(2): 5–22.

Dessler, G. 1999. "How to earn your employees' commitment." *Academy of Management Executive*, 13(2): 58–67.

Doran, G.T. 1981. "There's a S.M.A.R.T. way to write management's goals and objectives." *Management Review*, 70(11): 35–36.

Doyle, P. 1994. "Setting business objectives and measuring performance." *Journal of General Management*, 20(2): 1–19.

Drucker, P. 1954. *The Practice of Management*. New York: Harper & Row.

Dua, A., Heil, K., and Wilkins, J. 2010. "How business interacts with government: McKinsey global survey results." *McKinsey & Company*, accessed August 29, 2022, www.mckinsey.com/industries/public-and-social-sector/our-insights/how-business-interacts-with-government-mckinsey-global-survey-results.

Due Diligence. 2022. "HSBC feels the heat from its biggest shareholder." *Financial Times*, accessed September 4, 2022, www.ft.com/content/67a82191-58e8-40d2-8c7a-aa480f34cfbf.

Edgecliffe-Johnson, A. 2022. "Companies cannot win America's culture wars." *Financial Times*, accessed August 29, 2022, www.ft.com/content/248941e5-c95c-439a-a160-1ea344ddd2c0.

Elder, B. 2022. "What now for Peltz-powered Unilever?" *Financial Times*, accessed September 4, 2022, www.ft.com/content/a0494db5-c38b-45b9-b3e6-01cab87a9e23.

Espinoza, J. 2017. "Private equity is about hard work and building something." *Financial Times*, accessed August 26, 2022, www.ft.com/content/05374d3c-a8e4-11e7-ab55-27219df83c97.

Etiennot, H., Vassolo, R., Diaz Hermelo, F., and McGahan, A.M. 2013. "How much does industry matter to firm performance in emerging countries?" *Academy of Management Annual Meeting Proceedings*, 2013(1): 1–10.

Etzioni, A. 1960. "Two approaches to organizational analysis: a critique and suggestion." *Administrative Science Quarterly*, 5(2): 257–278.

Faelten, A., Driessen, M., and Moeller, S. 2016. *Why Deals Fail and How to Rescue Them: M&A Lessons for Business Success*. London: Profile Books.

Felin, T. and Powell, T.C. 2016. "Designing organizations for dynamic capabilities." *California Management Review*, 58(4): 78–96.

Ford, J. and Ford, L. 2009. "Decoding resistance to change." *Harvard Business Review*, 87(4): 99–103.

Frank, F.D., Finnegan, R.P., and Taylor, C.R. 2004. "The race for talent: retaining and engaging workers in the 21st century." *Human Resource Planning*, 27(3): 12–25.

Franklin, D. 2013. "Managing big change." *Credit Union Management*, 36(7): 14–15.

French, S. 2009. "Action research for practicing managers." *Journal of Management Development*, 28(3): 187–204.

Galpin, T.J. 1996a. "Connecting culture to organizational change." *HR Magazine*, 41(3): 84–90.

Galpin, T.J. 1996b. *The Human Side of Change: A Practical Guide to Organization Redesign*. San Francisco, CA: Jossey-Bass.

Galpin, T.J. 2018. "Realizing your strategy's potential: a seven-step model for its effective execution." *Strategy & Leadership*, 46(6): 35–43.

Galpin, T.J. 2020. *Winning at the Acquisition Game: Tools, Templates, and Best Practices across the M&A Process*. Oxford: Oxford University Press.

Galpin, T.J. and Herndon, M. 2014. *The Complete Guide to Mergers and Acquisitions: Process Tools to Support M&A Integration at Every Level*. San Francisco, CA: Jossey-Bass.

Galpin, T.J., Hilpirt, R., and Evans, B. 2007. "The connected enterprise: beyond division of labor." *Journal of Business Strategy*, 28(2): 38–47.

George, B., Walker, R.M., and Monster, J. 2019. "Does strategic planning improve organizational performance? A meta-analysis." *Public Administration Review*, 79(6): 810–819.

Ghemawat, P. 1986. "Sustainable advantage." *Harvard Business Review*, 64(5): 53–58.

Ghemawat, P. 2002. "Competition and business strategy in historical perspective." *The Business History Review*, 76(1): 37–74.

Ghemawat, P. and Siegel, J. 2011. *Cases about Redefining Global Strategy*. Boston, MA: Harvard Business Review Press.

Gilligan J. and Galpin, T.J. 2022. "Rethinking the M&A process: learning private equity's secret to outperforming corporate strategic acquirers." *Strategy & Leadership*, 50(3): 21–28.

Goldman, E.F. 2006. "Strategic thinking at the top: what matters in developing expertise." *Academy of Management Annual Meeting Proceedings*, 2006(August): F1–F6.

Goulet, P.K. and Schweiger, D.M. 2006. "Managing culture and human resources in mergers and acquisitions." In G.K. Stahl. and I. Bjorkman (Eds.), *Handbook of Research in International Human Resource Management*. Cheltenham: Edward Elgar, 405–429.

Green, A., Barbin, C., and Schmidt, M. 2007. "Stars and keepers." *Chief Executive*, 230(December): 44–47.

Griffin, R. 1982. *Task Design: An Integrative Approach*. Glenview, IL: Scott, Foresman and Company.

Grimes, C., Germano, S., and Fontanella-Khan, J. 2022. "Activist investor Third Point urges sweeping changes at Disney." *Financial Times*, accessed September 4, 2022, www.ft.com/content/5bfa9fd6-5df9-41d9-9309-85e50c9ee431.

Groth, A. 2011. "Companies that put tons of money into R&D aren't more innovative than those that don't." *Business Insider*, accessed August 21, 2022, www.businessinsider.com/booz-and-cos-innovation-study-2011-10?r=US&IR=T.

Haberman, M. 2016. "Future Friday: can you tell the difference between fads, micro trends, macro trends and megatrends?" *The SHRMblog*, accessed June 5, 2022, https://blog.shrm.org/blog/future-friday-can-you-tell-the-difference-between-fads-micro-trends-macro-t#:~:text=Micro%20and%20macro%20trends,5%20to%2010%20year%20range.

Harter, J.K., Schmidt, F.L., and Hayes T.L. 2002. "Business-unit-level relationship between employee satisfaction, employee engagement, and business outcomes: a meta-analysis." *Journal of Applied Psychology*, 87(2): 268–279.

Hartley, K. 1965. "The learning curve and its application to the aircraft industry." *The Journal of Industrial Economics*, 13(2): 122–128.

Haslett, S. 1995. "Broadbanding: a strategic tool for organizational change." *Compensation and Benefits Review*, 27(6): 40–46.

Henderson, B. 1970. "The product portfolio." *BCG*, accessed June 29, 2022, www.bcg.com/publications/1970/strategy-the-product-portfolio.

Herbst-Bayliss, S. 2021. "Activist investors post strong returns with board campaigns in first quarter." *Reuters*, accessed September 4, 2022, www.reuters.com/business/finance/activist-investors-post-strong-returns-with-board-campaigns-first-quarter-2021-04-29.

Hillman, A.J. and Hitt, M.A. 1999. "Corporate political strategy formulation: a model of approach, participation, and strategy decisions." *The Academy of Management Review*, 24(4): 825–842.

Humes, P. 2016. "2016 milestone anniversary: Newport News Shipbuilding, 130 years." *Inside Business*, accessed May 5, 2022, www.pilotonline.com/inside-business/special-reports/article_4e0676d5-ff21-5e2f-90c1-39039bd88ee8.html.

Hunker, D.A. 2021. "What boards need to know about shareholder activism." *EY*, accessed September 4, 2022, www.ey.com/en_us/board-matters/what-boards-need-to-know-about-shareholder-activism.

Jackson, T. 2017. "56 strategic objectives for your company to copy." *Clearpoint Strategy*, accessed June 18, 2022, www.clearpointstrategy.com/56-strategic-objective-examples-for-your-company-to-copy.

Jacob, J., Bond, J., and Galinsky, E. 2008. "Six critical ingredients in creating an effective workplace." *The Psychological-Manager Journal*, 11(1): 141–161.

Jacopin, T. and Fontrodona, J. 2009. "Questioning the corporate responsibility (CR) department alignment with the business model of the company." *Corporate Governance*, 9(4): 528–536.

Jansen, H. 2016. "94 mind-blowing strategy execution stats." *Boardview*, accessed May 16, 2022, https://boardview.io/blog/strategy-execution-stats/#execution.

Jevtic, M., Jovanovic, M., and Krivokapic, J. 2018. "A new approach to measuring the correlation of organizational alignment and performance." *Management: Journal of Sustainable Business & Management Solutions in Emerging Economies*, 23(1): 41–52.

Jiang, B. and Koller, T. 2006. "A long-term look at ROIC." *McKinsey Quarterly*, accessed May 27, 2022, www.mckinsey.com/business-functions/strategy-and-corporate-finance/our-insights/a-long-term-look-at-roic.

Johnson, G., Whittington, R., Scholes, K., Angwin, D.N., and Regner, P. 2017. *Exploring Strategy*, 11th edition. Harlow: Pearson.

Joo, B.K. and Mclean, G.N. 2006. "Best employer studies: a conceptual model from a literature review and a case study." *Human Resource Development Review*, 5(2): 228–257.

Kaplan, R.S. and Norton, D.R. 2005. "The balanced scorecard: measures that drive performance." *Harvard Business Review*, 83(7/8): 172–180.

Kim, W.C. and Mauborgne, R. 1997. "Fair process: managing in the knowledge economy." *Harvard Business Review*, 75(4): 65–75.

Kim, W.C. and Mauborgne, R. 2005. *Blue Ocean Strategy: How to Create Uncontested Market Space and Make the Competition Irrelevant*. Boston, MA: Harvard Business School Publishing Corporation.

Kjaer, A 2014. *The Trend Management Toolkit: A Practical Guide to the Future*. New York: Palgrave Macmillan.

Knoll, S. 2008. *Cross-Business Synergies: A Typology of Cross-Business Synergies and a Mid-Range Theory of Continuous Growth Synergy Realization*. Wiesbaden: Gabler-Verlag.

Knott, P.J. 2015. "Does VRIO help managers evaluate a firm's resources?" *Management Decision*, 53(8): 1806–1822.

Koller T., Goedhart, M., and Wessels, D. 2020. *Valuation: Measuring and Managing the Value of Companies*. Hoboken, NJ: John Wiley & Sons.

Kotter, J.P. 1996. *Leading Change*. Boston, MA: Harvard Business Review Press.

Kotter, J.P. and Heskett, J.L. 1992. *Corporate Culture and Performance*. New York: The Free Press.

Kristof-Brown, A., Zimmerman, R., and Johnson, E. 2005. "Consequences of individuals' fit at work: a meta-analysis of person-job, person-organization, person-group, and person-supervisor fit." *Personnel Psychology*, 58(2): 281–342.

Kullman, E. 2012. "DuPont's CEO on executing a complex cross-border acquisition." *Harvard Business Review*, 90(7/8): 43–46.

Laurie, D.L., Doz, Y.L., and Sheer, C.P. 2006. "Creating new growth platforms." *Harvard Business Review*, 84(5): 80–90.

Lawrence, P. 1954. "How to deal with resistance to change." *Harvard Business Review*, 32(3): 49–57.

Leana, C.R. and Feldman, D.C. 1989. "When mergers force layoffs: some lessons about managing the HR." *Human Resource Planning*, 12(2): 123–140.

Learned, E.P., Christensen, C.R., Andrews, K.R., and Guth, W.D. 1965. *Business Policy: Text and Cases*, 1st edition. Homewood, IL: Richard D. Irwin, Inc.

Leinwand, P. and Mainardi, C. 2011. "Stop chasing too many priorities." *Harvard Business Review online*, accessed June 18, 2022, https://hbr.org/2011/04/stop-chasing-too-many-prioriti.

Lewin, K. 1943. "Psychology and the process of group living." *Journal of Social Psychology*, 17(1): 113–131.

Lewis, A. and McKone, D. 2016. "So many M&A deals fail because companies overlook this simple strategy." *Harvard Business Review online*, accessed August 26, 2022, https://hbr.org/2016/05/so-many-ma-deals-fail-because-companies-overlook-this-simple-strategy.

Liedtka, J. M. 1998. "Strategic thinking: can it be taught?." *Long Range Planning*, 31(1): 120–129.

Lipton, M. 1996. "Demystifying the development of an organizational vision." *Sloan Management Review*, 37(4): 83–92.

Little, B. and Little, P. 2006. "Employee engagement: conceptual issues." *Journal of Organizational Culture, Communication and Conflict*, 10(1): 111–120.

Longman, A. and Mullins, J. 2004. "Project management: key tool for implementing strategy." *Journal of Business Strategy*, 25(5): 54–60.

Longo, S.C. 1996. "Has reengineering left you financially stronger?" *CPA Journal*, 66(1): 69.

Luft, J. and Ingham, H. 1955. "The Johari window, a graphic model of interpersonal awareness." *Proceedings of the Western Training Laboratory in Group Development*. Los Angeles, CA: University of California Los Angeles.

Lundqvist, S. 2012. "Post-merger integration issues: the importance of early appointment of new managers for successful PMI." *Problems of Management in the 21st Century*, 3(1): 62–80.

Mallon, W.T. 2019. "Does strategic planning matter?" *Academic Medicine*, 94(10): 1408–1411.

Mankins, M.C. and Steele, R. 2005. "Turning great strategy into great performance." *Harvard Business Review*, 83(7/8): 64–72.

Marr, B. 2018. "What is industry 4.0?" *Forbes*, accessed May 30, 2022, www.forbes.com/sites/bernardmarr/2018/09/02/what-is-industry-4-0-heres-a-super-easy-explanation-for-anyone/?sh=5f2a5d909788.

Maslow, A.H. 1943. "A theory of human motivation." *Psychological Review*, 50(4): 430–437.

Matzler, K., Uzelac, B., and Bauer, F. 2014. "Intuition: the missing ingredient for good managerial decision-making." *Journal of Business Strategy*, 35(6): 31–40.

May, D. and Kettelhut, M.C. 1996. "Managing human issues in reengineering projects." *Journal of Systems Management*, 47(1): 4–11.

McGahan, A.M. and Porter, M.E. 1997. "How much does industry matter, really?" *Strategic Management Journal*, 18(S1): 15–30.

McGrath, R.G. 2013. "Transient advantage." *Harvard Business Review*, 91(6): 62–70.

McKinsey & Company. 2020. "Growth and innovation." *McKinsey & Company*, accessed August 21, 2022, www.mckinsey.com/business-functions/strategy-and-corporate-finance/how-we-help-clients/growth-and-innovation.

McKinsey & Company. 2021. "The impact of agility: how to shape your organization to compete." *McKinsey & Company*, accessed May 16, 2022, www.mckinsey.com/business-functions/people-and-organizational-performance/our-insights/the-impact-of-agility-how-to-shape-your-organization-to-compete?cid=eml-web.

McKinsey & Company. 2022. "History of our firm." *McKinsey & Company*, accessed May 4, 2022, www.mckinsey.com/about-us/overview/history-of-our-firm.

Mihalache, A. 2017. "Project management tools for agile teams." *Informatica Economica*, 21(4): 85–93.

Miles, L. and Rouse, T. 2012. "After the merger, how not to lose customers." *The Wall Street Journal*, accessed July 17, 2022, www.wsj.com/articles/SB10001424052702304450004577279383547481476.

Miller, C.C. and Cardinal, L.B. 1994. "Strategic planning and firm performance: a synthesis of two decades of research." *Academy of Management Journal*, 37(6): 1649–1655.

Miner, K. 2010. "The four levels of innovation." *Graziadio Business Review*, 13(4): 1–5.

Mintzberg, H. 1987. "Crafting strategy." *Harvard Business Review*, 65(4): 66–75.

Morsing, M. and Oswald, D. 2009. "Sustainable leadership: management control systems and organizational culture in Novo Nordisk A/S." *Corporate Governance*, 9(1): 83–99.

Naranjo-Valencia, J.C., Jimenez-Jimenez, D., and Sanz-Valle, R. 2017. "Organizational culture and radical innovation: does innovative behavior mediate this relationship?" *Creativity & Innovation Management*, 26(4): 407–417.

Nieminen, J. 2018. "50+ statistics on innovation: what do the numbers tell us?" *Viima*, accessed August 21, 2022, www.viima.com/blog/innovation-stats.

Nippa, M., Pidun, U., and Rubner, H. 2011. "Corporate portfolio management: appraising four decades of academic research." *Academy of Management Perspectives*, 25(4): 50–66.

Oakley, T. 2015. "Coca-Cola: Ansoff matrix." *The Marketing Agenda*, accessed August 22, 2022, https://themarketingagenda.com/2015/03/28/coca-cola-ansoff-matrix.

Palich, L.E., Cardinal, L.B., and Miller, C.C. 2000. "Curvilinearity in the diversification-performance linkage: an examination of over three decades of research." *Strategic Management Journal*, 21(2): 155–174.

Peck, R.L. 1995. "Reengineering: full speed ahead." *Nursing Homes*, 44(9): 10.

Peloso, A. 2020. "Leveraging the power of micro-macro trends in contemporary organizations." *Journal of Applied Business and Economics*, 22(4): 168–174.

Phelps, B. 2015. "Behavioral perspectives on personality and self." *Psychological Record*, 65(3): 557–565.

Pisano, G.P. 2015. "You need an innovation strategy." *Harvard Business Review*, 93(6): 44–54.

Poister, T.H., Edwards, L.H., Pasha, O.Q., and Edwards, J. 2013. "Strategy formation and performance: evidence from local public transit agencies." *Public Performance & Management Review*, 36(4): 585–615.

Porter, M.E. 1979. "How competitive forces shape strategy." *Harvard Business Review*, 57(2): 137–145.

Porter, M.E. 1980. *Competitive Strategy: Techniques for Analyzing Industries and Competitors*. New York: The Free Press.

Porter, M.E. 1985. *Competitive Advantage: Creating and Sustaining Superior Performance*. New York: Simon and Schuster.

Porter, M.E. 1987. "From competitive advantage to corporate strategy." *Harvard Business Review*, 65(3): 43–59.

Porter, M.E. 1996. "What is strategy?" *Harvard Business Review*, 74(6): 61–78.

Porter, M.E. 2008. "The five competitive forces that shape strategy." *Harvard Business Review*, 86(1): 78–93.

Posner, B.Z. 2010. "Another look at the impact of personal and organizational values congruency." *Journal of Business Ethics*, 97(4): 535–541.

Powell, T.C. 2017. "Strategy as diligence: putting behavioral strategy into practice." *California Management Review*, 59(3): 162–190.

Prahalad, C.K. and Hamel, G. 1990. "The core competence of the corporation." *Harvard Business Review*, 68(3): 79–91.

Pretz, J.E. 2008. "Intuition versus analysis: strategy and experience in complex everyday problem solving." *Memory & Cognition*, 36(3): 554–566.

Ramirez, R., Churchhouse, S., Palermo, A., and Hoffmann, J.M. 2017. "Using scenario planning to reshape strategy." *MIT Sloan Management Review*, 58(4): 30–37.

Ransom, P. and Lober, D.J. 1999. "Why do firms set environmental performance goals? Some evidence from organizational theory." *Business Strategy and the Environment*, 8(1): 1–13.

Robbins, S. and Judge, T. 2012. *Essentials of Organizational Behavior*, 11th edition. Upper Saddle River, NJ: Pearson Prentice Hall.

Robertson, K. 2018. "Southwest Airlines reveals 5 culture lessons." *Human Synergistics*, accessed June 15, 2022, www.humansynergistics.com/blog/culture-university/details/culture-university/2018/05/29/southwest-airlines-reveals-5-culture-lessons.

Rumelt, R.P. 1991. "How much does industry matter?" *Strategic Management Journal*, 12(3): 167–185.

Rumens, L. 2002. "Measure of success." *Works Management*, 55(11): 25.

Ryan, G. 1989. "Dealing with survivors of a reorganization." *Research Technology Management*, 32(2): 40–42.

Schein, E. 1990. "Organizational culture." *American Psychologist*, 45(2): 109–119.

Schein, E.H. 1985. *Organizational Culture and Leadership*. San Francisco, CA: Jossey-Bass.

Schweiger, D.M. and DeNisi, A.S. 1991. "Communication with employees following a merger: a longitudinal field experiment." *Academy of Management Journal*, 34(1): 110–135.

Schwenk, C.R. and Shrader, C.B. 1993. "Effects of formal strategic planning on financial performance in small firms: a meta-analysis." *Entrepreneurship Theory & Practice*, 17(3): 53–64.

Selznick, P. 1957. *Leadership in Administration: A Sociological Interpretation*. Evanston, IL: Row, Peterson & Co.

Sherman, S. 1993. "A master class in radical change." *Fortune*, 128(15): 82–90.

SICE. 1990. "United States: restrictions on the importation of sugar and sugar-containing products applied under the 1955 waiver and under the headnote to the schedule of tariff concessions." *SICE*, accessed August 30, 2022, www.sice.oas.org/dispute/gatt/89sugarc.asp.

Skinner, B.F. 1953. *Science and Human Behavior*. New York: Free Press.

Skinner, B.F. 1974. *About Behaviorism*. New York: Random House.

Slater, R. 1999. *Jack Welch and the G.E. Way: Management Insights and Leadership Secrets of the Legendary CEO*. New York: McGraw-Hill.

Sloan, A.P. Jr. 1963. *My Years with General Motors*. New York: Doubleday.

Smith, A. 1776. *An Inquiry into the Nature and Causes of the Wealth of Nations*. London: Strahan and Cadell.

Society for Human Resource Management. 2007. "Change management survey report." *SHRM*, accessed July 17, 2022, www.shrm.org/hr-today/trends-and-forecasting/research-and-surveys/documents/2007%20change%20management%20survey%20report.pdf.

Steigenberger, N. 2017. "The challenge of integration: a review of the M&A integration literature." *International Journal of Management Reviews*, 19(4): 408–431.

Taleb, N. 2007. *The Black Swan: The Impact of the Highly Improbable*. New York: Random House.

Teece, D.J. 1996. "Firm organization, industrial structure, and technological innovation." *Journal of Economic Behavior & Organization*, 31(2): 193–224.

Thaler, R.H. and Sunstein, C.R. 2008. *Nudge: Improving Decisions about Health, Wealth, and Happiness*. New York: Penguin.

The Economist. 2015. "Capitalism's unlikely heroes: why activist investors are good for the public company." *The Economist*, accessed September 4, 2022, www.economist.com/leaders/2015/02/05/capitalisms-unlikely-heroes.

Thorndike, W.N. 2012. *The Outsiders: Eight Unconventional CEOs and Their Radically Rational Blueprint for Success*. Boston, MA: Harvard Business School Publishing.

Toppenberg, G., Henningsson, S., and Shanks, G. 2015. "How Cisco Systems used enterprise architecture capability to sustain acquisition-based growth." *MIS Quarterly Executive*, 14(4): 151–168.

Treacy, M. and Weirsma, F. 1995. *The Discipline of Market Leaders*. Boston, MA: Addison-Wesley.

van Ark, B. 2019. "Highly innovative companies outperform the market but are not insulated from global risks." *Forbes*, accessed August 21, 2022, https://www.forbes.com/sites/washingtonbytes/2019/07/03/highly-innovative-companies-outperform-the-market-but-are-not-insulated-from-global-risks/#3c6bc596425b.

Vantresca, M. 2022. "Strategy core primer." White paper. Oxford: University of Oxford.

Vazirani, N. 2012. "Mergers and acquisitions performance evaluation: a literature review." *SIES Journal of Management*, 8(2): 37–42.

Vermeulen, F. 2013. "Corporate strategy is a fool's errand." *Harvard Business Review*, accessed August 22, 2022, https://hbr.org/2013/03/when-it-comes-to-corporate-str.

Wernerfelt, B. 1984. "A resource-based view of the firm." *Strategic Management Journal*, 5(2): 171–180.

Wheelen, T.L. and Hunger, J.D. 2008. *Concepts in Strategic Management and Business Policy*, 11th edition. Upper Saddle River, NJ: Pearson Education, Inc.

Whittington, J.L. and Galpin, T.J. 2010. "The engagement factor: building a high-commitment organization in a low-commitment world." *Journal of Business Strategy*, 31(5): 14–24.

Withenshaw, J. 2003. "Successful termination." *Canadian Manager*, 28(3): 20–22.

Wright, P.M. and McMahan, G.C. 1992. "Theoretical perspectives for strategic human resource management." *Journal of Management*, 18(2): 295–320.

Zollo, M. and Singh, H. 2007. "Deliberate learning in corporate acquisitions: post-acquisition strategies and integration capability in U.S. bank mergers." *Strategic Management Journal*, 25(13): 1233–1256.

Index

Tables and figures are indicated by an italic *t* and *f* following the page number.